Palgrave Studies in the Enlightenment, Romanticism and Cultures of Print

Palgrave Studies in the Enlightenment, Romantic
work that does not fit comfortably within estab
periods or between disciplines. Uniquely, it will ... the power and materiality of print with explorations of gender, race, and class. By attending as well to intersections of literature with the visual arts, medicine, law, and science, the series will enable a large-scale rethinking of the origins of modernity.

Titles include:

Melanie Bigold
WOMEN OF LETTERS, MANUSCRIPT CIRCULATION, AND PRINT AFTERLIVES IN THE EIGHTEENTH CENTURY
Elizabeth Rowe, Catharine Cockburn, and Elizabeth Carter

Katey Castellano
THE ECOLOGY OF BRITISH ROMANTIC CONSERVATISM, 1790–1837

Noah Comet
ROMANTIC HELLENISM AND WOMEN WRITERS

Ildiko Csengei
SYMPATHY, SENSIBILITY AND THE LITERATURE OF FEELING IN THE EIGHTEENTH CENTURY

Alexander Dick
ROMANTICISM AND THE GOLD STANDARD
Money, Literature, and Economic Debate in Britain 1790–1830

Elizabeth Eger
BLUESTOCKINGS
Women of Reason from Enlightenment to Romanticism

John Gardner
POETRY AND POPULAR PROTEST
Peterloo, Cato Street and the Queen Caroline Controversy

George C. Grinnell
THE AGE OF HYPOCHONDRIA
Interpreting Romantic Health and Illness

David Higgins
ROMANTIC ENGLISHNESS
Local, National, and Global Selves, 1780–1850

Anthony S. Jarrells
BRITAIN'S BLOODLESS REVOLUTIONS
1688 and the Romantic Reform of Literature

Emrys Jones
FRIENDSHIP AND ALLEGIANCE IN EIGHTEENTH-CENTURY LITERATURE
The Politics of Private Virtue in the Age of Walpole

Jacqueline M. Labbe
WRITING ROMANTICISM
Charlotte Smith and William Wordsworth, 1784–1807

April London
LITERARY HISTORY WRITING, 1770–1820

Robert Morrison and Daniel Sanjiv Roberts (*editors*)
ROMANTICISM AND *BLACKWOOD'S MAGAZINE*
'An Unprecedented Phenomenon'

Catherine Packham
EIGHTEENTH-CENTURY VITALISM
Bodies, Culture, Politics

Murray G.H. Pittock
MATERIAL CULTURE AND SEDITION, 1688–1760
Treacherous Objects, Secret Places

Jessica Richard
THE ROMANCE OF GAMBLING IN THE EIGHTEENTH-CENTURY BRITISH NOVEL

Andrew Rudd
SYMPATHY AND INDIA IN BRITISH LITERATURE, 1770–1830

Seth Rudy
LITERATURE AND ENCYCLOPEDISM IN ENLIGHTENMENT BRITAIN
The Pursuit of Complete Knowledge

Sharon Ruston
CREATING ROMANTICISM
Case Studies in the Literature, Science and Medicine of the 1790s

Yasmin Solomonescu
JOHN THELWALL AND THE MATERIALIST IMAGINATION

Richard Squibbs
URBAN ENLIGHTENMENT AND THE EIGHTEENTH-CENTURY PERIODICAL ESSAY
Transatlantic Retrospects

David Stewart
ROMANTIC MAGAZINES AND METROPOLITAN LITERARY CULTURE

Rebecca Tierney-Hynes
NOVEL MINDS
Philosophers and Romance Readers, 1680–1740

P. Westover
NECROMANTICISM
Travelling to Meet the Dead, 1750–1860

Esther Wohlgemut
ROMANTIC COSMOPOLITANISM

Palgrave Studies in the Enlightenment, Romanticism and Cultures of Print
Series Standing Order ISBN 978–1–403–93408–6
hardback 978–1–403–93409–3 paperback
(*outside North America only*)

You can receive future titles in this series as they are published by placing a standing order. Please contact your bookseller or, in case of difficulty, write to us at the address below with your name and address, the title of the series and the ISBN quoted above.

Customer Services Department, Macmillan Distribution Ltd, Houndmills, Basingstoke, Hampshire RG21 6XS, England

---

Writing Romanticism

Charlotte Smith and William Wordsworth, 1784–1807

Jacqueline M. Labbe
Pro Vice Chancellor and Chair of Romantic Period literature, University of Sheffield, UK

palgrave
macmillan

First published in hardback 2011
First published in paperback 2015 by PALGRAVE MACMILLAN

Palgrave Macmillan in the UK is an imprint of Macmillan Publishers Limited, registered in England, company number 785998, of Houndmills, Basingstoke, Hampshire RG21 6XS.

Palgrave Macmillan in the US is a division of St Martin's Press LLC, 175 Fifth Avenue, New York, NY 10010.

Palgrave Macmillan is the global academic imprint of the above companies and has companies and representatives throughout the world.

Palgrave® and Macmillan® are registered trademarks in the United States, the United Kingdom, Europe and other countries.

ISBN 978–0–230–28549–1 hardback
ISBN 978–1–137–46510–8 paperback

A catalogue record for this book is available from the British Library.

Library of Congress Cataloging-in-Publication Data
Labbe, Jacqueline M., 1965–
Writing romanticism: Charlotte Smith and William Wordsworth, 1784–1807/Jacqueline M. Labbe.
p. cm.
Includes bibliographical references and index.
ISBN 978–0–230–28549–1 (cloth) 978–1–137–46510–8(pbk)
1. Smith, Charlotte Turner, 1749–1806—Criticism and interpretation. 2. Smith, Charlotte Turner, 1749–1806—Contemporaries. 3. Wordsworth, William, 1770–1850—Criticism and interpretation. 4. Wordsworth, William, 1770–1850—Contemporaries. 5. English poetry—18th century—History and criticism. 6. Romanticism—Great Britain. I. Title.
PR3688.S4Z75 2011
823'6—dc22 2011012056

Typeset by MPS Limited, Chennai, India.

Transferred to Digital Printing in 2014

To my children, Indie and Nathan

Contents

Acknowledgments

This book is deeply indebted to all the scholars of Smith's and Wordsworth's work who have established the depth and the durability of their poetry. In researching it I have learned vaster amounts than have made it into this study. As literary fashions have come and gone, what is remarkable is the enduring consensus about Wordsworth's pre-eminence. The corollary is Smith's centrality to the study of Romantic-period women's writing, which found its own consensus as soon as feminist literary critics found her. It is my fervent wish that this book will do something to merge these agreements and place Smith and Wordsworth on the same page, critically, thematically, poetically.

As always, I am immeasurably grateful for the tutelage and scholarly example shown by Stuart Curran. By asking me to edit Smith's poems for the Pickering and Chatto *Works of Charlotte Smith*, he allowed me to get inside her poetry. I am grateful, as well, to Stephen Gill for his edition *The Oxford Authors: Wordsworth*, and to the varied editors of the Cornell editions of Wordsworth which have given all readers and scholars of Wordsworth such confidence in the texts they study.

Some portions of this book have already appeared in print. I am grateful to the following, both for publishing the work in the first place, and for allowing its revision and republication:

- A section of Chapter 1 appeared as "The hybrid poems of Smith and Wordsworth: Questions and Disputes." *European Romantic Review* 20 (2009), pp. 219–26.
- A section of Chapter 3 appeared as "At the Intersection of Artifice and Reality." *Romantic Localities*, eds. Jacqueline Labbe and Christoph Bode. London: Pickering and Chatto, 2010, pp. 25–38.
- Versions of Chapter 4 appeared as "Revisiting the Egotistical Sublime: Smith, Wordsworth, and the Romantic Dramatic Monologue." *Women and Men Romantic Poets*. Ed. Beth Lau. Aldershot: Ashgate Press, 2009, pp. 17–38; and as "Smith, Wordsworth, and the Model of the Romantic Poet." *Romanticism and Victorianism on the Net* 51 (2008); http://www.erudit.org/revue/ravon/2008/v/n51/index.html?lang=en.

As I have worked on this book I have benefited tremendously from the insightful comments of colleagues who have listened patiently at

North American Society for the Study of Romanticism conferences, British Association for Eighteenth-Century Studies conferences, British Association for Romantic Studies conferences, and other venues. I am extremely grateful to the two anonymous readers for Palgrave, whose generous and intellectually challenging responses have made this book more than it otherwise would have been. I am also indebted to Anne Mellor and Cliff Siskin, not only for their scholarship, which has enriched Romanticism, but for accepting this book for their series.

Finally, as both Smith and Wordsworth would say, this book is dedicated to my children, Indie and Nathan, who so carefully "watched out for the books!"; and as Wordsworth might say but Smith most definitely would not, to my spouse, Rod, who always makes the time.

Jacqueline Labbe
Coventry, April 2011

List of Abbreviations

DS	*Descriptive Sketches*
EW	*An Evening Walk*
LB	Lyrical Ballads, *and Other Poems, 1797–1800*
P2V	Poems, in Two Volumes, *and Other Poems, 1800–1807*
Poetry	Charlotte Smith, *Poetry.*
RC	*The* Ruined Cottage *and* The Pedlar
SP	*The Salisbury Plain Poems*

Introduction

Romanticism is in a constant state of flux. For a good twenty years, it has been undergoing regular adjustments: re-visionings, re-evaluations, re-statings, re-workings. Many critical studies open by making the claim for novelty and new visions. What is most interesting about the regular claims to innovation, however, is how much actually stays the same. Books tend still to discuss the usual figures: the familiar six in poetry, an increasing number for prose but nearly always including, for instance, Godwin, Scott, de Quincy, Hazlitt: the familiar essayists and fiction writers. Or they are self-consciously going off piste, covering the still not fully mapped terrain of the huge and growing numbers of women writers, in both poetry and prose (but mainly prose) of the period. The two segments don't seem, very often, to overlap; that is, books about the male writers may put forward theories useful to authors of books about female writers, but there is not a lot of traffic the other way. For some reason, arguments about specific male writers can be applied more generally across the field, while arguments about the group "women writers," as well as individual authors, remain useful only for that ring-fenced specialism. Many books still rely on a familiar set of assumptions about the period: divisions into "high" and "low" Romanticism, or discussions of first and second generations, or a gendering of genre (women mainly wrote novels, men mainly wrote poetry and politics). And, of course, the Habermasian separate spheres are still pretty rigidly assumed, as well.

In some ways this book is no different. I am arguing for a new understanding of Romanticism, and I am focusing on one of the well-known, major figures: Charlotte Smith, whose poetry ranges over the Romantic interests in how Nature and culture collide, in how memory functions to fulfill one's potential through a creative (re)writing of one's personal past, in how the landscape of childhood and of the domestic affections can create an imaginative geography, in how political and revolutionary events invite the leavening of artistic intervention to lead to a fuller understanding of the worlds of the self and of society. However, despite Smith's centrality to the formation of Romantic-period poetics and also the culture we call Romanticism, this book also takes on a more up-and-coming figure, one who has featured increasingly commonly in studies that focus on the personalized experiences poetry so often seems to project so seamlessly, whose poetry stands as exemplary of a responsive form of writing that recognizes a mainstream literary culture and writes sometimes within, sometimes against it. This figure, William Wordsworth, is familiar nowadays to most readers of Romantic-period poetry, even if he has yet to emerge as a fully fledged major writer (the subject of his prominence usually takes on a gendered tinge). It is my contention that if we read Smith alongside her important, if understudied contemporary, then something truly novel happens: we begin to understand more, not just about the Romantic writing each undertook, but about how each undertook to write the Romantic. In other words, despite the legible shorthand that mandates a common reading of the Smithian, it is time to see what happens if we unpick this to find how much of the "Wordsworthian," to coin a term, cohabits the construct.

Smith was important to Wordsworth from an early age. As Duncan Wu notes, even as a schoolboy in Hawkshead Wordsworth was reading Smith: "the master of Hawkshead Grammar School ... was among Wordsworth's mentors, and lent his precocious charge ... Charlotte Smith's *Elegiac Sonnets* ... when they were first published."[1] Later, Wordsworth is among the subscribers to the fifth edition of the *Sonnets*, which he read repeatedly to the point that they become a familiar stand-by: "beloved William is turning over the leaves of Charlotte Smith's sonnets," writes Dorothy Wordsworth in 1802.[2] Smith serves as a touchstone for Wordsworth's earliest conceptions of himself as a poet: many of his 1780s poems were Smith-style sonnets, and his often-mentioned but seldom-studied first publication, the "Sonnet on Seeing Miss Helen Maria Williams Weep," is an overblown version of a Smithian sonnet, palpating with emotion yet hemmed in by its strictly observed Shakespearian rhyme scheme. By 1787, when this poem is published in the *European Magazine*, Smith had established herself as the sonneteer à la mode, and was just about to make her first big splash as a novelist with *Emmeline* (1788). Wordsworth's sonnet, with its layers of not-seeing and theatrical over-feeling, places itself within a mode of sensibility that draws from, yet over-writes, Smith's as it was then read (by 1787 the *Elegiac Sonnets* were in their fourth edition).[3] The speaker of Wordsworth's sonnet presents a visual relationship with Williams, herself by the mid-1780s a prominent author, and whose 1786 "To Sensibility" fosters a "trembling" that encourages Wordsworth's image. In Wordsworth's sonnet, however, the vision is not of Williams but rather of a speaker whose own immersion in vicarious feeling aligns him with the emotional state permeating the poem. Overcome with the thrill of the scene thus set, the speaker's "full heart" has no room left for life itself: "life left my loaded heart, and closing eye" (l. 5). "A sigh" calls it back, and the poem projects the solace that sensibility provides even in the face of "misery's midnight hour," shining like those stars whose light is overwhelmed, during the day, by the sun's "malignant power" (ll. 6, 12). Luxuriant in its imagery, the poem challenges its readers to identify the feeling subject that inhabits it; in fact, *who* feels seems less important than the feeling felt. The poem draws on the trope of the wanderer, itself important in Smith's sonnets, and features the phrase "dear delicious pain" (l. 4), not identical to, but not far from, the "dear delusive art" by which Smith identifies poetry-making itself in her Sonnet I.[4] Wordsworth's sonnet displays not merely his sense of the attractions of a genre, but more meaningfully his understanding of the potential contained in its Smithian model.

At the start of his poetic career, then, Wordsworth wrote with a style and a tone that drew on that of an eminent public figure. The standard literary history of the late eighteenth century, however (as opposed to that I offered above), has not itself been founded on the Smithian but rather on the Wordsworthian. This book sets out to explore the interconnectedness of these paradigms within the period 1784–1807, the early Romantic period, and to discuss how the work of these two poets not only responds to, but in many ways sets, the tone of the age. Wordsworth has for generations been studied as the major maker of the varying major modalities of the period, whether these are defined as the abstract philosophies of memory, imagination, and Nature that were key in the nineteenth and twentieth centuries, or the more concrete engagement with, or avoidances of, history, politics, and ideas of class and gender that became important by the end of the twentieth century. It was during this latter period that Smith became newly visible on the critical stage, but for many years only in isolation or as a member of the generic group "women writers." Periodically, notice has been taken of the two poets' similar projects; in 1970, Bishop Hunt, Jr. outlined their commonalities, charting the similarities of approach and imagery they shared.[5] More recently, Stuart Curran has noted that her "most direct beneficiary among the more canonical male poets was William Wordsworth, who seems to have felt her impact from the first."[6] My own book on Smith concluded by discussing, briefly, the poetic relationship they shared.[7] These approaches, however, have been cursory and merely comparative. By investigating in detail the poetry, philosophies, and cross-fertilizations of the two poets, this study will establish a complex inter-weaving of themes, ideas, and philosophies that, taken together, create a more nuanced, and more historical, understanding of Romanticism.

Smith and Wordsworth perform perhaps the most creative partnership of the many that flourished within the period. They met only once, in November 1791, when the young Wordsworth, on his way back to France, called on Smith in Brighton and received from her a letter of introduction to Williams. Smith makes her only mention of Wordsworth in her voluminous correspondence: "I was ... detained by Mr. Wordsworth (whom I could not take leave of, till he embark'd) till it was too late" to visit her friend Lucy Hill Lowe.[8] It has not, perhaps, been adequately discussed how unusual this visit is. Smith's prominence as a poet may well have attracted Wordsworth, and Judith Stanton notes that he "was distantly related to her by marriage" through a rather complex lineage (p. 39, n. 4). Even so, Smith implies a visit of some length, extended by the necessity of awaiting Wordsworth's embarkation, which goes well beyond the politeness owed to a stranger, distantly related through marriage as he might be. This slight and tantalizing mention, in other words, carries with it the suggestion of a better acquaintance than the record evidences: Smith's correspondent seems expected to know who "Mr. Wordsworth" is (no description or explanation is offered), and Mr. Wordsworth seems to be given much more hospitality than courtesy alone would dictate. Indeed, both Wu and Hunt suggest that the sonnets inscribed on the endpapers of Wordsworth's copy of *Elegiac Sonnets*, poems not found in the volume itself, were shown in manuscript to him by Smith during this visit, another intimacy not required by common politeness.[9] It is impossible to say whether the two knew each other better than the record attests, or whether they simply recognized in each other a kindred poet; thereafter, their partnership seems to have been purely textual. Smith never mentions him again in her letters, and Wordsworth himself keeps rather quiet until 1833, when he observes in a note to his poem "Stanzas ... Off St. Bees' Head" that

> The form of stanza in this Poem, and something in the style of versification, are adopted from the 'St. Monica', a poem of much

> beauty upon a monastic subject, by Charlotte Smith: a lady to whom English verse is under greater obligations than are likely to be either acknowledged or remembered. She wrote little, and that little unambitiously, but with true feeling for rural nature, at a time when nature was not much regarded by English Poets; for in point of time her earlier writings preceded, I believe, those of Cowper and Burns.

Thus by 1833 Smith has become a footnote to Wordsworth's own compositions, but in associating her with Cowper and Burns, whose texts he read, along with Smith's, as a schoolboy, he embeds her formative influence subtextually, despite his offhand tone.[10]

That Wordsworth, nearly twenty-five years after Smith's death, pulls from her posthumous 1807 volume *Beachy Head: with Other Poems* both the form and style of "Saint Monica," however, attests to her continued textual presence in his poetic life.[11] Although unremarked by Dorothy, this suggests another instance of *interleaving*, of a weaving of poetics that, in this case, draws from Smith. It also hints that by the 1830s Wordsworth understands not merely the place Smith takes in his own poetics, but her standing, however unheralded, within "English verse." His statement is often taken to indicate the centrality of Smith's oeuvre to the development of his: that in it, he acknowledges, however obliquely, his own obligations even as he also consigns them, and her, to a forgotten past. While Wordsworth's phrasing "English verse," however, is often read as code for "my verse," it also suggests that for Wordsworth, the state of British poetry itself, as it currently stood in 1833, was indebted to Smith as an originary voice – a parent, a creator, an authority. Further, because "English verse," for Wordsworth, would mean poetry *like* his (a more nuanced version of "my verse"), then his judgment becomes even more meaningful. Wordsworth assigns explicitly to Smith, and implicitly to himself, the responsibility for shaping "English verse" into its contemporary form, that which by the twentieth century was understood as *Wordsworthian* Romanticism. As this book will show, however, this formulation is only half the story. The real interest lies not in how a form of poetics was derived from the evaluations that Wordsworth and his readers and critics attached to his work, but rather in how that poetics developed from a continual cross-reading between Smith and Wordsworth and the enriched writing that resulted.

For that reason this book is deeply interested in the construct "Romanticism," specifically the Wordsworthian version: what it means, how we read and define it, where it has come from. This

Nature-, memory-, and self-based form owes as much to readerly interpretation as it does to an intangible spirit of the age, with one of the main readers being Wordsworth himself. His Fenwick notes, for instance, tend to be received as allowing unmediated access to Wordsworth's poetic process. While this may be true of his very late work, it seems less convincing that reminiscences in the 1840s can give direct access to the imaginative processes of the 1790s and early 1800s. They do show, however, part of the process by which a certain understanding of Wordsworth's/English verse became commodified as the nineteenth century progressed. A key component of the poetry of the Romantic period comes to be defined through the exemplary figure of Wordsworth, who has himself been written into being as much as he has been read. The "Wordsworthian," however, has been based on an understanding of Wordsworth's aesthetics and poetics that lacks recognition of his great affinities with Smith.[12] This book aims to establish how much of the Wordsworthian develops from the Smithian, but it is not a simple influence study. As the chapters demonstrate, these two poets actively read each other, and, although the chain begins with Smith as the elder writer, from the 1790s onwards there are key moments of the meeting of poetic minds and texts. The complex interfusion that begins as Wordsworth absorbs Smith through the sonnets continues as a cross-fertilization. As this book contends, Wordsworth becomes the poet we read most frequently – that is, the poet of the Arnoldian, Levinsonian "great period" – through his reading of Smith. Smith, for her part, matures and develops through her reading of Wordsworth. The two of them cultivate and innovate the ideas that underpin "Wordsworthian Romanticism" in the burst of creative co-writing that gets underway in the mid-1790s until Smith's death in 1806, an endpoint marked by the publication of *Beachy Head: with Other Poems* and *Poems, in Two Volumes* in 1807. The Romanticism that is written by Smith and Wordsworth shows their creative writing partnership to be the most fertile within the period, but the difficulty in fully seeing this is a legacy of critical and other readerly assumptions and constructions about what they do. *How* they are read, and the conclusions we draw from this, in many ways reflects a critical indebtedness to nineteenth-century reconstructions of Romanticism. It will not be the task of this book entirely to debunk such reconstructions, since the emphasis on the centrality of, for instance, personal memory as a catalyst for poetry draws directly from the texts. However, an important aspect of the argument that follows is that the Victorian value placed on the integrity and sincerity of the poet arose from misreading, misprision, and that this is due not merely to a misunderstanding of Romantic irony, but to a misinterpretation of the techniques essayed by Wordsworth in conjunction with Smith.[13] This becomes visible not only by returning to the texts, but by returning to the double act that wrote the textbook.

What Is Romanticism? Moreover, Who Are Smith and Wordsworth?

There is no simple answer to the first question. When Rene Wellek and A. O. Lovejoy took it up, their thoughtful descriptions functioned just as much to give other critics definitions to work against as within. Romanticism becomes itself through comparisons with not-Romanticism. L. J. Swingle worked through this in 1978, defining "Romanticism" through defining it as a problem of definition (that is, Romanticism is itself because it is not the Enlightenment). Swingle follows Morse Peckham in focusing on the problems that arise if Romanticism is only ever *not* what went before, although in seeing this as an obstacle Swingle nonetheless finds it difficult to evade: "Romanticism's problem is an eighteenth-century proliferation of systems and, following from that, a multiplication of seemingly viable but conflicting alternatives."[14] In inheriting an over-abundance of eighteenth-century systems of thought and philosophy, "Romanticism" found itself under the necessity of distilling and identifying the most effective aspects of its legacy. Thus, the "Romantic emergence" is that of a number of mutually unaware systems, each operating independently as "best" and oblivious to those around it. This more or less re-inscribes a reactive Romanticism; hence Wordsworth writes *Lyrical Ballads* against the forceful flow of stilted Enlightenment artifice (although Swingle's argument is not as crude as this). The strength of Swingle's approach is that it destabilizes certainties, but in the end it comes back to a "thing" Romanticism does: "the inclination of Romanticism is to rise beyond enticing solutions and to occupy spaces wherein the persistence of alternatives seems to offer promise of the soul's freedom" (p. 283). The reference to the soul's freedom reifies a need for Romanticism to be a pure form, a conduit to absolutes, to Truths.

This is the kind of Romanticism that arises from mystical, or perhaps mystified, readings of Wordsworth. This Wordsworth is the "true artis[t who] work[s] alone," the "king-poet of our times," as Elizabeth Barrett referred to him in 1841.[15] He is the poet-prophet, the poet-philosopher, the poet of Nature, the poet of social reform. He is the poet of childhood, validating its special essence; he is a priest of Nature; he is a "Poet-priest" (another label of Barrett's); he is morally elevated, alert to the beauties of landscape (indeed, creating them), an icon of simplicity; he is a Poet-philosopher, an icon of complexity. He fulfills expectations and also disappoints them; thus Carlyle moves from anticipation to anti-climax, noting repeatedly to various correspondents his sense that Wordsworth did not live up to his own poetry. He is "natural" and akin to streams and mountains, and sincere with flashes of insight, but in the end diminished by his own self-regard and egoism, "a genuine kind of man, but intrinsically and extrinsically a *small* one," an "*earth*-born *well*" but "astonishingly *diluted*."[16] Carlyle's reaction is important not so much for what he says as for how many times he says it, to himself and to others. His tone shifts from scorn to humor, but what emerges is an incredulity, that the poet who by the 1830s had become a national institution and treasure could be so, well, unsatisfying. Whether king and prophet or small, thin, and prolix, before his death Wordsworth had become a touchpoint for a style of writing that soon became academically codified, and in which he participated through his conversations with Isabella Fenwick. The poet and prophet of Nature won out: he was more convenient to maintain after Wordsworth's death, when admirers no longer found themselves having to reconcile grandeur with humanity. And this codified figure subsequently informs attempts to codify a major form of Romanticism, even as the construction of Romanticism involves the (re)construction of Wordsworth. As Zachary Leader has charted, for instance, editions of Wordsworth reflect specific ideas of who he was and specific interventions in how he desired to be seen and read.[17] To this may be added Wordsworth's centrality when critical understandings of the writing of the period develop: hence he is central to New Criticism, New Historicism, New Formalism, and so on.[18]

The conflation of Wordsworth and Romanticism, however, tends to overstate and understate both. Although the older Wordsworth heartily desires to represent his younger self as coterminous, and although his Victorian and later readers also frequently "confound ... present feelings with the past," the poet-in-training of the 1790s writes from a different space even than that of 1802.[19] And yet, his position as "the inevitable poet for anyone concerned with Romanticism" continues to authenticate the sense that "Wordsworth" *is* Romanticism and the other Romanticisms are adjuncts, specific forms derived from, say, Blake or Byron.[20] As Alan Richardson notes, the statement "'Wordsworth cannot properly be considered a Romantic poet'" operates entirely differently to "'Blake cannot properly be considered a Romantic poet'":

> [The second] sentence ... begin[s] an argument about Blake – and arguments that Blake seems eccentric in relation to British Romanticism

> have often been made, even at the height of his reputation as a "Romantic" poet. The [first] sentence, however, will be taken as leading to an argument deconstructing the category of Romanticism altogether: if Wordsworth can't be considered a Romantic poet, who can?[21]

So that even as critical understandings of the role of nineteenth- and twentieth-century literary culture gain greater nuance, the conclusion that Wordsworth contains Romanticism, and vice versa, maintains itself. And from here, critical shorthand that confounds the early and later Wordsworth and that reads the (relative) present into the past creates a poet and a style that begin with some kind of revolutionary break and end with the most recent text on Wordsworth and Romanticism.

Where is Smith in all this? Mainly, she is operating in a separate critical space, one populated predominantly by female and other "minor" writers. As Wordsworth is being canonized in the nineteenth century, something rather different, although equally culturally imposed, applies to Smith. The sharp change in gender dynamics that accompanies the move from "Romantic" to "Victorian" has not yet been fully charted, but one effect is a more thoroughly applied, and culturally enforced, identification of the female writer as a *female* writer. Throughout her life, Smith was well aware of the limitations her sex imposed, particularly regarding such public activities as her frequent interactions with lawyers, trustees, and publishers, and she referred often to her maternal worries and anxieties. Unlike some of her contemporaries, however (Mary Robinson would be an example), she avoided troping her femininity within her poetry; as I have shown previously, her play with gender roles means that the identity, and hence the gendering, of a sonnet's speaker is frequently fluid, and this obtains throughout her oeuvre. Smith clearly saw herself as a writer who was a woman, rather than a "woman writer"; although she occasionally used the term "authoress" regarding her novel-writing, "poetess" was anathema. First and foremost, she was a poet, and she regarded her poetry as the expression of her highest ambitions as a writer.[22] Smith joined other writers of her period, notably Mary Wollstonecraft, in querying the cultural conclusion that women were rendered other, irrational, lesser by virtue of their sex, and she expected those around her to respect her autonomy as an adult, rational being. To some extent, in the 1780s and 1790s and early nineteenth century, this was possible; but as Louise Duckling has shown, almost as soon as Smith died she began to be repositioned as foremost a woman, secondarily a writer. Duckling surveys the major anthologies of writing women that appeared in Britain and America in the nineteenth century and finds that Smith is represented either as an "idealized specimen of womanly excellence, a suffering paragon of a wife, gentlewoman and 'mother-martyr,'" or as a woman with an unfortunate habit of tainting her otherwise exemplary poems and novels of sensibility with unseemly political opinions and too-open expressions of bad temper, disappointment, and disdain for her husband.[23] Either identity strips her of any claim to be remembered as a *poet*, although each could, and did, justify transmitting her biography as a kind of female cautionary tale.

Even, then, as Wordsworth was being constructed by his nineteenth-century readers, whether admiringly or not, as a poet-priest and an avatar of Nature, Smith was being rewritten as exactly the poetess she would have decried. And as this was happening, the burgeoning culture of literary studies consistently undervalued her achievements, or else re-assigned them elsewhere. Hence, by the 1830s Wordsworth is hailed as the master of the modern sonnet by R. F. Housman in *A Collection of English Sonnets*, who lauds his attention to generic convention, while the general representation of Smith's work as "embodying" the "quality" of the woman ensured its increasing association with a biography that, by mid-century, had solidified into cliché (Duckling, pp. 205, 207). For a century interested in "the exultation that was associated with the poetry of the Victorian poet-prophet, William Wordsworth," the poetry of such a woman could only be, at best, a curiosity (Duckling, p. 214). By the early twentieth century, when the Viscount St. Cyres noted disapprovingly Smith's "irresponsible treason," he colors it in comprehensively gendered terms: "miracles of feminine logic" "loudly asserted" by a "Charlotte [who] took a very high line."[24] The story of her transformation from poet to poetess to silly is not confined to Smith, of course; it is the main plot that affects nearly every female writer and was the first obstacle to be met by feminist critics. Thus it took more than twenty years for a newly recovered Smith to move from "minor" poetess (as in Hunt's explication) to "the first poet in England whom in retrospect we would call Romantic," and another decade before her work was comprehensively available across her many genres.[25] What has not yet been undertaken, however, is detailed critical scrutiny of her work fully within her field of Romantic-period poetry, rather than women's writing; the "English verse" that Wordsworth referenced. To be more specific, the verse and poetics critically assigned to and associated with Wordsworth since the nineteenth century must now be understood within a corpus that not only includes Smith, but acknowledges both her formative position on Wordsworth and on "Wordsworthian" Romanticism, and the complex of imaginative interaction that weaves their work together.[26]

Writing in 1784 and 1793

Christopher Nagle relates that the young Wordsworth "takes the liberty of editing her published work" when he revises some lines of Smith's Sonnet XLIV: "Written in the Church-Yard at Middleton in Sussex" in his copy of the fifth edition of *Elegiac Sonnets* (1789) (pp. 51–4). From very early on, there is evidence that the two writers read and revised each other. As already noted, Wordsworth's first published poem was a sonnet in the Smith mold, appearing in the periodical she most favored, the *European Magazine*. Her own first publications were in this forum: Sonnets I, II, V, VII, and XI appeared, most under the pseudonym "S.C.," in September, October, and December 1782.[27] When *Elegiac Sonnets* appeared in 1784, they immediately caught the interest of the reading public, including that of a boy at school in the northwest of England, and although his schoolmaster's gift of Burns and Cowper proved to be formative as well, it is Smith whose work lasts in Wordsworth's imagination. Charles Ryskamp, perhaps unsurprisingly given the period in which he writes (1965), asserts that Wordsworth "felt that Cowper and Burns were the two 'great' authors who helped him"; Smith is not visible to Ryskamp as "great," although the emphasis placed on the word suggests the presence of the "not-great" as well.[28] Smith's sonnets begin one of the great Romantic projects, that of "stag[ing] a Romantic persona for whom loss and recovery and diffusion are the rhetorical work at hand and the labor of poetic speech" (Kelley, p. 285); they also, in the forty-eight sonnets and other poems that make up the fifth edition to which Wordsworth subscribed, explore the imagery of sound, place, and affect, and the creation of modes of poetical transport that provide a tone and a vocabulary for Wordsworth in 1793.

Descriptive Sketches and *An Evening Walk* do not attract much of the attention of Wordsworth scholars. One recent exception is Christopher Miller's *The Invention of Evening: Perception and Time in Romantic Poetry*, which in passing notes that "Tintern Abbey" is "a poem of sentimental return reminiscent of pilgrimage-sonnets by William Lisle Bowles and Charlotte Smith" without "their pensive nocturnal atmospherics."[29] He turns to *An Evening Walk* as the precursor to "Tintern Abbey": "together, these poems form a chiasmus of separation and reunion" (p. 84). Despite her similar poetics, Smith is laid to one side, and picked up again as the chorus to Keats' "Ode to a Nightingale" (she "wrote several nightingale poems," p. 157). For Miller, evening enables Fancy: "seeing in the dark" (p. 85). *An Evening Walk*, however, provides a telling example of Wordsworth, and his readers and critics, first noting, then removing, Smith from the frame. The poem contains a number of verbal echoes of Smith, two of which have come into and out of focus since publication. Line 19 appeared in 1793 with quotation marks around the phrase "a happy child," which draws on Sonnet V: "To the South Downs" ("Oh! hills belov'd – where once a happy child ..." [l.1]). By 1849, Wordsworth has eliminated the quotation marks, though not the quotation, which is not re-ascribed to Smith until F. W. Bateson does so in 1954. Then, in l. 55 the poem describes "shades of deep embattl'd clouds with lights between." In 1977, John O. Hayden in *William Wordsworth: The Poems, Volume One* noted that "deep embattl'd clouds" is quoted from Smith's Sonnet LIX: "Written September 1791"; unlike "a happy child," Wordsworth did not allude to his quotation in *An Evening Walk*, and the 1984 Cornell edition of *An Evening Walk* assigns the phrase to James Beattie's *The Minstrel*, even though in that poem we find only "embattled clouds" (*EW*, p. 34).[30] In 1793, then, Wordsworth makes semi-public his debt to Smith for one phrase, and obscures another; near the end of his life he eliminates evidence of the debt; by the second half of the twentieth century the debt is partially restored.

Interestingly, although Sonnet LIX is dated 1791, it does not appear in *Elegiac Sonnets* until the seventh edition of 1795. Does Smith, then, owe the phrase to Wordsworth? Does she perform the complicated maneuver of disguising her debt by dating her poem to before *An Evening Walk*? At this point the strangely extensive visit Wordsworth paid to Smith in November 1791 comes to mind, and along with it Nagle's observation that Wordsworth's copy of the 1789 *Elegiac Sonnets* "includes additional sonnets not published in the volume, apparently inscribed by Wordsworth on the back endpapers" (p. 176, n. 26). Wu confirms that Sonnets XLIX and LI, both originally found in Smith's 1791 novel *Celestina*, are those to which Nagle refers.[31] Did Smith show these newest poems to her visitor, including the one with its memorably amended line from Beattie? That both independently sought inspiration in Beattie is an unlikely coincidence, and yet the Cornell elision of Smith is also misleading, as is the lack of comment by Haydon on the publication dates.[32] A close look at *An Evening Walk* in fact reveals other allusions that have, so far, gone unnoticed: line 148's "viewless plank," which evokes Sonnet XXXIX: "To Night. From [the novel of Emmeline]" ("viewless wind," l. 8). Or line 218's use of "mantling," which recalls Sonnet XXX: "To the River Arun" ("mantling bindwith," l. 6). Or the "sportive chase" of line 347, which calls to mind Sonnet XLVII: "To Fancy," with its "sportive pencil" (l. 2). Things are even more intriguing if one examines the unpublished 1794 version of *An Evening Walk*, which, much like Smith's 1793 *The Emigrants*, "explores social, ethical, and religious issues" (*EW*, p. 13). Here, the allusions seem to go the other way: hence, in one short section Wordsworth mentions "infant Zephyrs" (l. 395) and "low-muttering" "shapes of Solitude and Death" (ll. 406, 407). In Sonnet LXXVIII: "Snowdrops," Smith describes the "infant Zephyr's wing" (l. 2), and in "A Descriptive Ode" "storms" are "low-muttering" (l. 11); both of these poems appear in Volume II of *Elegiac Sonnets*, first published in 1797.[33] Finally, Smith uses the phrase "shagg'd with woods" in Book II of *The Emigrants* (1793), just as Wordsworth describes a bridge "half-shagg'd with ivy" in the 1793 *An Evening Walk*.

Given the general silence of the historical record, not much more can be done with such echoes and allusions than to note them. However, they suggest that as early as 1793 Wordsworth and Smith were reading *each other* attentively, with an eye open for and an ear attuned to striking images. Even if they are both merely consulting and borrowing from common sources, this in itself hints at a communal poetic project. As compelling as the repeated overlaps of lexis is the narrative tone of *An Evening Walk*, with its "attentive and warm regard" for Nature that, says the *Gentleman's Magazine*, marks the "true poet," but that marks, as well, Smith's sonnets.[34] Equally striking are the verbal similarities between *Descriptive Sketches* and both *Elegiac Sonnets* and *The Emigrants*. Again, there are unnoted allusions: Wordsworth's "weak and more weak" (l. 396), which calls so strongly to mind Smith's "faint and more faint" (Sonnet XII, l. 13) and "loud, and more loud" ("Elegy," l. 9); his "love to stray" of l. 664, so like Sonnets IV and XLVIII ("delight to stray," l. 2, and "attempts to stray," l. 1); his "vain regret" of line 743 and her "vain regret" of Sonnets XXXIV (l. 8), XLI (l. 12), and XLVIII (l. 2). There is the general elegiac tone of much of the poem ("When the poor heart has all its joys resign'd,/ Why does their sad remembrance cleave behind?" [ll. 622–3], for instance). And again, there is a kind of read-back by Smith of a figure highly like the Shepherd of the Hill who occupies lines 506–671 of "Beachy Head": "The maidens eye him with an enquiring glance,/ Much wondering what sad stroke of crazing Care/ Or desperate Love could lead a wanderer there" (*EW*, ll. 42–4), which morphs into "village maidens thought/ His senses injur'd; and with pity say/ That he, poor youth! must have been cross'd in love" ("Beachy Head," ll.

519–21). And finally, there is an overlap of thematics and imagery between *Descriptive Sketches* and *The Emigrants* that suggests a common project: the mother who succumbs to the elements with her baby and falls prey to wolves in Book II of *The Emigrants* (ll. 254–91), and the gypsy mother whose baby's "small cry" entices "the famish'd wolf" (*DS*, ll. 242, 240); an embedded reference to Paine in *Descriptive Sketches* that accords with the vocabulary of "rights of man" in *The Emigrants* ("Pain's wild rebellious burst proclaims her rights aloud," *DS*, l. 653); the turn to declamation that ends both poems with mutual appeals to God, Liberty, Freedom, and Justice against Oppression and Avarice (among a host of other figures[35]).

These early Wordsworth poems engage in Smithian ways with Nature and politics as well as constructions of self and other. They participate in the kind of socially progressive conversation that distinguishes the late eighteenth century, especially that current before the repressive moves of the mid-1790s. But these poems also combine with Smith's in their concern with "the vexed question of language, the symbol, and materiality."[36] The poems of 1784 and leading up to 1793 contain in embryo a joint poetic project that will do more to create and establish the parameters of the most familiar of Romanticisms than any single poet or other, more physically evident partnership achieved. What happens after 1793, and as a result of the poetry that both wrote in and before 1793, shapes succeeding understandings of poetic possibilities. To view this development as "Wordsworthian" reflects a cultural myopia that is only recently clarifying, and then only in fits and starts, within literary studies. What Smith and Wordsworth write in the first ten years of the period this book discusses creates the incipient shape of "Romanticism."

Methods, Modes, Models

The Romanticism with which this book engages is one specific kind: that which has been labeled Wordsworthian. Hence, this book also meets up with the tradition of naming and constructing an ineffable something with, nonetheless, an identifiable structure. It is my contention that "Wordsworthian Romanticism" elides 1) the centrality of Smith to the formation of Wordsworth's poetics; 2) the necessity of recognizing Smith's poetry as pursuing "Wordsworthian" thematics before Wordsworth began to, and in a productive parallel fashion once he joined in; 3) the lack of credibility of discussing this kind of Romanticism without discussing, in full and not tangentially, Smith's poetics. As the chapters in this book demonstrate, when we read the two poets together we can begin to understand how a form or mode of poetics that stood and still stands for so many later readers as a new, innovative, socially aware (even socially responsible) intervention came to be. The Romanticism that comes to be written by Smith and Wordsworth starts out, in the 1780s and 1790s, by elaborating and commenting on models that had attained a literary currency by the century's end: using poetry to express and contain emotional states, demonstrating a perfect grasp of form, finding one's place within a community of writers. Their Romanticism, however, also talks back to these traditions, and writes into being a curiosity about what, and how, poetry can mean that resonates throughout their period of co-writing. Emphasizing the experimental nature of Romantic writing is not new, and Wordsworth has consistently been read as a major innovator, but as this book argues, the Romanticism undertaken by Smith and her contemporary is not only experimental, it uses novelty and the (re)consideration of poetic possibilities as its basis. This is expressed in a number of ways: through actual poetic innovation (that is, experiments with form and content), through a productive suspicion about the nature of poetry and of the Poet, through a scrutiny of poetic ideals, through a kind of play with roles and approaches. Some of this play hardens for later readers into evidence of a poetic certainty about speaker and mimesis, and here I am thinking of readerly efforts to interpret figuration as autobiography: Smith's sonnets uncover states of being female, or Wordsworth's lyrical ballads voice his *direct* concern with the plight of the rural poor. While these stances underpin some of the poems, they are nonetheless stances, two among many. The poets explore how sincerity *cannot* be written, in other words, just as much as they write (of) themselves. However, experiments sometimes escape the control of their dreamers, and in this case the conviction of authenticity over-writes the poems' internal conflicts. What strikes the reader who reads Smith and Wordsworth together is their common interest in presenting such an approach, as it were, philosophically: something to question, something to pursue and try to understand, not necessarily something to endorse.

From the start of his career as a poet, Wordsworth recognizes the utility of experiment. From her first publications, Smith demonstrates her understanding that powerful poetry results when the poet "strays." Wordsworth's early reading of Smith showed him what could be done, and how to do it, and from the moment their mutual reading began, in the early 1790s, they function as co-inventors with specific interests in form and its reforms, place, persona and voice, and the poetry of event.

The two are exemplars, innovators, teachers, and originators, and, as this book shows, between 1793 and 1807 they create a poetics as a joint project, if only virtually so. Experimentation is threaded throughout their works to 1807, with specific points of convergence that enable the establishment of Romanticism.[37] However, as this book contends, it is also necessary to rewrite, or reconceive, critical understandings of that Romanticism that have been predicated on only half the story, have read only half the writing. Reconstituting the pair not only renders their co-writing newly visible, but illuminates aspects of Wordsworth's initial poetic development, and both poets' subsequent creative movements, that have been overlooked. The two poets inaugurate a kind of poetry that we call Romantic, but they also write against a set of critical assumptions that have built up around the cultural figure of "Wordsworth" and "his" Romanticism. Paul Keen observes that Wordsworth "mimics the language of Enlightenment reform in order to legitimize his own, very different emphasis on the social role of literature as poetry, and what is inseparable from that, on the status of the author as poet"; he "inverts rather than rejects the dominant literary preoccupations of his day."[38] He learns how to do this from reading Smith; moreover he, and Smith, not only invert, they revert, convert, and otherwise remold such preoccupations, in the process laying the groundwork for the new ones that have preoccupied, separately, their critics. It is the aim of this book to bring them together, productively.

In discussing how Smith and Wordsworth write Romanticism, I have had to select aspects of what is, even in its Wordsworthian form, a baggy monster. I have opted to focus on their shared, fruitful interest in and forwarding of the rewards, and the distractions, of experimentation. Experimentation does not always produce the expected results, and in some of the discussion in this book I explore what happens when things go awry. But for the most part I posit that both poets maintained a control over their methods, and a constructive insight about the possibilities even of failure. I see them as active poets, not in thrall to their poetics but rather deeply interested and invested in the potentialities of poetry. This extends to an interest in the figure of the poet as a Figure: pulling author away from speaker as an aspect of their experimentation. Their poetry nonetheless galvanizes the appeal of the personalized speaker, which becomes attractive for many poets of the period (Coleridge, Robinson; later, Shelley, Landon) and which develops, in the later nineteenth century, into the Victorian fascination with poetical narrators, and later still provides a focal point for criticism. I do not reject readings of Wordsworth's ethical frustrations of the

1790s, for instance, nor do I seek to overturn analyses of Smith's proto-feminism (indeed, I have made some of these latter arguments myself). And it would be foolish to argue that Smith and Wordsworth only write as a double act, and that studying them as individuals somehow yields worthless results. I contend, however, that reading them in tandem uncovers a vital underpinning to Romanticism, that they are equally central to the formation of Romanticism, and that their contributions are shaped and influenced by their reading of each other's work. Theirs is a cross-fertilization even more rich than the more familiar pairing of Wordsworth with Coleridge. The Wordsworth/Coleridge relationship was fueled by rivalries, spoken and unspoken; the Smith/Wordsworth concatenation shows a continuing meeting of minds and imaginations, from which "English verse" flowered.

Chapters concentrate on exploring how Smith and Wordsworth write into Romanticism some of its familiar aspects (place, the subjectivity of the Poet, political or historical disturbances, for instance), troubling them on the way; they re-situate the agenda of progressive poetic development (the when and how of the lyrical ballad, for instance); they suggest new approaches that arise specifically from re-orienting Romanticism toward their partnership (the vital year of 1807, for instance). Chapter 1 discusses how the two poets engage with the rules of poetry in order to bend, tweak, or reject them. It explores the development of an exemplary Romantic poetic form, the lyrical ballad, and shows the centrality of self-reflexivity to this experimental process. Beginning with the premise that the hybrid nature of Smith's elegiac sonnet presages the formal experiment of the lyrical ballad, the chapter also discusses Smith's poems from the early 1790s that bear a strong resemblance to the poems composed by Wordsworth for the 1798 *Lyrical Ballads*. Finally, it situates the *Lyrical Ballads* as a key text for Smith's subsequent poetic developments. Chapter 2 turns to poems on war and deprivation that characterize Smith's and Wordsworth's output in the mid-1790s. By grappling with their complex presentations of suffering and the moves such poetry makes to understand or mediate suffering through poetic devices, I show one of the failures their poetry sustains: the mismatch between emblematicizing artifice and what might be read as the poeticizing of real events. The meanings and value of transcendence and symbolism become especially important.

Chapter 3 reads Smith's and Wordsworth's presentations of place and space through their poeticizing of the mechanics of poetry-making and of the dangers of solipsistic solitude. The poets' geographically specific poems – those with dates and places in titles – act as innovations on the Enlightenment convention of the loco-descriptive poem. Exploring in particular the resonances of the "written" and the "composed" as well as the complexity of solitude, the chapter proposes a poetics of spatial and compositional geographies, where not only the poet's locale matters, but also who the poet purports to be. Chapter 4 considers the poets' use of autobiographical feints to explore anew the concept of Romantic egoism. Both Wordsworth and Smith have attracted especial attention as self-centered egoists, and this chapter reads their presentations of pseudo-autobiography as the model for the Victorian dramatic monologue, on the one hand, and explores their troping of sincerity and authenticity, on the other. For both poets, critiques of a seamless Poet-persona overly reliant on visions and versions of selfhood are embedded in poetic form. Finally, Chapter 5 closes the experimental circle. Reading *Beachy Head: with Other Poems* and *Poems, in Two Volumes* specifically as collected miscellanies or compendiums of display, and focusing on the scientific poetics this enables, the chapter suggests that the result of the experimental hybridizing of the 1790s is, at least in part, the rule-setting of 1807.

Stuart Curran has noted that Smith's *The Emigrants* "point[s] directly toward the achievement that Wordsworth will shortly wrest from making himself the eyes and ears of an interiorized natural scene."[39] As this book shows, however, the achievement is an outcome of a shared poetic project, and the pointing goes both ways. Even as Wordsworth is indebted to Smith, so too Smith is indebted to Wordsworth. And Romanticism itself, as invested in explorations of selfhood, subjectivity, and solipsism; memory, childhood, and history; landscape, nature, and pantheism; composition, innovation, and experiment, owes its disposition to the Smith/Wordsworth complex.

1
Writing the Lyrical Ballad: Hybridity and Self-Reflexity

The proposal that the Romantic period sees experimentation across genres and cultures is not a new one. The common tale of social upheaval resulting from the French Revolution and literary upheaval following the publication of *Lyrical Ballads* is fundamental to the critical understanding of the period, even if 1798 is no longer fully accepted as the "start date." Wordsworth has always been central to this formulation: "Wordsworth in his early years was drawn into paths of speculation and experiment," says David Bromwich in his justly celebrated study of the poetry of the 1790s.[1] For Bromwich, the experimentation was social and philosophical, centered on enduring questions about the interrelationships between authority, oppression, and cultural ownership. Crucially, "personal identity" is both expressive through poetry and "coherent and irreducible by analysis," and Wordsworth's experimental impulse lay in finding and working through a variety of "images of Wordsworth" (pp. x, 43). This reading chimes with the contemporary understanding, within natural history, that forms – whether species, classes, orders, or other words denoting coherent groups – were themselves "coherent and irreducible." Once discovered, they were known; and once known, they were fixed. From at least the middle of the eighteenth century onward, naturalists, following Carolus Linnaeus and Georges Louis Leclerc, comte de Buffon, concentrated on finding difference and instituting order. Although Linnaeus and de Buffon diverged, with Linnaeus concentrating on "morphological differences" while de Buffon favored a more comprehensive understanding of interrelated aspects of being, their approaches required an acceptance of a neat and distinct web, rather than chain, of being.[2] The Wordsworth who may subdivide self-images but who maintains a self-focus functions as his own species, his poems as branches from the main stem of being.

This kind of experimentation operates in the service of establishing the knowable, understanding the world and its natures. In the 1780s and 1790s, as Melissa Bailes shows, this understanding "of fixed biological forms ... tended to see newness as divisible into two categories: those of originality and hybridity" (p. 106). Bailes focuses on Anna Seward's need to follow an "order of poetics" that, like the orders of natural history, led to fixed and irreducible forms of poetry; from this, in turn, Seward believed she could discern the poet, as long as she or he observed hierarchies and conformed to *unmixed* style. As this chapter will suggest, poetic hierarchies and insistence on definable styles and definitions were prevalent in the period. Coexisting with Linnaeus and de Buffon, John Newbery and Hugh Blair (for example) constructed poetic history, dividing poetry into fixed forms and assigning status to each, avoiding the chaos of unmoored structure: "that which does not fit" (Bailes, p. 114). As Bailes makes clear, the analogous natures of natural and poetic history enable their overlap; hence, as "natural historians stressed the discovery of new forms," so too poets could develop new classes, as long as they were "legitimate," unmixed, composed of themselves only, *original* in the sense of originary. The real problem was hybridity: Seward hated, for instance, what she saw as Charlotte Smith's monstrous mixings of sources into mishmash verse, "unclassifiable" plagiarisms (Bailes, p. 121 *passim*).

The allusions and quotations that Smith incorporates in her *Elegiac Sonnets*, however, act more like splices, and this process does not result in hybrids so much as coupled forms. The spliced parts will never cohere into a new species; they will simply grow together, although distinctly. Seward was perceptive nonetheless in her understanding that Smith somehow violated an order of poetics, since *Elegiac Sonnets*, as this chapter will discuss, instituted a new possibility for poetry: that in engaging with the rules of poetry, the poet may also bend, tweak, or reject them altogether. This is more than a mere intellectual exercise; as Bromwich argues, Wordsworth's 1790s poetry pursues images of the poet – or rather, *a* poet, a figure who writes poetry visibly, for whom composition becomes part of the point of the poem. The Wordsworth who "discovers" the lyrical ballad in fact participates in a joint endeavor with another investigator of poetry, the Smith who discovers the elegiac sonnet. For both, experimentation with the shape and form of poetry, putting together different, and differing, parts to form new and unusual wholes, results in what for some are the poetic equivalent of monstrosities: the "hackneyed scraps of dismality" that so offend Seward, the "worthles[s] ... design" that belies "excellen[t] ... execution" in

Southey's equivocal phrase.[3] Nevertheless, readerly attention is drawn *to* the poems, because as hybrids they effectively announce their own creativity, their enacting of process.[4] This is, of course, one of the hallmarks of Romantic poetry: self-reflexivity.

Smith and Wordsworth, for whom the raw material is words and form, use their poetry to converse, figuratively, with extant methods and conclusions. Their starting point is the fixed order of poetics, with its knowable divisions and rules. Their conclusions arise from the activity of writing, since what they write illustrates both their method and their outcomes. They use the language of experiment, which is also the language of philosophical inquiry. As this chapter will show, the result is a form of poem that perpetually escapes classification even as it invites definition: the lyrical ballad, something that first emerges in nascent form in 1791. Hybridity, as this chapter will suggest, allows Smith and Wordsworth to demonstrate the viability, and the necessity, of poetic experimentation.

When, in 1798, the anonymous author of the new volume of poems, *Lyrical Ballads*, expressed his conviction that "Poetry" is "a word of very disputed meaning," he offered his volume as a means by which the question may be further pursued. Readers

> should ask themselves if [the book] contains a natural delineation of human passions, human characters, and human incidents; and if the answer be favorable ... they should consent to be pleased in spite of that most dreadful enemy to our pleasures, our own pre-established codes of decision.
>
> Readers of superior judgment may disapprove of the style in which many of these pieces are executed ... It is apprehended, that the more conversant the reader is with our elder writers, and with those in modern times who have been most successful in painting manners and passions, the fewer complaints of this kind will he have to make.
>
> An accurate taste in poetry ... is an acquired talent, which can only be produced by severe thought, and a long continued intercourse with the best models of composition ... [I]f poetry be a subject on which much time has not been bestowed, the judgement may be erroneous, and ... in many cases it necessarily will be so. (*LB*, p. 739)

I have quoted this at length because to do so shows how, after we move past the initial assertion that the poems within the volume "are to be considered as experiments," it is remarkable, although often unremarked, how the majority of the Advertisement argues not for the novelty of the poems to come, but for their conformity to the best habits of "elder writers." The nameless Author wants to be read by those who know what constitutes the poetic, as established and recognized by tradition and talent; rather than needing readers to re-educate themselves before they can appreciate the poems now before them, he asks merely that they *educate* themselves, that they be prepared for poetry as it is meant to be. And this in turn suggests that when he notes the "disputed" nature of the meaning of Poetry, he does not refer to a lack of agreement among authorities, but rather points merely to the existence of *disputations* on the subject. Such debates underpin his own efforts, with the Advertisement functioning as a concise *disputatio* of its own. The Author seeks to bring out the truth about Poetry via his efforts, which are only experiments in the academic sense; that is, they are tests of his own theory of Poetry, itself based on successful existing attempts at "painting manners and passions."

For Wordsworth and Samuel Taylor Coleridge, both university educated, the implications of using the language of academic rhetoric would not be lost. The Author takes the place of a Master whose expertise has been honed, in practice, through virtual disputations with other Masters, those "elder writers" and accomplished contemporaries who are named as the most likely to understand the nature of this new book of poems. "Taste," ineffable yet necessary, is not inherent but must be learned over a long period of sustained study. The *Lyrical Ballads*, then, will not appeal in an instinctive and naturalized way, but will require the appreciation of the dedicated student of Poetry, the frequent reader, and the knowledgeable authority. Looked at this way, the Advertisement does not announce the newness of its contents, but rather seeks to insert the poems into the roster of true – that is, *un*disputed – Art. The multiple references to "taste" reify the inference that *cultivated* readers will appreciate the poems' worth; those who wish to attain such levels of taste are invited to set aside their "pre-established codes of decision" and accept the tutelage the poems offer. And this, perhaps, underscores the need for the fiction of unity the Advertisement's "Author" allows; in a *disputatio* there can be only one Master, who constructs the dialectic necessary to enlighten his students. The theoretical question (*quaestio*) that emerges in the later, openly authored *Preface* – "What is a Poet?" – is here embedded in the Advertisement's selling point: "what is a Poem?" The debate ensues as the poems progress. The Author can thus "hope for readers only among the few, who, to sensibility of heart, join simplicity of taste"[5] – those fit though few who have either already "severe[ly] thought," or are prepared to do so.

Lyrical Ballads, with a Few Other Poems thus joins a debate rather than initiating one. Moreover, it is rather belated; the question of what constitutes a poem was key to the eighteenth century. It is one reason why Charlotte Smith, publishing fourteen years earlier, opens her collection with its own dispute:

> The little Poems which are here called Sonnets have, I believe, no very just claim to the title; but they consist of fourteen lines, and appear to me no very improper vehicle for a single Sentiment. I am told, and I read it as the opinion of very good judges, that the legitimate Sonnet is ill calculated for our language. (*Poetry*, p. 10)

Following at least one Master, Samuel Johnson ("it is not very suitable to the English language"), Smith implies her *quaestio* when she declines to accept wholeheartedly what she is told and what she has read, and when she begins her internal discussion about the nature of her "little Poems" with "what are herein contained?" "What is a Poem?" In rhetorical terms, it is significant that in the Preface to the Third and Fourth Editions, she writes, "I have attempted [a few poems] on the Italian model; with what success I know not; but I am *persuaded* that, to the generality of readers, those which are less regular will be more pleasing" (*Poetry*, p. 11). The desired end of a *disputatio* is to persuade; further, having acknowledged an existing dispute about the suitability of English to the "legitimate" sonnet, she now introduces the "less regular" to her readers. For, like the Author of the *Lyrical Ballads* after her, she depends on the existence of readers for the continuance of the debate: a Master requires students as well as peers. And since, unlike a "lyrical ballad," there is little confusion over what a "sonnet" *is*, Smith's Preface suggests that she is thinking past the simplicities of genre to the intricacies of Art. Indeed, as Daniel Robinson has made plain, this is exactly the implication of Smith's original title: *Elegiac Sonnets, and Other Essays*; "essays" implies experiments, which here extends to the new category of the "elegiac sonnet."[6] So, like the *Lyrical Ballads'* Author after her, Smith's poems serve to test their own validity: they are the constituent parts of the dialectic *disputatio* begun in their respective prefaces.

Both Smith and Wordsworth seem alert to the historical nature of the debate they enter. Both use their collections to explore the nature of the poetic and use their poetry to push the boundaries of genre and style. For both, the questions that occupy their Master-personas are the same that concern earlier theorists of the "art of poetry" such as John Newbery and Hugh Blair. Although Blair's probable influence on Wordsworth has been noted,[7] Newbery's has not; and neither has been suggested as at all prominent in Smith's development. However, this has more to do with the dominant strain of Smith studies, which sees her as, primarily, a woman writer reacting to and critical of masculine culture. As I suggest in my Introduction, this view of Smith makes it harder to situate her as a philosophical writer and poet functioning *within* her literary culture. At any rate, it is instructive to return to Newbery and Blair, since each asks the same question that occupies Smith and Wordsworth in their "experimental" volumes: What is poetry? What forms a poem? For each, both the questions they pose and the forms they choose to compose in their collections interrogate – *dispute* – Poetry as well as write it.

This chapter will argue that Smith and Wordsworth engage with the history of poetry not by writing treatises – although of course by 1800 Wordsworth does that as well – but by writing poetry, that within the *Elegiac Sonnets* and *Lyrical Ballads* they put to the test hypotheses about the nature and fitness of its art. In beginning a study of this kind with the *Lyrical Ballads*, I am immediately confronted with a bulky tradition of scholarship that seeks mainly, it seems, either to prove the utter novelty of the poems or to show how, in fact, the poems neatly fit into patterns of poetic dramatic technique, popular publishing, or political endeavors. Similarly, most scholarship on the *Elegiac Sonnets* concentrates either on how they exemplify Smith's female experiences or how they ventriloquize the experiences of others.[8] Wordsworth's poetic project has received enough attention that it may seem redundant to approach it again. Nevertheless, the critical conviction persists that this project is in and of itself "Wordsworthian," that others may follow but that the pathless track to *Lyrical Ballads* is blazed by Wordsworth at some point between 1793 and the explosion of writing that began in 1797.

As I will suggest throughout this book, something happens if we bring a text like *Elegiac Sonnets* and a poet like Smith into the picture. Smith provides not simply a model to be perfected or an influence to be developed; the poetic relationship between the two is dynamic and vital rather than one-way and static. And yet, since Smith begins her *Elegiac Sonnets* in the early 1780s and begins to publish them from 1782 onward, when Wordsworth is a young adolescent, impressionable as well as, to use Duncan Wu's word, "precocious," there is, as the Introduction illustrated, an initial flowing of ideas from the South

Downs to the Lakes. Smith's practical applications of theories of poetry inform the young Wordsworth, who by the early 1790s had been exposed to increasingly developed versions of the *Elegiac Sonnets* as well as the "other essays" the volumes contained. When he begins his own dispute, one established Master has provided a model. What makes the relationship dynamic, however, is how this elder Master responds to the questions posed in 1798.

On one level, then, Smith and Wordsworth pick up on the philosophies of poetic form current to the second half of the eighteenth century. But this alone would not distinguish their writing. Beyond merely reiterating poetically what Newbery and Blair say in prose, they use form and style to develop ideas of poetry as an art. Although, as many literary historians note, the late eighteenth century saw an explosion of poetic publishing – to the despair and derision of readers and critics – overwhelmingly writers published "poems," "odes," "sonnets," "pastorals," and other generically safe works.[9] The *Lyrical Ballads* struck out on what seemed to be an entirely new line: combining two genres, the lyric and the ballad, and puzzling readers ever since about what, exactly, such an appellation meant. Smith's *Elegiac Sonnets* may be easier to define, but their introduction of a named hybridity signals one aspect of the *disputatio* her volume undertakes. The *quaestio* of what kind of poetry results is worked out within the volume itself, as it is in the *Lyrical Ballads*. If the two collections are paired, then their mutual originality is even more startling: Why should poetic forms be combined? What is the benefit of hybridity? Since both poets were writing for money as well as status, why produce poetry that risked alienating or confusing readers when straightforward *Sonnets* or *Ballads* would be so much more likely to sell?[10] And even if artistic merit is the guiding force, what enabled these two poets to recognize the possibilities that would arise once the art resident in poetry was pushed beyond the bounds ratified by time and authority?[11]

I would like first to look at two of the types of texts likely to have informed Smith's and Wordsworth's understanding of the kinds and functions of poetry defined as art, rather than doggerel, in the late eighteenth century. John Newbery's *The Art of Poetry* was published in two volumes in 1762, while Hugh Blair's collected *Lectures on Rhetoric and Belles Lettres* first appeared in 1783 and went through multiple editions by the end of the century.[12] Both texts sought to lay down the foundations of good poetry as well as to define and interrogate the different styles and genres of poetry. Both relied heavily on established masters of poetry like Milton, Pope, Thomson, and Dryden, with smatterings of less canonized names like Phillips, Smart, and Warton.[13] Both used a method that described the rules of good poetry and then followed this with examples to be emulated and those to be avoided. The detail available in each text suggests the general concern felt in the period that poetry be rescued from the bondage of poetasters and rehabilitated to its pure and essential form. For each, the need to differentiate styles and modes of poetry is paramount. Because of the complex ways in which Smith and Wordsworth respond to and develop the theories of poetry such as those put forward by Newbery and Blair, it will be illuminating to explore these two model texts in more detail.

Writing at much the same time as Newbery and Blair, Thomas Warton in *The History of English Poetry* (1774–81) noted that the proposed studies of poetry by his peers Pope and Gray was based on the "observance of arrangement; and in the place of the satisfaction which results from a clearness and a fulness of information, seemed only to substitute the merit of disposition, and the praise of contrivance." The "mechanical attendance to this distribution" Warton hoped to avoid by concentrating more on the "gradual improvements of our poetry" and, along with it, the English language. Warton's emphasis on generic and linguistic evolution highlights a key late-eighteenth-century interest in the language and diction of poetry. For Warton, his own time represented "perfection in a polished age," with poetry having reached its ultimate function of mirroring "human society ... faithfully recording the features of the times, and ... preserving the most picturesque and expressive representations of manners."[14] Emphasizing poetry's responsibility to substitute "human passions, human characters, and human incidents" for "gaud[y] and inane phraseology" ("Advertisement," *Lyrical Ballads*), Warton's Preface suggests a consensus view of which the Advertisement's is another version. Newbery, too, anchors his discussion of poetry within images of social evolution, noting the relationship between poetry's origin and early societies' wishes to record their histories in music and dance. However, he also considers the nature of the poet:

> A true poet is distinguished by a fruitfulness of invention, a lively imagination tempered by a solid judgment, a nobleness of sentiments and ideas, and a bold, lofty, and figurative manner of expression. He thoroughly understands the nature of his subject; and, let his poem be never so short, he forms a design or plan, by which every verse is directed to a certain end, and each has a just dependence on the other; for it is this produces the beauty of order and harmony, and gives satisfaction to a rational mind. (I: 7)

Newbery focuses on the thought that underlies the poetic process, and the ability to recollect ideas, images, and expressions and convey them in their most evocative form. Rationality and imagination ("invention") ally to enliven "sense ... thought ... [and] diction" (I: ii, 7). "A poetical genius is the *gift of nature*, and cannot be *acquired*," but poetry's "rules and directions" may be (I: 8). Thus Newbery distinguishes between the Poet and the Poem, suggesting that even genius requires the regulation of knowledge.

For Newbery, true poetic knowledge consists of an understanding of poetic structure, rhyme, meter (which he calls poetry's "sorts"), the necessity of "thought," the varieties of style, and the divisions of "species." "Epithets" – that is, modifiers – are to be used sparingly: "a luxuriancy of epithets tends to make the style prolix and flaccid, and robs it of ... strength and force," especially where "the passions" are concerned (I: 43, 44). The poet's intuition must be bolstered by an acquired habit of stylistic restraint and expressive control: "we would have the poet, like a good architect, distinguish ornament from strength, and put each in its proper place" (I: 45). Poems, like buildings, must be built judiciously, with consideration given to structural necessity before the addition of ornament; indeed, Newbery's words suggest that ornament resides in the integrity of structure. For that reason, the true poet understands the different species of poems, but also comprehends the value of flexibility and diversity and structural innovation: "if ... there are poems of considerable character which are essentially different from those [traditionally defined: the Epigram, the Elegy, Pastoral, the Ode, the Satire, the Comedy, Tragedy, and the Epic,] and are not to be resolved into any of them, another distribution may be justified" (54). Hence, Newbery adds to the usual list the Epitaph, the Epistle, the Descriptive Poem, the Preceptive Poem, Tales and Fables, and the Allegorical Poem, and subsumes the Epic into the new category of the Heroic poem (I:55). Once the main discussion commences, further division emerges: the category of Lyric Poetry is introduced in Volume II, with its subcategories of the Sublime Ode, the Lesser Ode, the Divine Ode, and the Song.

Newbery is careful to delineate generic boundaries, and yet his argument also depends on a recognition that these boundaries are and must be permeable. Even as he enumerates the distinctions of the species, he also acknowledges the possibility, even the desirability, of crossing over:

> [i]f it be said, that the ... species of poetry often partake of all these different kinds, I answer, that is no objection; for this they occasionally [do] of each other: even the epic poem, with all its dignity, has

> sometimes the plaintive strain of the elegy, and the sarcasm and asperity of the satire. (I:55)

Newbery's text sets down "rules and directions" while also embedding crafty departures from such rules; that is, departures derived from the craft of poetry. It is this ability, it seems, that distinguishes the Poet from the mere copyist: natural genius allied with a knowledge of the art of composition produces poetry. The Poet, then, has a responsibility to truth without relying on mere reality, "not [things] *as they are*, but as they *seem to be*" (I:19). Newbery offers this as a kind of *quaestio*, since he does not mean that the poet embellishes or improves on reality; nor does he suggest that the poet deals in fantasy. Rather, the true Poet knows the difference between "*falshood* and *fiction*, between that which is really false, and that which is only so in appearance" (I:19). By invoking metaphor, hyperbole, irony, fable, and other figures, Newbery appeals to exactly the stylistic artifices of poetry that render it different from prose. They "have truth for their basis, which is recommended and rendered more amiable by those airy disguises" (I:19). It is the Poet's task to make such artifice acceptable, to ensure that "the thoughts [that] were not obvious to the reader before ... should appear so now" (I:41). The Poet, then, both understands and can achieve textual unity as well as variety; knows and understands generic boundaries as well as how to cross them; approaches poetry as an art that polishes and refines natural genius; and sees poetry as enabling truth as well as the development of the reader.

Newbery's precepts find general play in Blair, whose lectures on poetry close his three-volume treatise. Like Newbery, Blair divides poetry according to style and genre, focusing on the pastoral, lyric (subdivided into the ode, song, and hymn), didactic, descriptive, epic, and dramatic. Again like Newbery, Blair critiques the careless and unmeaning use of epithet: "[e]pithets are frequently brought in, merely to complete the verse, or make the rhyme answer; and hence they are so unmeaning and redundant; expletive words only..." (III: 184). Blair's chief opposition is between the Poet, who enlivens verse with "Imagination, and the Passions" (III: 104), and the poetaster, who seeks only to fill lines and find rhymes, mechanically. The Poet's "mind is supposed to be animated by some interesting object which fires his Imagination, or engages his Passions; and which, of course, communicates to his Style a peculiar elevation suited to his ideas; very different from that mode of expression, which is natural to the mind in its calm, ordinary state" (III: 105). The Poet can fire language with passion, and hence can elevate the bare outlines of form and genre above the "calm" and the "ordinary." The language of the passions derives from the infancy of poetry, when the "early Bard arose and sung ... in wild and disorderly strains ... the native effusions of his heart" (III: 117); the language of imagination provides the order and, for Blair, the "regular numbers" (III: 105) required for true art.[15]

For Blair, then, two things are necessary for true poetry: there must be shape and order, and there must be vitality. The one only achieves its worth if inhabited by the other. What Blair despises is the "Author" for whom only the words themselves matter: those who use epithets woodenly, or who "affect what they [do] not feel":

> Composing coolly in their closets, they endeavou[r] to imitate passion, rather than to express it; they tr[y] to force their imagination into raptures, or to supply the defect of native warmth, by those artificial ornaments which might give Composition a splendid appearance. (III: 117)

Where Newbery saw knowledge as allowing for the most effective expression of genius, Blair requires genius to promote mere knowledge into art. But for both, the two modes are required elements of true poetry, and the fundamental tools of the true Poet. It is imagination – genius – that allows the Poet to understand, for instance, the requirements of meter ("the proper mixture and succession of long and short syllables"), the essence of punctuation within meaning ("[an] essential circumstance ... is the caesural pause ... [and] it is a distinguishing advantage of our English verse, that it allows the pause to be varied ... By this means, uncommon richness and variety are added ..."), and the relationship between rhyme and genre ("An Epic Poem, or a Tragedy, would be fettered and degraded by [rhyme]. It is best adapted to compositions of a temperate strain, where no particular vehemence is required in the sentiments, nor great sublimity in the Style") (III: 120, 123–4, 128). For Blair, the central question in his *disputatio* seeks to disentangle the product from the producer, to illuminate the most necessary ingredients for poetry, and then to derive from that the essential qualities of the Poet. Hence, while poetry is made up of images put together using meter, rhyme, and other aspects of style that conform to recognizable structures, nonetheless it only achieves the status of art once wielded by the Poet.

Both Newbery and Blair settle on rules for poetry and poeticizing that rely on clear boundaries, observing rules and order. Nevertheless, each also allows for small overlaps. This emerges when Newbery describes the need to create new categories of poetry, precisely to *avoid* mixture, or when Blair notes how description "seldom form[s] a separate species of writing, yet into every species of Poetical Composition ... it both enters, and possesses in each of them a very considerable place" (III: 173). Both, however, privilege the idea of separate and recognizable genres, each of which has distinguishing elements, all of which are brought to life by the mastery of the Poet. And yet the hints of generic sharing in their texts speak to an implicit understanding that one of the most enlivening aspects of true poetry is precisely this kind of flexibility. Traditional forms have themselves evolved, in their accounts, from the desires of poets to find ways to represent events, emotions, and relationships convincingly; imagination continually pushes the boundaries on which custom relies. For Smith and Wordsworth, hybridity itself is predicated on the very generic boundaries that Newbery and Blair describe. Their poems in *Elegiac Sonnets* and *Lyrical Ballads* exemplify the elegy, song, lyric, pastoral, and so on even as they explore the effects of mixture. In turning to their collections I will discuss their transformations of genres, not focusing on what an elegiac sonnet or a lyrical ballad *is* (although this will form part of the discussion), but rather tracing how these experiments explore the *quaestio* of poetry and further the "disputes" undertaken by Newbery and Blair.

Newbery is clear about the makeup of an elegy:

> The *Elegy* is *mournful* and *plaintive*, but yet a sweet and engaging kind of poem ... [N]ot only matters of grief, but joy, wishes, prayers, expostulations, reproaches, admonitions, and almost every other subject, were admitted ... however, funeral lamentations and affairs of love seem most agreeable to its character.
>
> ... [N]one of those *fine things* which most people are so fond of in every sort of poem, can be allow'd in this, but must give place to nobler beauties, those of *Nature* and the *Passions*. Elegy rejects whatever is facetious, satirical, or majestic, and is content to be plain, decent, and unaffected; yet in this humble state is she sweet and engaging, elegant and attractive. This poem is adorn'd with frequent *commiserations, complaints, exclamations, addresses to thing or persons,* short and proper *digressions, allusions, comparisons, prosopoeias* or feigned persons, and sometimes with short *descriptions*. The diction ought to be free from any *harshness; neat, easy, perspicuous, expressive of the manners, tender,* and *pathetic*; and the numbers should be *smooth* and *flowing*, and captivate the ear with their uniform sweetness and delicacy. (I: 70)

From this description it is clear how closely Smith hews to generic requirements. Newbery's highly gendered language (the elegy is nothing short of an idealized kind of maiden) works in her favor as well, since the public persona she cultivated from the first was, if not maidenly, then fully feminized.[16] By casting the sonnet as elegiac, Smith in effect takes a short-cut to Newbery's details of meter and imagery. Smith seems only to miss out "joy" in Newbery's list of suitable subjects, but even here she signals her awareness in the anti-joy of Sonnet XXIX: "To Miss C— on being desired to attempt writing a comedy": "[I] .../... used to long to tread/ the gloomy paths of Sorrow's cypress shade..." (*Poetry*, p. 34, ll. 1, 2–3). The funerary, of course, finds play in Smith's presentations of loss at all levels: personal, public, private, material, emotional. And after the death of her beloved daughter Anna Augusta in 1795, grief obtains a more tangible object, as does love, for Smith writes about her daughter as a lost love, inscribing her death as devastating through language usually reserved for the bereft lover.[17] As much as the sonnets express personalized grief, however, they also, in their overt ventriloquisms (the translation sonnets, the novel sonnets) and in their more subtle theatricalisms enact the "feigned," introducing "persons" who are not and could not be Smith, and yet whose complaints, exclamations, addresses, and so on chime closely with those voiced by the "person" of Smith herself.[18] Proving herself a fit pupil, then, Smith on one level conforms to and reifies the strictures of the Master, here Newbery, by writing elegies, sonnetized or not, that reflect the question as he sees it.

It is significant that in the first editions of the *Elegiac Sonnets* Smith also includes a "song"; for Newbery, songs were a subset of the lyric, while also functioning, as with Blair, as a lingering example of one of the earliest forms of verse, the sung poem. Smith's "Song. From the French of Cardinal Bernis," as a translation, deflects responsibility for its subject matter to its original author, which is emphasized in the first and second editions of the *Elegiac Sonnets* by the inclusion of the French original alongside Smith's version. In 1792, in the Sixth edition, Smith inserted another "Song," which addresses the mysterious Clara as both responsible for, and pitying of, the speaker's "hapless love." And in 1797, in Volume II of the *Elegiac Sonnets*, Smith returns to French for a "Song. From the French," which equates Louisa with all of Love's virtues. This has the effect, for students of Newbery, of allowing the lyric to make the occasional appearance among the elegies, and by relying on translations to provide her "songs" Smith also suggests a kind of linguistic combining; French, as the language of love, becomes also the appropriate language of song, while the translated songs allow English to partake of the "easy, natural, and flowing" (Newbery, II: 43) rhythm of the French originals.

The song to Clara, however, suggests that Smith also realizes the importance of exploring the linguistic possibilities of this style of lyric shorn of a French model. This "Song" is notable for the questions it leaves unanswered: Who is the speaker? Who is Clara? If a song is meant to be "easy" and "natural" so that "poetry and music may be agreeably united," it seems noteworthy that in this song Smith creates a speaker for whom language – the verbal – has become a hindrance in the expression of authentic emotion. The speaker pleads with Clara to "speak – with those expressive eyes!/ Let one low sigh escape thine heart" (ll. 3–4). Surrounded by a "gazing crowd," Clara exists publicly, but her love, to the "watchful" speaker, is conveyed through "soft looks" and "sigh[s]." "Words are useless, words are vain," exclaims the besotted speaker, who interprets Clara's sigh and looks as he sees fit (l. 9). Lurking within the speaker's knowledge of Clara's meaning is a desire that needs no verbal affirmation; in building up an alternative mode of expression the speaker exhibits, contrary to his own verbalizing of love, a silencing of Clara and, more, a concentration verging on obsession, in a move that anticipates the twisted logic of Porphyria's lover.[19] In other words, when Smith writes what seems to be her own song, she moves well beyond the minor ornamentation Newbery assigns to this lyric mode and begins to associate lyric expression with a darkened subjectivity.

This "Song," superficially one-dimensional and uni-generic, to coin a word, reflects the sonnets' more extensively worked out methods of combining differing subjective modes within genres that simultaneously conform to and challenge existing definitions. Even as Smith faithfully adheres to the Newberian model, she also institutes her own questioning of the possibilities afforded by its generic confines. Taking another look at the funerary elements of the sonnets, it becomes clear that when Newbery mentions the elegy's "funeral lamentations" it means exactly that: lamentations uttered at the death of a loved one. For Smith to substitute for this lamentations at the death of hopes, dreams, desires, and aspirations means that the outward, other-focused trajectory of the elegy becomes an inward and circular spiral of grief that enlarges the subjectivities created in each sonnet. The unceasing woe associated with Smith's sonnets is by no means always her own, but the ease with which readers have assumed it is speaks to their successful creation of an elegiac modality, dependent, here, on the apparently confined and restrictive space afforded by the genre Smith chose to exploit: the sonnet. Remembering that Smith described the sonnet as "no improper vehicle for a single Sentiment" opens the question of the singularity of each individual poem. The propriety, for which we may read the rightness or fitness, of containing a sentiment within the vehicle of a poem becomes one of the questions Smith poses within her sonnets. In this sense, propriety acts as a synonym for a rule system: Smith both invokes the existence of the system and uses her sonnets to expand it. Once the elegy is allied to the sonnet, a new genre is created, one that relies on the formalities of each pre-existing form while also hybridizing each. The resulting composite leads generic definitions in new directions; it maximizes the possibilities of each *and* amalgamates their structures. The *Elegiac Sonnets*, then, begin a process of experimentation that responds to the rules of structure laid down by masters such as Newbery, but that pushes the dispute in directions only possible once the new *quaestio* has been formulated; that is, does generic mixture produce a fertile offspring, or will it only lead to a sterile end in itself?

No other poets in the 1780s and early 1790s are posing such questions; no other poets are doing something as daring as mixing poetic matter.[20] With the sonnets, Smith begins a process that teaches the value of thinking about form and structure both within and outside of the traditional box. And as early as 1789, with "Elegy," she begins to question specific generic boundaries.[21] Although, strictly speaking, this poem voices an elegy's complaint (exclamation, address) to another person, it also offers a narrative framework that, in providing details of background and situation, elevate the poem into another kind of hybrid: an elegiac narrative with a summary final stanza that both moralizes on and commemorates the preceding lines.[22] Before the poem begins, a note to the title explains that

> This elegy is written on the supposition that an indigent young woman had been addressed by the son of a wealthy yeoman, who resenting his attachment, had driven him from home, and compelled him to have recourse for subsistence to the occupation of a pilot, in which, in attempting to save a vessel in distress, he perished.
>
> The father dying, a tomb is supposed to be erected to his memory in the churchyard mentioned in Sonnet the 44th ["Written in the church-yard at Middleton in Sussex"]. And while a tempest is gathering, the unfortunate young woman comes thither; and courting the same death as had robbed her of her lover, she awaits its violence, and is at length overwhelmed by the waves. (*Poetry*, p. 52)

Smith uses her note to offer two possibilities for the subject of the elegy, neither of which the poem takes up. Both the dead lover mourned and the dead father redeemed would be an expected narrative path. Instead, the poem enacts the death-in-progress of the young woman herself, who, having lost her lover's body, throws away her own. The note, further, offers the untold tale, which would be a fitting ballad, of the young, heroic pilot, as well as the unnarrated romance – another ballad? – of the young woman and her star-crossed love. And the intertextual reference to a sonnet concerning a real graveyard afflicted by gothic disinterments effectively places this poem, though fiction, within the realm of reality. There is no narrative need for the two graveyards to be the same; therefore, the note seems to infer a structural need to reaffirm the reality, or perhaps the feasibility, of the situation dramatized by "Elegy." Within the note, then, Smith bundles the essential ingredients of at least four other narratives, two additional genres, and several competing modes of representation.

The poem itself, mainly spoken by the bereft young woman and accompanied by a plate showing her actively seeking annihilation, carries the reader from life to death. The young woman's emotional desolation is matched by the "threatening storm" and the "desart beech," while another nature-based identification is created when the narrator comments on the "rugged nature" of the hard-hearted father (ll. 16, 18). Nature, in other words, responds to and mirrors the speaker's grief *and* provides the model for the generator of her grief. Throughout the poem, the young woman, unlike Clara, seizes vocality; without an auditor or observer, it seems she speaks to herself, and by extension to the reader, but by speaking at all she redirects the force of the elegy from the mourned object to the mourner, in the process inscribing herself *as* the mourned object. Unable to maintain the image of her lost beloved – "'I see him rise the whitening waves above,/ .../ Yet, powerful Fancy! bid the phantom stay,/ Still let me hear him! — "Tis already past!'" – she is equally incapable of believing her own image-making – "'Ah! wild Illusion .../ He hears not, comes not...'" (ll. 42, 53–4, 57–8). Under the guise of grief, the poem presents the loss of creative energies and imaginative force; unable to conjure up her beloved, the young woman instead submits to the "resistless sweep" of the waves which "tear from its base the proud aggressor's tomb,/ And bear the injured to eternal sleep!" (ll. 74, 75–6). The narrative voice's closing summary claims the imaginative power lost by the young woman; where her attempts to call up her lover are illusory, the last stanza refers to "the embodied waters" which "bear" the woman to "sleep" and by extension to bed.

The poem thus offers consummation outside of its own boundaries. Its note, and the three stanzas spoken by the narrating voice, also work to carry it beyond the strictures of the elegy. And the young woman, as both mourner and mourned, voices an awareness of the power, and the limitations, of the imaginative process. The poem, then, tells a story while also telling a story about story-making; it is self-reflexive, aware of its function *as* poem. Stepping outside its own boundaries seems to enable a generic development: rather than a closed narrative, the poem offers a multivalent spiral.

"The Peasant of the Alps," a transplanted poem from *Celestina* (1791), uses a more conventional story-telling style, with an third-person narrator relating the peasant's tale of love and loss. It conforms in many ways to Newbery's precepts for a tale in verse, but telescoped: within eight stanzas the reader is introduced to the peasant and "the mistress of his heart" (l. 13), given insights about his contentment with his lot, allowed glimpses of his cottage and garden and a privileged view of the conjugal bed, and finally witnesses the destruction of all this from an avalanche and the peasant's despairing suicide.[23] This pseudo-conclusion signals an important departure from precept, since suicide, a mortal sin, can hardly be seen as a "useful lesson" (Newbery, I: 235). However, Smith does more than merely add sensation to her tale. First, as indicated, she delivers a conclusion to the tale that is, nonetheless, not the conclusion to the poem. The last stanza transforms a tale into another kind of elegy:

> A fate too similar is mine,
> But I – in lingering pain repine,
> And still my lost felicity deplore!
> Cold, cold to me is that dear breast become
> Where this poor heart had fondly fix'd its home,
> And love and happiness are mine no more! (ll. 49–54)

The third-person narrator emerges as a speaker in the last stanza, but not before then, and the story of natural disaster suddenly transforms into a metaphor for the speaker's own emotional sense of loss. What began as a tale now takes on elements of a fable or an allegory, with the "useful lesson" focused not on the peasant's exemplary life (which in itself lends a pastoral air to the narrative, even if a mountain is substituted for a pasture) but rather on the speaker's recognition of abandonment. The speaker, in other words, constructs the tale in order to obscure her (or his – the poem is not gendered) emotional state, only for those emotions to break their narrative bounds at the last minute. As with "Elegy," this more than anything elevates the poem beyond its generic requirements; the poem has become as much about the power of poetry to uncover and liberate "powerful feeling" as it has been about the peasant's catastrophe.

As Smith explores the compositional possibilities of these reformulated narratives, she is also continually writing sonnets; each new edition of the *Elegiac Sonnets*, expanded to two volumes in 1797, contains reams of new work. The earlier sonnets – those written in the 1780s and early 1790s – use the hybrid form to push the idea of personalized subjectivity, showing the ways in which the apparently autobiographical "I" can mask an evolving series of voices and selves. In the 1790s, interestingly, the sonnets, through loco-descriptive titles and identifiable autobiographical content, do more than the earlier ones to convey a sense of the grieving poet; there is less dodging an ultimate identification with the poet herself, and a more intensive testing of the elasticity of the sonnet form, its rhyme scheme and structure. Alongside this, Smith explores facets of subjectivity and narration, building on the gains made in "Elegy" and "The Peasant of the Alps." In "The Female Exile," Smith embeds a poetic pre-history, by rewriting a segment of the blank-verse *The Emigrants* in rhyme.[24] Although Blair had cautioned against the use of rhyme in poems of a "highly pathetic strain," noting that only blank verse could capture their "dignity and force" (128), Smith reconsiders her adherence to this precept. As her note to the poem says, in blank verse the narrative reached only the level of "sketch," but now, in rhyme, it has become a "Poem" (*Poetry*, p. 91). Its "highly pathetic" subject, the plight of the destitute émigrée who daily waits for news from France on the quayside at Brighton while her oblivious children play, gains more currency from the moves the narration makes away from pure description toward psychological realism. Although the diction is balladic and even courtly, the effect is to allow observers to read the woman's state of despair and abandonment from her physical self-placement and "unregarded" dress. But although she does not regard her appearance, she "beholds" her children, and as she does so, we both regard and behold her, invited implicitly by the narration and explicitly by the plate that accompanies the poem.

This readerly stance is constructed by a narration that not only embodies the woman but also, in a "Peasant"-like move, introduces a speaker in the last stanza:

> Poor mourner! – I would that my fortune had left me
>   The means to alleviate the woes I deplore;
> But like thine my hard fate has of affluence bereft me,
>   *I* can warm the cold heart of the wretched no more! (ll. 33–6)

Again, a tale becomes an elegy, but it also reaffirms its realism, since here the speaker has not composed the tale to stand in for personal grief, but rather draws personal knowledge from observing and writing about another grief-stricken figure, a person as real as the speaker is. The female exile thus does double duty: she emblematizes her own loss and that of the speaker, while remaining naïvely unaware of her poetic function. The speaker is able to draw a parallel that relies on and remains within the realm of poetry, while also invoking the world wherein poetic precepts have no legitimacy. The reader is left to wonder: Which figure, exactly, is the true female exile? The identification that the speaker creates with the émigrée does not, actually, benefit either, at least not materially; but the poem serves to create an association that enriches the speaker, whose isolation is leavened temporarily, while within the poem. Not much changes for the female exile, it is true, but in poetic encounters of this kind little does change for the emblematic other. The function of the poem is to allow for the development, the evolution, of the speaker. *This* speaker has gained an analogue whose trials and sorrows serve to legitimate the speaker's own "woes."

The narration that allows for the flowering of subjectivity in these poems comes itself to fruition in "The Forest Boy." It is interesting to note, here, Newbery's precepts for the epic poem:

> An Epic or Heroic Poem is a Discourse formed upon a Story partly real and partly feigned, representing some one glorious and fortunate action, that is distinguished by a variety of wonderful, yet probable and pleasing events, and delivered in verse by way of Narration, in a sublime and flowing stile, to form the manners, and inflame the mind with the love of virtue.
>
> What distinguishes an *Epic* from a *Dramatic* Poem is, its being a *Narration* that comes immediately from the Poet... (II: 180–81)

"The Forest Boy" concerns Will of the Woodlands, his attempts to support his mother after his father's death, and the development of his relationship with "his sweet Phoebe." Although Will "toil'd from the dawn, and at evening ... hied/ .../ To supply all [his mother's] wants from the town," his mother remains "sad and distrest"; even Phoebe, nature's child ("Her form like the aspen.../ And [her] eyes .../ As the skies of the Summer were blue!") cannot cheer her (ll. 18, 20, 24, 28–30).[25] But Phoebe's presence compensates Will for his hard labor: "whatever she said/ Was more sweet than the voice of the dove" (ll. 44–5). The pastoral tone of the poem carries some hints of the "real," in that the hardship of the characters' lives is only partly alleviated by love, but the first quarter seems to indicate that the poem will dramatize Will and Phoebe's love and eventual retirement to a happy cot along the lines of that already lost in "The Peasant of the Alps."[26] However, the probable enters when Will goes to town for supplies and fails to return:

> The clock in her cottage now mournfully told
> The hours that went heavily on;
> 'Twas midnight; her spirits sunk hopeless and cold,
> And it seem'd as each blast of wind fearfully told,
> That long, long would her William be gone.
>
> Then heart-sick and cold to her sad bed she crept,
> Yet first made up the fire in the room
> To guide his dark steps; but she listen'd and wept,
> Or if for a moment forgetful she slept,
> She soon started! – and thought he was come.
>
> 'Twas morn; and the wind with an hoarse sullen moan
> Now seem'd dying away in the wood,
> When the poor wretched mother still drooping, alone,
> Beheld on the threshold a figure unknown,
> In gorgeous apparel who stood.
>
> "Your son is a soldier," abruptly cried he,
> "And a place in our corps has obtain'd,
> Nay, be not cast down; you perhaps may soon see
> Your William a captain! he now sends by me
> The purse he already has gain'd."
>
> So William entrapp'd 'twixt persuasion and force,
> Is embark'd for the isles of the West ... (ll. 71–92)

The allure of quick money overcomes the Forest Boy, who soon regrets his decision, anticipates his mother's exasperation, Phoebe's wedding another, and "anguish now sped/ The dart of disease – With the brave numerous dead/ He has fall'n on the plague-tainted shore" (ll. 113–15).

Saved neither by Nature nor nurture, Will succumbs to his culture's war-mongering. His mother dies, "unable to bear/ *His* loss," and in the grave "has both him and her sorrows forgot" (ll. 118–19, 120). The last victim, Phoebe, both unable to die and unable to forget, goes gently mad and "weaves/ Reed garlands, against her dear William appears" (ll. 127–8). This poem, with its pastoral/tragic narration; its gestures to grand events that are here rendered as destructive; its mixture of the wonderful (the fairy-tale forest setting, the "figure unknown"), the pleasing (Phoebe's relationships with the mother and Will), and the probable (Will's impressment, the effects on the others) functions as a miniature epic, fulfilling Newbery's precepts while reconfiguring them through poetic narration. The final stanza brings in the heretofore invisible narrator, but without the personalizing force of the previous poems; this narrator wants only to make sure that the tragic elements of this pastoral mini-epic are plain:

> Ah! such are the miseries to which ye give birth,
>   Ye statesmen! ne'er dreading a scar;
> Who from pictured saloon, or the bright sculptured hearth,
> Disperse desolation and death thro' the earth,
>   When ye let loose the demons of war. (ll. 131–5)

Plainly, the truly epic wonder is the criminality of these magus-like figures, whose actions undo the contentment that might have been possible in the poem. The social critique, and the emphasis placed on the experiences of the common soldier as well as those he leaves behind, signal a new focus on those who actually fight wars (or, in Will's case, don't) rather than the officers and gentlemen in the "gorgeous apparel." Although the poem in part dresses up Will and Phoebe in pastoral guise, it also, as noted, contains real-world aspects that compromise what would otherwise be a purely literary world – after all, what shepherd or swain needs to visit the grocery store? This is the poem's great strength: to preserve poetic convention on the one hand and undo it on the other. The themes of loss, despair, and man's inhumanity to man (which, here, impinges directly on women), as well as the suggestive way in which Will's emotional regret has such a debilitating bodily effect, lift the poem to a level not foreseen by Newbery, not definable by precepts. The Smithian hybrid, from the elegiac sonnet on, proves fertile; each version feeds into another and leads poetry away from "single sentiments" to an abundance of interacting forms.

These extended readings demonstrate that Smith is not merely writing elegies, tales, or sonnets; she is also expanding the definitions of each, creating hybrid verse that functions on narrative, formal, and metaphorical levels to demonstrate, actively, a new direction for poetry.

The poems themselves advance the parameters of poetry, while the experimental subgenre of the *Elegiac Sonnets* provides a new model, a new strand to an ongoing *disputatio*. Indeed, "Elegy," "The Peasant of the Alps," "The Female Exile," and especially "The Forest Boy" push the narrative poem into a shape most closely associated with Wordsworth: the lyrical ballad, and many of the terms of my analysis of Smith will resonate for any student of the *Lyrical Ballads* themselves. This is deliberate, since one aim of this chapter is to show how, in introducing the notion of the hybrid poem through the *Elegiac Sonnets*, Smith explores its usefulness further in these other poems, and lays the groundwork for Wordsworth's management of the form in his writings of 1797/8. As noted, for most critics, the *Lyrical Ballads* represent either a stunning departure from existing poetic practice or the usual subjects dressed up in a new lyricism.[27] Although there have been studies that place the poems historically, that read the poems as expressions of genderboundedness or gender explorations, and that acknowledge certain kinds of generic indebtedness, none has connected the experiment in hybridity that Wordsworth undertakes with the model provided by Smith. And yet the *Lyrical Ballads* take up the same issues of generic history, lyric expressiveness, and disputations on the art of poetry that underpin the *Elegiac Sonnets, and Other Essays*. The *Lyrical Ballads* have stood for so many readers and critics as the harbinger, if not of a new development in poetry, then at least of Wordsworth's poetic maturation that their intricate connections with Smith have gone unremarked.

Mary Jacobus has situated Blair's definitions of poetry and poetic language centrally to Wordsworth's project in the late 1790s, noting that Coleridge and he read the *Lectures* and showing how closely Wordsworth assimilated Blair's ideas about passion and imagination. For Jacobus,

> Wordsworth was not alone, either in his primitivism or in his search for an alternative idiom. What set him apart was his extension of Blair's theory of poetry to the world immediately around him – his belief that ordinary people ... expressed themselves undisguisedly and forcefully in a language which poetry could use. (p. 191)

However, the 1798 *Lyrical Ballads* contain few poems written in the voice of the "ordinary" person; mad mothers, idiot boys, superstitious sea captains, and local landowners are inherently extraordinary. The majority of the "other poems" are voiced by a speaker *attuned* to the extraordinary. Wordsworth's phrases, like "the real language of men," resonate so strongly that they overshadow the aspects of the poetry that Wordsworth himself did not pick out, their "real language of poetry." Wordsworth's poeticizing, like Smith's, follows on from Masters such as Newbery and Blair; Wordsworth as poet seems to understand the central *quaestio* of the *Elegiac Sonnets*, and the dispute in which he enrols his work is the same: What is Poetry? Despite his professed focus on the language of men, the poems in *Lyrical Ballads*, like those in *Elegiac Sonnets*, explore the possibilities of the language of poetry, specifically a language of mixture and hybridity.

Like Smith, Wordsworth shows in his titles and forms that he understands the components of the art of poetry. Newbery, who divides the lyric into the sublime ode, the lesser ode, and the song, notes the sung aspect of the ancient lyric, but in his precepts lays out rules for the lyric that emphasize its "natural, just, and pleasing" language, the "harmony, and often uniformity" of its versification, and the "pathetic" and "affecting" nature of its subjects (II: 50, 47, 49). In the *Lyrical Ballads*, Wordsworth imports the elements of the song, ode, and other forms to the ballad, a form not found in Newbery's list of poetic "species."[28] Of course, whether by "ballad" Wordsworth meant to invoke literary history or street culture has never been clear, but it seems plain that, like Smith with the sonnet and the elegy, Wordsworth means a specific poetic form modified by an emotive or structural state.[29] Newbery does, however, supply precepts for a form not explicitly evoked by Wordsworth, but which seems resident in his *Lyrical Ballads* nonetheless: the pastoral.[30] Newbery considers that the pastoral, in presenting a rural setting and "shepherds or other rusticks" as its main characters, "gives great delight ... since innocence and simplicity generally please":

> The character of the Pastoral consists in simplicity, brevity, and delicacy: the two first render an eclogue *natural*, and the last *delightful*. With respect to nature, indeed, we are to consider, that as a pastoral is an image of the ancient times of innocence and undesigning plainness, we are not to describe shepherds as they really are at this day, but as they may be conceiv'd to have been ....
>
> To make it natural with respect to the present day, some knowledge in rural affairs should be discovered, and that in such manner, as if it was done by chance rather than by design ... for what is so engaging in this kind of poetry proceeds not so much from the idea of a country life itself, as in exposing only the best part of a shepherd's life, and concealing the misfortunes and miseries which sometimes attend it. (I: 85–6)

Variety in scene or prospect is also necessary, and

> is in a great measure obtained by frequent comparisons drawn from the most agreeable objects of the country; by interrogations to things inanimate; by short and beautiful digressions; and by elegant turns on the words, which render the numbers more sweet and pleasing. (I: 86)

By factoring Newbery's precepts into Wordsworth's appreciation of poetic form, what emerges is his consistent *overturning* of the requisite beauties of pastoral, his insistence on exactly the miseries and misfortunes the pastoral should mask, and his understanding that "the numbers" are enlivened not by elegance but by trauma. Wordsworth engages with these "elder writers" *so that* he may challenge their precepts.

Blair follows Newbery in his description of the pastoral, noting that

> in every Pastoral, a scene, or rural prospect, should be distinctly drawn, and set before us ... [O]bjects must be particularised ... A single object, happily introduced, will sometimes distinguish and characterise a whole scene ... [The Poet] must diversify his face of nature ... We expect to be entertained by Shepherds, or persons wholly engaged in rural occupations ... [The Shepherd] may have good sense and reflection; he may have sprightliness and vivacity; he may have very tender and delicate feelings ... [but] he must not deal in general reflections, and abstract reasonings.... (III: 137–40)

By allowing pastoral characters to think and feel, Blair lifts them above the caricatures found in so many highly stylized depictions of "Colins" and "Phyllises," and opens a space wherein a shepherd may become a "statesman," for instance, or may mourn the last of his flock; or where a rustic speaker's familial feelings of community may over-rule absence through death; or where good sense may be found outside general definitions of such, baffling interlocutors.[31] Wordsworth shows his understanding of Blair's argument: he assigns feelings and speeches to his rustic characters, but he reserves "general reflections, and abstract reasonings" for the observing speaker of a poem. However, this is not to say that he privileges their stance – often, of course, more questions are raised by the speakers' stolid perspective than the rustics' innate understanding. Rather, he suits the tenor of expression to the station of the speaker. The dispute arises from the wordscape of the poem: if Smith's hybrids display their fertility, in part, as self-reflexivity, do Wordsworth's?

Wordsworth, like Smith, acknowledges the rules set down by Masters, incorporates them, and then engages in his own *disputatio*. For instance, in "The Female Vagrant," he returns to a story he had included in his 1793 poem *Salisbury Plain*. As Smith does with her Female Exile, Wordsworth mines his earlier politicized work for an excerpt that would reduce its concerns to a single sentiment; the Female Vagrant, a familiar poetic figure in the 1790s as Mayo has shown, nonetheless introduces readers of the 1798 *Lyrical Ballads* to Wordsworth's conception of her plight.[32] As Smith does, he uses rhyme, thereby signaling the regrettable everydayness of his subject matter, while also asserting the elevating qualities lent by rhyme. The Female Vagrant contains elements of "Elegy" and "The Forest Boy" as well as "The Female Exile"; Wordsworth draws from pre-existing narratives the pathos of suffering under petty tyranny, the domestic destruction visited by war, and the despair and alienation felt by the woman left behind.[33] The Female Vagrant has the kind of rural upbringing experienced by Will and Phoebe, yet idealized in a way that the earlier poem, with its recurrent theme of grocery shopping, avoids. However, once the greedy master is introduced the poem takes on a gothic tinge: within five stanzas the woman and her father are evicted, taken in by the woman's lover, live for "four years" by dint of "constant toil and constant prayer," and experience death and destitution, until "We had no hope, and no relief could gain./ But soon, with proud parade, the noisy drum/ Beat round, to sweep the streets of want and pain./ .../ To join those miserable men [my husband] flew;/ And now to the sea-coast, with numbers more, we drew" (ll. 92–4, 98–9). Where Will abandons his mother and lover, this young man effectively enlists with his family, but the result is the same: husband and children all die "by sword/ And ravenous plague" (ll. 132–3), and the woman is left on her own, to become a memento mori and an emblem, as well, of the disenfranchised. Wordsworth begins in pastoral mode and swiftly introduces the tragic, dramatizing the action through the woman's first-person narration. This, however, is a poetic feint; the aside in line 2 that "(The Woman thus her artless story told)" is reified in the last lines when "She ceased" (l. 267).

Wordsworth voices feminine anguish, but given the familiarity of the figure in the poem, it seems less important that he does this than that he gives her a voice at all. This woman seems consumed by the same kind of loss and grief that affected the speaker of "Elegy." Both are rural figures whose "tender and delicate feelings" drive their actions. Both narrate their tragedies but lack an ability to transcend them. The woman in "Elegy" gives herself over to death-dealing Nature, while the woman in Wordsworth's poem survives, although her survival is predicated on the telling of her story:

> She ceased, and weeping turned away,
> As if because her tale was at an end
> She wept; – because she had no more to say
> Of that perpetual weight which on her spirit lay. (ll. 267–70)

A "perpetual weight" suggests perpetual voicing; the narrating voice, which only partly subsumes its physical presence via parentheses and dashes, interprets the tale's existential weight on the basis of weeping, a physical condition. The "as if" immediately links to "because," which then substitutes itself entirely. This forces a reading of the poem which pushes it past the anti-pastoral, a simple formulaic riposte to the precepts of Newbery and Blair; the poem now functions both to tell a story and to read it. The Vagrant's sorrows inhabit her almost physically, so that her tears are rendered, by the narrator, as all she is capable of producing if she is not actually speaking. But this interpretation has the effect of privileging the narrator's thoughts and feelings over those of the vagrant's, so that her 265 lines of story-telling become submerged in the narrator's five lines of reflection. This lyrical pastoral ballad, then, reverses at the last minute into a kind of soliloquy, less about the Female Vagrant than about the interpretative needs of her listener.

By composing a poem that enforces its own interpretation, Wordsworth makes use of a Smithian effect of hybridity: linearity can be manipulated by a poem aware of itself as a poem. He also, like Smith, inserts personalized speakers in poems such as "Lines Written in Early Spring," "We Are Seven," and "Anecdote for Fathers." "Lines" again follows "The Forest Boy" in its recognition of the depradations wrought on natural humanity by uncaring men. The speaker, already infected by a shuddering despair, opens the poem in a paradoxical "sweet mood when pleasant thoughts/ Bring sad thoughts to the mind" (ll. 3–4). Presented as a natural state of mind, this sweet sadness operates rather in contrast to the "thousand blended notes" of the birds and the nature-scape of the poem; indeed, the "fair works" of nature are canceled out by the speaker's grief at "what man has made of man" (ll. 1, 5, 8). The speaker is unable to resist the onslaught of thought, although he attempts to mask it with further thought: "And I *must* think, do all I can,/ That there was pleasure there" (ll. 19–20, emphasis added). "Must" acts to its own contrary, as it is plain that the pleasure of l. 3 has been lost in "thoughts [he] may not prevent": "Have I not reason to lament/ What man has made of man?"

(ll. 21, 23–4). This speaker, akin to that in "Peasant," composes a nature that leads inexorably to his own emotional state. Nature provides not solace, but a constant reminder of what has been lost. The speaker seems to seek an auditor, but finds only his own poem, and the poem can do little more than reflect his state of paralysis. Something has happened, something exists that feeds the speaker's anxiety, but what it is remains oblique. "What man has made of man" suggests its own unanswerability.

Similarly, in "Anecdote" and "We Are Seven," the speakers' need to force the children into delivering answers they recognize as truthful leads them to bullying and bafflement respectively. The naïfs offer an understanding of the world that conforms to Blair's enhanced pastoral character, but Wordsworth here shows the risk involved in reflections and "abstract reasonings." Edward, goaded by the speaker, learns not to lie, but rather to deny the validity of his native truthfulness; the little girl, oblivious to the speaker's need for clarity, causes him to "thro[w] words away" (l. 67). If a poet throws words away he abandons the tools necessary to his trade; if a poet creates a scene in which abstract reasoning is denuded of its weaponry – words – then he writes a poem in which innate understanding is privileged. In both poems, Wordsworth explores scenarios wherein poetry almost becomes redundant, while simultaneously acting as the only medium by which wordless knowledge can be suggested. The voicelessness that underlays Smith's "Song" comes to mind. Wordsworth shows his ability to learn from and overtake Masters like Newbery and Blair, working with the same tools of poetic art as does Smith. The *Lyrical Ballads* thus act as the fruits of his *disputatio* with Smith.

In their work of 1800, there is intriguing evidence that the two poets implicitly recognize the debate in which they are engaged. In the second volume of the *Lyrical Ballads*, for instance, Wordsworth includes a "Song," one of the Lucy poems that have so captivated readers.[34] With Newbery and Blair in place, this "Song" takes on a categorical tinge not usually discussed, and with Smith's "Song" in place, Wordsworth's version seems less about the mystery of Lucy's identity. As a lyric, the poem should be "easy" and "natural." Wordsworth literalizes the idea of "natural" when he creates Lucy as embedded within images of unknown, unknowable Nature: the "untrodden ways," the "half-hidden" "Violet," the single shining star (ll. 1, 6, 5). Wordsworth subverts the idea of "easy": the poem is neither easeful nor readable. Making a virtue of its obscurity, the poem uses Lucy as shorthand for the speaker's need: "But she is in her Grave, and Oh!/ The difference to me," he sighs, leaving it up to the reader to decipher "difference" (ll. 11–12). As much as Smith's "Song" privileged the emotional state of the speaker, while also revealing his inability to assert it ("Clara mourns my *hapless* love," l. 2, emphasis added), so too Wordsworth's "Song" gives the speaker's emotions primacy while also relegating them firmly to the past ("She is in her Grave"). The poem's mystery and obscurity revolve around the speaker, not Lucy; she, like Smith's Clara, functions only as a foil for the speaker's emotional state. And even as Smith's "Song" has, at its heart, silence, so too is Wordsworth's built on unknowability. Silent, unreadable songs; the simplest lyric affords, for Smith and Wordsworth, an opportunity for the greatest complexity.

In 1800 Smith also publishes a second edition, of Volume II of the *Elegiac Sonnets*, and she closes it with a poem called "Lydia." As she does with "Elegy," Smith underpins the poem with a note that gestures toward one form of generic pedigree, here the ballad as ghost story. Her scene-setting reference to "the Horseman's ghost" is underpinned with information gleaned from rural legend:

> Some years ago a strange notion prevailed among the people occasionally passing over one of the highest of the South Downs, that a man on horseback was often seen coming towards those who were returning from market on Saturday evening. This appearance, the noise of whose horse's feet they distinctly heard, vanished as soon as it came within an hundred yards of the passengers who often tried to meet it. At other times it was seen following them. They have stopped to let it approach, but it always melted into air. I have been present when a farmer not otherwise particularly weak or ignorant, said, that he had seen it, and distinctly heard the horse galloping towards him. (*Poetry*, p. 114)

The length and detail of the note suggest that the Horseman will play an important part in the poem, and that this story, based on "well-authenticated fact" (*Lyrical Ballads*, Advertisement), has inspired the poem. And yet the Horseman features only twice, and is first invoked by a speaker who, "a lonely wanderer," has climbed the "high down" to "gaze around" (ll. 9, 1, 10). The speaker does not show the same interested detachment of the speaker of the note; indeed, the poem-speaker seems to accept the viability of the Horseman, just as he/she accepts the presence of "hapless Lydia," who has "lain" "thro many a drear and stormy night" on the high down among the "Juniper and scathed Yew" (ll. 8, 7, 3). It is Lydia who next mentions the Horseman, asserting that his ghost "I often see" as she keeps her vigil (l. 34) for her lover Edward.

While the note offers the story of the Horseman as local legend, and slyly suggests that his appearances may coincide with the particularly susceptible state of farmers on their way home from market on a Saturday night, the poem's speaker and Lydia agree on the reality of this supernatural figure. Further, while the speaker disguises this, the poem also indicates his complicity in Lydia's predicament. His opening lines imply that he has come upon Lydia by chance, and yet if she has become a fixture on the down and the speaker "love[s] to climb and gaze around," then his encounter seems less by chance and more by design. Lydia, whose eyes are "wild yet vacant," is inhabited by unthinking nature and obeys only one imperative: her lover's instruction that she await his return when "the tenth blessed moon arise[s]" (ll. 21, 55). She tells her story by rote to a speaker who already knows that "'long since thy wandering Lover died,/ The moon returns in vain!'" (ll. 59–60), but who declines to tell her so, since "why awaken her to pain?" (l. 58). For the speaker, Lydia's presence on the down is an essential part of the landscape he/she loves to explore, just as the Horseman is. Less essential, it seems, is the humane act of leading Lydia out of her delusions and back to "the villag[e] below" (l. 15). Lydia animates the landscape just as Martha Ray does for the superstitious sea-captain in "The Thorn," whose narrative seems to inform this speaker's. His own superstition, and desire to keep Lydia where she is, evolve directly from Wordsworth's presentation in "The Thorn" in 1798. But Smith takes her speaker one step further. Where Wordsworth makes it clear that his "loquacious narrator" is neither himself disguised, nor any aspect of himself ("not ... in the author's own person" [*LB*, p. 739]), Smith devises a speaker whose ending exclamation evokes, not a colorful local character, but the personalized philosopher who concludes a poem like "Anecdote for Fathers."[35] Having decided against enlightening Lydia about her lover's death, the speaker concludes "– The hopes of half the World, poor Maid!/ Are not more rational than thine!" (ll. 63–4).

Smith's playful, or pointed, shift in characterization suggests her careful reading of the *Lyrical Ballads*, which in turn implies the fertile nature of Wordsworth's own hybrid. In tone and content, "Lydia" is like the lyrical ballad that Wordsworth forgot to write, but its force resides, again, in a self-reflexive move that invites the reader to question the speaker's version of things: his/her meeting with Lydia, his/her motives in merely listening to her story, the nature of his/her love of climbing and gazing. The speaker's ability to construct a class difference between him/herself and Lydia (she is "the maid," the "wretched Girl," ll. 12, 60) and his/her gesture toward the "rational" in the last line function to elevate him/her while settling Lydia firmly in the position of the "other." Is Lydia's the "language of conversation"? Is the speaker's? Or is Smith subtly calling into question the idea that language can be so delineated? The poem invites scrutiny of its very status: are we reading a ballad, or are we reading something more developed? If Smith and her elegiac sonnets led Wordsworth to the lyrical ballad, then Wordsworth's lyrical ballads leads Smith further still, to a deconstruction of the form itself. Thus each Master becomes, in turn, the student; thus they use their poetry to form new questions and enliven the ongoing *disputatio*.

In allowing their poetry to embody the *quaestio* of "What is a Poem?," Smith and Wordsworth push the genre past the stark divisions and species laid down by writers such as Newbery and Blair, responding instead to the hints toward flexibility such texts suggest. The *Elegiac Sonnets, and Other Essays* and the *Lyrical Ballads, with a Few Other Poems* signal from the title page onward their understanding of generic divisions, while also refusing to follow this tradition of categorization. And it is their titular creations of new genres that allow their poetry to be read as new and in new ways.[36] Through their development and mutual appreciation of poetic hybridity, Smith and Wordsworth achieve what is truly, excitingly novel about Romantic poetry: self-reflexivity. By engaging in a *disputatio* with and questioning the very nature of poetry – its makeup, possible parameters, potential powers – both poets create the model Romantic poem.

2
Mediating History: War Poetry[1]

> Ah! Too soon
> From the gay visionary pageant rous'd,
> See the sad mourner start! – and, drooping, look
> With tearful eyes and heaving bosom round
> On drear reality ....
>
> Smith, *The Emigrants*, 1793

> ... what we feel of sorrow and despair
> From ruin and from change, and all the grief
> The passing shews of being leave behind,
> Appeared an idle dream that could not live
> Where meditation was.
>
> Wordsworth, *The Ruined Cottage*, 1797–8

As the previous chapter showed, for Smith and Wordsworth poetry was fertile ground for experimentation and for investigation into how form responded to manipulation and the questioning imagination. As they develop the style that came to be known as the lyrical ballad, moreover, they pursued a poetics more and more invested in worldly concerns: the hybrid poem as a reflection of their interests in the social. Running parallel to this poetics of innovation was another responsive form: the poetry of the 1790s that was directly concerned with war and its effects on people, place, and art. The events of 1792–7 – the September Massacres, the execution of Louis XVI, the declaration of war, the execution of Marie Antoinette, and the rise of a new French martial imperialism; the reactive political movements in Britain such as the Seditious Libel Act, the Treason Trials, suspensions of habeus corpus, an increasing conservatism that made pro-Revolutionary writing more and more suspect – resonate strongly in the literature of the period, as a variety of scholars have shown.[2] As she has become more securely embedded in the canon of familiar literature, Smith's *The Emigrants* has featured more and more in this scholarship; Wordsworth, thanks mainly to his pithy "Bliss was it in that dawn to be alive,/ But to be young was very Heaven," has been a key author for most who seek to show the trajectory of enthusiasm fading to disillusion and despair on the part of liberal thinkers in the 1790s. Many readers of Wordsworth work backward, using his hindsight as established in *The Prelude* as indicative of his 1790s literary politics, to establish a movement from the critique of *Salisbury Plain* to the disengagement evident at the close of *The Ruined Cottage*. Meanwhile, Smith's readers locate her political writing, other than in *The Emigrants*, in her novels, charting a move from the brashly pro-Revolutionary *Desmond*, through the more cautious *The Old Manor House*, to what has been seen as the reactionary *The Banished Man*.[3] Such readings, however, overlook the ahistoricity of reading the Wordsworth of the 1790s as if he already has the vision of the later Wordsworth; they miss the political tinge of the later poems in the second edition of the *Elegiac Sonnets*, in particular those carefully dated to 1792. Moreover, by studying them separately they miss how both writers struggle in similar ways with the impingement of the "real" on the poetic.

In this chapter I will discuss how Smith and Wordsworth play with art, artifice, and symbolism in their war poetry of the 1790s, and how each is defeated by the intrusion of the real. *The Ruined Cottage*, for instance, has been identified by many scholars as the poem in which Wordsworth learned how to "do" transcendence: the final turn from the affecting tale of the bereft Margaret to "the forms of things" anticipating the "life of things" of "Tintern Abbey" and signaling Wordsworth's rejection of the corporealities of the real world. In turn, the poems in the second volume of *Elegiac Sonnets* that have tended to receive the most attention are those in which Smith presents herself as a grief-stricken mother; an aspect of reality, to be sure, but a domesticated, only subtly politicized one. The "other poems" in the volume, some of which were discussed in the previous chapter, are overlooked, including the group significantly dated to November 1792. This has the effect of presenting a Smith whose post-*Emigrants* poetry is uninterested in the "real." And yet for both poets the war and its effects on certain classes of people – women, the poor, poets – characterize their 1790s poetry, and for both the "real" demonstrates its pervasive hold. *The Emigrants*, the 1792 short poems, *Salisbury Plain*, and *The Ruined Cottage* are placed firmly in landscapes disrupted by war, violence, and destitution, and despite the poets' strategies of displacement (turns to emblem, art, the symbolic), efforts to transcend the historical moment rupture rather than ensure coherence. Alan Liu, whose work in many ways supplies a bedrock for this chapter, has noted that the "Romantic imagination was a mediation between the worldly and otherworldly whose definitive act was the *simulation* of transcendental release."[4] Whereas Liu sees this simulation as a form of denial, I am interested in the ways in which simulation becomes part of the praxis of the poetry; in other words, the poet may attempt transcendence but in so doing shows its impossibility. I see this as historically located: it is part of the 1790s confusion over what can and can't be written (or even, following John Barrell, imagined). Smith and Wordsworth write the "real" through its parts, a collection of approaches that, in these poems, establish the relentlessness of the "real" in a time of war. But they also try out, through turns to the artistry of poetry, alternatives to the "real." Their war poems "arouse [the] expectation that there is a secure logic to be discovered for their perplexing circumstances ... [but then] frustrate such modes of discourse even as they put them forth."[5] Moments of pure art in the poems cannot, in the end, disguise the poems' inability to escape the "real."

There is an obvious difficultly in examining poems through the lens of the "real," which obtains in defining what "real" means. The events of the 1790s and their human cost heightened a sense that humanity was on a cusp, and yet how to identify that cusp fluctuated (as ever) according to individual and social points of view. Representing the "real" is heavily genre dependent: reportage or documentary *may* record events without mediation, but can poetry? In fiction, the 1790s is the decade where romantic tales of sensibility are beginning to give way to what comes to be labeled the realist novel: a text populated by recognizably human characters who react to the world in recognizable and plausible ways, and whose "adventures" move further and further from the coincidence and allegory of earlier decades. William Godwin's *Caleb Williams*, for instance, provocatively subtitled *Things as they are*, delves into psychologically feasible states of paranoia, anxiety, and surveillance, even though the plot resonates within the tradition of the romance. And Smith's own novels of the 1790s narrate stories of war, disenfranchisement, social and familial breakdown, and personal disenchantment that ring with the tones of modernity. In fact, Smith's novels pull into the last decade the full flowering of Frances Burney's 1778 phrase regarding her character Evelina: she is "true to nature if not to life." That is, she is a fully fleshed out, plausible character akin to the "real thing." Readers of *Evelina* may take some issue with the statement, but it glosses well a strategy both Smith and Wordsworth follow. Where their hybrid poetry demonstrated what was possible when formal regularity and tradition were put under the figurative microscope in the interest of recombination, their poetry of the real sets up another form of experimentation: Can poetry, in fact, contain or narrate the real? Can what David Bromwich identifies as the moment of encounter with the damaged other survive its transformation into poetry?[6]

In *The Artifice of Reality*, Karl Kroeber defines modern historians as

> those who examine the inner life of men's [sic] societies; focussing upon the interior life of events, they deduce the pattern of invisible forces of economics, ideologies, customs, and so forth, which are not visible at any one instant or at any single place but can be perceived only by finding the logic or coherence which binds together many separate phenomena.[7]

Although, based on his reading of "The Old Cumberland Beggar," Kroeber determines that Wordsworth is not a modern historian, embedded in his description is the conviction that the job of the modern historian is to establish the logic of event, to find the coherence that is otherwise invisible. The modern historian, in other words, exits history itself in order to make it. The problem with Kroeber's version of the historian is that logic and coherence are often not a part of event, even in its "interior life"; however, this is not to say that historians such as he describes don't still attempt to uncover it. The "Wordsworth" who narrates *Salisbury Plain* and *The Ruined Cottage* is exactly Kroeber's modern historian, but he is also the poet whose skepticism about the efficacy of rising above event creates a conflict of interest. Smith, too, narrates events in *The Emigrants* as if they have an internal logic, an invisible pattern, but as I have noted elsewhere, this poem is only superficially coherent; in its very susceptibility to breakdown it demonstrates its permeability to event, and its refusal to acquiesce to an expectation of the meaningful force of historical facts' "hidden relationships" (Kroeber, p. 128). In part, Kroeber's modern historian embodies a version of Romantic hermeneutics as advanced by Gerald L. Bruns. For Bruns, "we cannot know another's pain." This is not due to a lack of empathy, or indeed of trying, but is because the unknowability of others derives from "an untranscendable doubt produced by the limits of reason ... the limits of the human itself."[8] The attempt to overcome this unknowability mirrors Kroeber's historian diligently seeking invisible patterns.

For Bruns, this doubt is eased by a fantasy of overcoming boundaries, of imaginatively "knowing the other from the inside out," even though in so doing one risks the loss of the self in the other; as he puts it, "the dispossession of madmen, murderers, and sinful women" (p. 403).

The historian who rises above event in an attempt to find the pattern to which it conforms may be said to transcend the limitations of the experience of history. Philosophical transcendence, the act of surpassing or overcoming existent categories, here combines with the metaphorical process of exceeding, of rising above, so that finding the pattern transforms into finding a kind of solution. The catastrophes poeticized by Smith and Wordsworth in the poems this chapter discusses beg for resolution, for consolation, that which might conceivably be supplied by, say, the objective or unimplicated historian. This figure nominally speaks the poems, and searches for transcendence – that is, solutions – within the arts of poetry.[9] Rather than locating an efficacious pattern that can essentially overwrite disaster, however, the speaker finds him- or herself retreating into symbol, substituting one story for another, and failing to encounter either the real event or the needs of the sufferer. In other words, "transcendental release" cannot even be simulated, and mediation is itself the problem: the poetry ultimately, and irresistibly, retreats from social and political intervention into mere effect. Both Bromwich and Simpson locate this in the moment of encounter and in the portrayal of the other; for my purposes it is necessary to draw back from the narration of event in the poem to the praxis this narration relies on – transcendence.[10] As a work of the imagination, and as a work of art, it is achieved, or attempted, through the willful imposition of a speaker's conviction that he or she can know the other, see into the life of things and of people, and hence comprehend forms of history. In Smith's and Wordsworth's war poetry, things and people focus the speakers' need both to know and to overcome the real: to be modern historians. And yet, as the poems show, history, or event, is precisely what makes this, in the end, an impossible task, even within fantasy. The attempt to interpret the real world through symbol, emblem, and art creates not a seamless transcendence of the world, but a crashing return to it. The poems' engagement with "things as they are," shaded by attempts to create "things as they should be," is a deeply fraught encounter.

The 1790s, of course, sees an outpouring of poetry as well as other literature that narrates the "real," or versions of it, so Smith and Wordsworth are not unique in writing poems featuring emigrants, dead beggars, vagrants, and ruined cottagers. They are, however, interesting in their mutual fascination with the instability of the war poem's artistry, its inability to maintain its symbolic order. It is as if the material (of the) world simultaneously provides material for the poem, encourages or dangles the lure of transcendence through the application of poetic art, and then reinstates its authority when that art shows itself to be heavy, gauche, clumsy, or callow – or simply unconvincing. This echoes Liu, who sees "rhetoric as the facsimile knowledge ... whose distinctive method is its tendency to lose its way at decisive moments ... [O]nly inner troping allows method to be perceived *as* rhetoricity in the first place ..." (pp. 81–2). In other words, it is both what Smith and Wordsworth write about and how they undermine, or even unwrite, their subject.[11] This is not to suggest a lack of commitment in the poets' political stance. However, as I argue throughout this book, Smith and Wordsworth write poetry *as* poetry, as a form of art and not as a form of biography. Therefore, while political liberalism and a certain amount of political disappointment may be seen to underlie the poems under discussion, what is more important is the way in which the poetry, rather than ideology, comes undone when asked to bear the weight of the real. Smith and Wordsworth seem to write war poetry in which the violence they poeticize comes to signify the poetry itself, through an "inner troping" of symbolic and emblematic art as weak and unsustainable. The rhetoric, then, is one of disruption, imposture, trauma, distress, and artifice, not conveyed simply through pictures of human suffering, but rather, and more importantly, through its impact on the poetry *as* poetry. In the 1790s, neither Smith nor Wordsworth can write poetry that can successfully or seamlessly transcend a world defined by violence, betrayal, and loss. Instead, the poetry is itself contained and defined by this world. The poet who attempts to move from documenting war-related misery finds that poetry *about* the world is inevitably drawn back *to* the world. In finding themselves unable to transcend the pull or weight of the material world, the real, in their war poems, Smith and Wordsworth show that poetry can neither resist the world nor rewrite it. The poetry, in other words, fails.

I have called the poems this chapter is concerned with "war poems," because they either dramatize aspects of war or narrate the effects of war on individuals. But we might also call them historical narratives, to differentiate them from the seemingly more personal poetry the two are also writing at this time: the sonnets, for instance, or some of the lyrical ballads. However, as I show elsewhere in this book, the "personal" is a vexed category for Smith and Wordsworth as they co-write, and even here their narratives gesture toward another kind of real: one poet's own experiences in November 1792/April 1793, for instance, or another's as he crosses Salisbury Plain in the summer of 1793. Nonetheless, what differentiates these poems from various sonnets or ballads is that they are given over to the stories of others; even *The Emigrants* does this, although Smith leavens her portraits with turns to the self. The stories narrate the anguish of those who suffer either directly or indirectly from the privations occasioned by war. They are spoken by one whose own sufferings, if they form part of the poem, are not due to war but to different forms of distress. The speaker tells a tale that is, first, real (or meant to be true to life), but is also characterized by poetic flourishes designed to elevate the poem's focal figure(s), transform them into something more than individual examples of despair. Through symbol or emblem the speaker wants to combat the material misery of the poem's sufferers, and yet each is defeated by the reassertion or intrusion of the real. The result is a poetics of damage: history does not ground but rather threatens to destroy a poetry that tries too hard to escape its own materiality. However much transcendence is sought, or even written into the poem, in the end it is the real that is reinstated.[12]

For Smith and Wordsworth, writing war poetry in the 1790s means writing poems that reflect on the effects of war. Both poets begin the decade fervently pro-Revolution; both write poems in which a strong anti-war ethos yet retains the tinge of a dedication to liberty and freedom, as defined by the underlying principles of the Revolution. Smith writes in the Dedication to *The Emigrants* that "the very name of Liberty has ... lost the charm it used to have in British ears, [and] many who have written, or spoken, in its defence, have been stigmatized as promoters of Anarchy" (*Poetry*, p. 122). This is in 1793; in 1797, she attaches a note to "The Dead Beggar" stating

> I have been told that I have incurred blame for having used in this short composition, terms that have become obnoxious to certain persons.[13] Such remarks are hardly worth notice; and it is very little my ambition to obtain the suffrage of those who suffer party prejudice to influence their taste; or of those who desire that because they have themselves done it, every one else should be willing to sell their best birth-rights, the liberty of thought, and of expressing thought, for the *promise* of a mess of pottage. (*Poems*, p. 90)

Freedom of thought may be more esoteric than freedom from the oppression of the *ancien régime*, but it is inherent to a Revolutionary ethos. Smith dates "The Dead Beggar" to November 1792, but she adheres to liberal principles well past that date. Wordsworth's political development perhaps makes the jump from enthusiasm to disillusion more starkly; Liu's characterization that Wordsworth "denies" history as he formulates an "ideology of self" in *The Prelude* – which is then, as I noted above, read back into the 1790s – is an astute and deceptively simple argument that recollects the Poet as deliberately, intentionally, and necessarily outside history.[14] In the pre-*Prelude* 1790s, however, Wordsworth, like Smith, wrestles with the war.

Stock figures of distress and the miseries of war

The most familiar distressed figure in 1790s war poetry is, of course, the bereft woman. Whether a threatened mother (*The Emigrants*), an abandoned or bereaved wife (*The Ruined Cottage, Salisbury Plain*), or a displaced emigrant ("The Female Exile"), she is a constant presence in the period. Smith and Wordsworth use her ubiquity in their poems as a trope of the real, her distress as a marker of general misery. The movement from the particular to the general is an attempt to instate the transcendent, to use the figure to berate the powers that be for their callous dismissal of those who suffer when they "let loose the demons of war" ("The Forest Boy," *Poetry*, l. 135). By the 1790s, the notion that women suffered particularly well was an established social conclusion, due in no small part to the tremendous popularity of the heroine of sensibility, defined by her ability to feel. And yet sensibility itself was beginning to lose some of its appeal; a generation of devoted readers was giving way to a new audience, skeptical about the inherent value of emotional dissolution.[15] As Smith and Wordsworth write the suffering female, then, they do so in an atmosphere where her suffering signals true social breakdown *and* a showy and not entirely plausible dedication to feeling. Stock characters can perform with the minimum of backstory because they are so familiar; the question for Smith and Wordsworth is whether this enables a turn to symbolism, or complicates it.

Smith's terrorized mother in Book 2 of *The Emigrants* stands simultaneously as an example and an exemplar ("the figure of the distraught mother is universal"[16]). "A wretched Woman, pale and breathless," she "flies" "to a wild mountain" pursued by "hostile footsteps" both real and imagined,

> clasping close
> To her hard-heaving heart her sleeping child,
> All she could rescue of the innocent groupe

That yesterday surrounded her – Escap'd
Almost by miracle! Fear, frantic Fear,
Wing'd her weak feet: yet, half repentant now
Her headlong haste, she wishes she had staid
To die with those affrighted Fancy paints
The lawless soldier's victims! (p. 143, II: 258, 254, 260, 264–72)

Surrounded by the blast of cannonballs, "overwhelm'd/ Beneath accumulated horror," she "sinks" into death; her "maternal tenderness" toward her baby is unavailing, and "Mother and Infant perish both!" (p. 143, II: 279–80, 282, 291). Smith clearly designs this Mother as a symbol.[17] Her melodramatic flight, almost literalized when she is given "wing'd" feet; her abandonment of all her children save one; and her blind fear render her both a dramatic device and an affecting individual. Certainly, as a mother she is ineffectual: the poem makes it plain that she leaves behind living children, which she only "half" repents; she takes her baby to certain death and probable devourment by the "prowling monsters" roaming the hills – a gothic image of wolves that suggests the lines are written as much from the mother's terrified point of view as they are the outraged speaker's. Indeed, Antje Blank has called this scene "true Gothic," its mountains "a Salvator Rosaesque landscape" (p. 84). Her stock credentials thus intact, the mother provides a shorthand image of the victim of war. Following Liu, as a "victim of violence" she easily "becomes a 'symbol,'" so that "the liberal intellectual, writing past scenes of strife as a simulacrum of praxis, [can] speak for it."[18] Smith, then, writes a recipe in which victimized mother is mixed with horrific scenes in order to symbolize the miseries of war: "Mother and Infant perish both!," wiping out the existing and the next generation. "Such are thy dreadful trophies, savage War!" (p. 144, II: 313).

The poem, however, paints its picture too starkly; the Gothic is not "true" but rather only a veneer. Smith provides details that pull the mother away from her exemplary mode. First, there is the "frantic Fear" that allows her to abandon her children, as noted. The poem delays confirming their death, first assigning it only to the mother's "affrighted Fancy," but in the next verse-paragraph it provides the "fatal truth": the mother's husband, a "feudal Chief," arrives home. "[O]'er a bleeding corse/Stumbling he falls; another interrupts his staggering feet .../... all his family/Lie murder'd in his way!" (p. 144, II: 304–7). The "true Gothic" *may* include such scenes of carnage, but it would not permit a devoted mother to run away. The point needs emphasizing: this mother leaves all but one of her children to be horribly killed. Symbolic transcendence would demand that at the least she succeeds in placing her baby in safety (a convent, perhaps?), but instead the poem makes sure to kill it too. A dead mother could still be symbolic, Liu's victim whose destruction enables the writer to draw the greater lesson. And certainly Smith writes as if she is making the mother (and her husband, whose grief transforms him into "a wild raving Maniac" [p. 144, II: 309]) emblematic of "woes [that] Man inflict[s] on Man" (p. 144, II: 319). However, murdered children slam the poem back to the material world. A baby eaten by wolves is too messy a prospect for symbolism. Smith's exemplar becomes *too* moving, her situation *too* true. The Gothic veneer cracks and the event reasserts itself.

Kari Lokke has argued that Smith devises a transcendence that "represent[s] a potentially emancipatory distance and detachment from what she perceives as the largely male-dominated economic and political struggles of her time."[19] This distance allows for the construction of a counter-public sphere; Smith "seeks a transcendent perspective as a vehicle through which to represent with utmost clarity, detachment, and compassion the precise contours of her contemporary political landscape" (p. 87). She opposes Smith's style to that of Wordsworth, who, she notes, "sought to displace socio-political struggles into an apolitical and ahistorical realm" (p. 87), and reads the eminent settings of the two books of *The Emigrants* as the "locus of detachment and potential transcendence" (p. 93).[20] Lokke is a perceptive and nuanced reader of Smith, but in reading a poem like *The Emigrants* from the perspective encouraged by the sonnets (that is, as a personalized examination of society from the disenfranchised point of view of the woman[21]) she misses the longer poem's movement from detached transcendence to failed transcendence, encoded in the failed symbolism of the terrorized mother and the maniac father. Her summary of critical views on Wordsworth is salutary, however, the more so because she works from approaches to "Tintern Abbey" and his later poetry. The transcendent Wordsworth, or the Wordsworth who writes transcendence, is a later development.[22] The Wordsworth who has just finished reading *The Emigrants* writes his own anti-war poem, *Salisbury Plain,* which as Terence Allan Hoagwood argues, "scarcely veils its lament for the failed revolution."[23] Its stock bereft female, the Female Vagrant, has been analyzed extensively, and her tale is, perhaps, more successfully symbolic than Smith's; indeed, as a character she is almost parodically emblematic. The elegant and fluent overstatement of her famous couplet "And homeless near a thousand homes I stood,/ And near a thousand tables pined and wanted food" almost undoes the deprivation that it expresses. Moreover, her body is blazoned in what is almost a burlesque:

> Gently the Woman gan her wounds unbind
> ...
> Like swans, twin swans, that when on the sweet brink
> Of Derwent's stream the south winds hardly blow,
> 'Mid Derwent's water-lillies swell and sink
> In union, rose her sister breasts of snow,
> (Fair emblem of two lovers' hearts that know
> No separate impulse) or like infants played,
> Like infants strangers yet to pain and woe.
> Unwearied Hope to tend their motions made
> Long Vigils, and Delight her cheek between them laid.
> (ll. 203, 208–16)

The female body becomes a social body, her parts emblematized so that social cohesion may be re-effected, her story exemplary of the privations suffered by many. Liu calls her "a passive register of hurt" (*Wordsworth*, p. 188). Stephen Gill's influential argument that *Salisbury Plain* is a poem of "mediating symbols," where "nature leads the sense beyond themselves, and imagination becomes aware of its autonomy," allows the poem to be placed as a kind of apprentice to the transcendence he sees Wordsworth achieving in his later, greater work.[24] And yet the poem is also a political call, since Wordsworth, like Smith, poeticizes the "political events" of his "historical moment" while also "engag[ing] in a criticism of the underlying and collective mental acts that constitute the human world in which politics and economic change take their place" (Hoagwood, p. 180). Neither of these approaches, however, can come to terms with an image of female breasts as snowy twin swans resembling two hearts beating as one; or are they playful, happy, innocent babies, watched over by Hope while cuddling Delight? The poet points the way to symbolism with the overt reference to the breasts as "fair emblems," but the cumulative effect of the breasts' competing emblematic identities is to dismantle the symbolism altogether. We are left, instead, with the original picture: "the Woman gan her wounds unbind." As much as the poem wants to veil this with complicated symbolism, the picture persists: a woman, showing us her wounds. Even as Smith's terrorized mother cannot be transcended, neither can such an action. The stock figure of the bereft woman does more than emerge from the miseries caused by war; she *is* the misery, she feels it and suffers it. Try as they might, the poems can't transcend such trauma; it drags this war poetry right onto the field. Praxis fails to illuminate any kind of overarching, detached theme.

Salisbury Plain's Traveller, who "measured each painful step" in an echo of *The Emigrants*'s narrator's "step,/ Mournful and slow" (p. 138, II: 3–4), is rewritten in *Adventures on Salisbury Plain* as a criminal sailor, but in his first incarnation resembles another stock figure, the beggar. *Salisbury Plain* is really the Female Vagrant's story; the Traveller is there to listen. At his death, his likely fate is that of Smith's "Dead Beggar," who is "buried at the Expense of the Parish" in a short poem, the thrust of which is to emblematize (transcendentalize?) him for the benefit of a "Lady" whose sensibility finds the burial "affecting" (*Poetry*, p. 90). Unlike the bereft woman, the dead beggar takes more easily to being emblematized as a symbol of the equality found in the grave and ensured by "Death, the Leveller" (l. 15). The poem is not overtly a war poem, although as noted above Smith makes effective use of the language of political liberalism. However, by date it is grouped not only with "The Female Exile" (redacted from *The Emigrants*) and "Written for the Benefit of a Distressed Player," but also Book One of *The Emigrants*. November 1792 thus stands out as a meaningful date: a scant two months after the September Massacres, on the eve of winter and of war. Since the poem was not published until 1797, its temporality is doubled: it cannot be "about" the coming war, and yet it cannot help but *meaningfully* predate it. The Dead Beggar, then, whose "Death vindicates the insulted rights of Man," is both a decomposing corpse and a symbol of want and neglect (l. 20). It is true that the poem presents death as the beggar's reward for a life of suffering: "he rests upon the mercies of his GOD" (l. 24). And yet the poem itself is quiescent; in offering death as the beggar's triumph it goes some way towards disagreeing with its own note: "in a country like ours, where such immense sums are annually raised for the poor, there ought to be some regulation which should prevent any miserable deserted being from perishing through want" (*Poetry*, p. 90). The poem finds consolation in religious quietism, albeit expressed in the language of Paine; the note expresses the opinion that the beggar should not have been permitted to die of starvation. So is death the reward or is death, more simply, more realistically, the result of a lack of care? The speaker, who applies Revolutionary principles emblematically, displays what Hoagwood calls the "enslaved mind" who "puts on like clothing the ideological (mental) fetters whose mental origin the slave soon forgets" (p. 182) – what Smith in *The Emigrants* puts thus:

> ... luxury wreathes with silk the iron bonds,
> And hides the ugly rivets with her flowers,

> Till the degenerate triflers, while they love
> The glitter of the chains, forget their weight. (ll. 278–81)

The speaker, in other words, attempts to transcend the material conditions that led to the beggar's death by turning his death into a moral lesson or emblem for the "Lady." The poem undoes this with its sideswipe at the inequities of the social system. The real does not allow us to forget its weight.

Voices Telling Tales

Smith and Wordsworth focalize their war poetry through others' voices as well as through versions of their own. Smith's efforts to anchor *The Emigrants* in what is insisted upon as actual experience has led readers to express some annoyance that, even when her subject is the suffering of others, her emphasis is on herself (as one review commented, she could be "discover[ed]" "almost at the bottom of every page, as [one might] the portrait of the most renowned painters in the corner of their most favourite pictures"[25]). But *The Emigrants* is narrated from a variety of perspectives, as suggested above; and these competing perspectives pertinently affect the coherence and the cohesion of the poem. *Salisbury Plain*, as it moves from version to version, changes its mind about whose is the dominant voice, but even the version under discussion in this chapter complicates the reader's ability to decide who tells the tale. Likewise, *The Ruined Cottage* cannot quite decide who to favor – the narrator, the Pedlar, or Margaret – to devastating effect. And "The Female Exile" and "Distressed Player" base their structure on forms of layered quotation, further undermining the poetic pursuit of transcendence. The ease with which Smith and Wordsworth create narrators that readers can identify closely with the poet requires that we approach their presentations of personalized speakers – speakers whose history aligns closely with the poet's – with some reservations.[26] Even as this voice might stand for the inclusion of the real, it also directs the poem(s) in the project of transcending the real. The intricate and not fully resolvable conflict that results from voice speaking and listening to voice, however, works against this.

As many critics have noted, myself included, Smith anchors *The Emigrants* in historical time in the "scenes" which open each book. In so doing, she *creates* historical time: November 1792 and April 1793 take on a historicized temporality that means something in the poem itself. The "Scenes" function as a version of voice, telling where and when we are. Moreover, the very specificity it offers – "a Morning in November, 1792," "an Afternoon in April, 1793" – signals a real-time operation for the poem. Historical time and real time vie. This spurs what Christoph Bode calls the "pretence" of Romantic writing: "the delusory nature of such linguisti[c] present tense speech act[s]." As Bode observes, "a considerable number of British Romantic poems highlight their *textuality* ... these poems are conspicuously and ostentatiously aware of their *mediality*, and the grounds of their being."[27] This conspicuous and ostentatious mediality, however, is emergent rather than declarative; we gradually become aware of the artifice, which is in part due to the strength and conviction of the voice who situates the poem with such clarity. As we read the two books of *The Emigrants*, therefore, we are transported to its "scenes": place is created wherein voice(s) can speak. However, Smith does not provide a speaker for Book I until more than thirty lines into the poem. As it opens, we are offered a seascape seemingly overlooked by no one: "Slow in the Wintry Morn, the struggling light/ Throws a faint gleam upon the troubled waves;/ Their foaming tops, as they approach the shore/ And the broad surf that never ceasing breaks/ On the innumerable pebbles, catch the beams/ Of the pale Sun ..." (p. 125, I: 1–6). When the speaker enters, it is to a fantasy: "How often do I half abjure Society,/ And sigh for some lone Cottage, deep embower'd/ In the green woods ... / .../ the short grass, strewn with fairy flowers" (p. 126, I: 42–4, 49). This speaker longs for anything *but* the real world, tainted as it is by "proud oppression," "legal crimes," and war. The real and fantasy are instantly in conflict: even as the speaker registers her[28] real-world existence and its miseries, she does so through allusion to "the fabled Danaïds" and "the wretch,/ Who ceaseless, up the steep acclivity,/ Was doom'd to heave the still rebounding rock" (p. 126, I: 68–70).

The speaker, then, the first voice, finds herself unable to inhabit either reality or fantasy completely; linguistically, she seems to choose both, and her shifts from one to the other provide the model for the poem's inherent indecisiveness. As the speaker turns to her putative subjects, the Emigrants, she does so via two images of social realism: the "buildings, new and trim" discussed above, and a parenthetical critique of the pointed landscaping of the rich – "the village Church (with care conceal'd/ By verdant foliage, lest the poor man's grave/ Should mar the smiling prospect of his Lord)" (p. 127, I: 82–4). This suggests a way to view the figures: as actual, real men (and one woman) pacing the beach. Smith embues each with a specific personality, while at the same time making each exemplary of his station: hence, the self-denying monk, "amaz'd" by the pity and charity of those he "condemn'd as Heretics"; the "haughty," high-ranking cleric, in despair as he "dwell[s] on all he lost"; the sanguine, flattering, smiling, self-deceiving Abbé; the mild, patient, submissive, sorrowing parish priest, dismayed by "his erring people"; the aristocrat with his "martial air" and "high consciousness of noble blood"; his wife, "a softer form," dreaming of the lost glories of Versailles (pp. 127, 128, 129, 130, 129; I: 120, 123, 125, 128, 197, 234–5, 202). They are, then, both real and imaginary: both people with whom the speaker shares the beach, and symbols or selected types of emigrants. Smith knows the difference: in "real life" she shelters and aids actual emigrants, and sees her daughter fall in love with and marry one. The emigrants that she writes into the poem are, therefore, exemplary because Smith wants them to be: they are meant as Figures rather than figures (I will return to this distinction below). They are spoken for rather than speak: the narrating voice operates a kind of functional free indirect discourse that is nonetheless tinged with her own need to see the emigrants symbolically, to associate with them as fellow victims. "I mourn your sorrows; for I too have known/ Involuntary exile"; that is, *because* the speaker has experienced what she characterizes as exile, she can empathize with the emigrants (p. 128, I: 155–6). She is *as* them: feeling proceeds from identification. This is the same speaker who could not decide between fantasy and reality; to reiterate the point, her abjuration of Society was only, itself, half-hearted ("half abjure"). Underlying the speaker's presentation of the exemplary emigrants, then, is her own vacillation between the real and the symbolic, the "here" in this particular Scene, and the "there" that transcends it.

The speaker's rhetorical strategies consistently misfire. Although she condemns the aristocrat's alienation from the real world of merit (he relies on "the splendid trophies/ Of Heraldry" with its "painted puns, and visionary shapes" as evidence of his "exalt[ation] ... from the crowd" [p. 131, I: 253–4, 257, 260]), she finds herself unable to maintain the detached tone that would allow a consistent turn to the immaterial. Despite Lokke's argument that "Smith's transcendence is a kind of self-doubling and self-awareness that allows one to see oneself from the outside, to appreciate one's worth as well as to practice self-criticism and to honor the common humanity even of one's ideological enemies" ("Moon," p. 98), the narrator of *The Emigrants* flits back and forth between these states. Lokke's point presents the flip side to Bruns':

> the problem of being human, of being certain of one's humanity or of one's real human existence ... is not a problem that goes away

> when one becomes full-grown, rather it gets worse, that is, one's humanness grows the more questionable so that one can no longer see in oneself, or rather feel in oneself, quite what (one thinks) one once saw and felt: one has to turn elsewhere, to someone else, some simulacrum or reconstruction of oneself ... (Bruns, p. 412)

Lokke finds that Smith is able to focus on the self *and* the other/self, hence the self-doubling. But in *The Emigrants* this seems abortive, since the poem presents only abjected and empty others, and a miserable and conflicted self. The voice who tells the poem cannot maintain the integrity of her images: hence the monstrousness of the terrorized mother, for instance, or "poor but peaceful hinds" who are, elsewhere and simultaneously, the "solitary Shepherd[s] [who shiv'ring ten[d/ Their] dun discolour'd flock" (pp. 138, 132; II: 63, I: 299–300). As Smith explains in a moment of clarity that directly confronts the real/art conflict, the shivering shepherd, who is real, is "unlike/ Him, whom in song the Poet's fancy crowns/ With garlands, and his crook with vi'lets binds" (p. 132, I: 300–302). Too true; which casts doubt on the subsequent pictures, where poverty exists but is leavened by peace. The poor but peaceful hind is joined by "the emaciate wretch," at first an exemplar of need, and, like the Dead Beggar after him, a symbol of national shame,[29] but within a few lines the poem is gratified by the fact that "Peace is here,/ And o'er our vallies, cloath'd with springing corn,/ No hostile hoof shall trample, nor fierce flames/ Wither the wood's young verdure" (p. 141, II: 196, 205–208).

The poem, so clearly anti-war, cannot find a consistent mode in which to present its sentiments. Veering from symbol to real and back again, sometimes with the same figure, it relies on a narrative voice itself unsure whether she is herself a victim or a savior, one with the emigrants or their source of succor. Perhaps this is one reason Smith returned to portions of the poem in the second volume of the *Elegiac Sonnets*. "The Female Exile" focuses on the one female emigrant of the group. Recast in anapestic tetrameter with frequent pyrrhics, the poem displays its status as art, as *versed poetry*, over its origin as what Smith in a note calls "a sketch ... in blank verse" (*Poetry*, p. 91). The poem paints a portrait in words, accompanied by a plate objectifying the female exile as young, winsome, and melancholy, simply but fashionably dressed, watching her children play childish games. The poem deletes the exile's regret over the lost graces of Versailles, instead taking the reader from "November's chill blast" to a seat "beneath that chalk rock" where the "poor mourner" "reclines" in elegant disarray (ll. 1, 5, 33, 5). Overall, the poem is more artifice than art, despite its formal pose; as self-quotation it emphasizes its status as (re)written, but it cannot quite transform the female exile into a symbol, nor can it render her a convincing example of the real. This is, in the end, due to the speaker, who enters in the last stanza: "Poor mourner! – I would that my fortune had left me/ The means to alleviate the woes I deplore;/ But like thine my hard fate has of affluence bereft me,/ *I* can warm the cold heart of the wretched no more!" (ll. 33–6). We learn that the exile is not so much a failed symbol of the miseries of war as she is an activated symbol of the speaker's misery, an element of the history she charts and a potential springboard to the bigger picture. But the picture is only as big as the speaker. If *The Emigrants* could not reconcile its speaker's varying forms of imagery, "The Female Exile" settles on one with a thump: the exile suffers so that we may understand that the speaker suffers, since she is unable to alleviate the exile's suffering. This provides us with an example of the English charity that so amazed the French clergy, but like "The Dead Beggar" it is quiescent; hardship and need are transferred from subject to speaker and rendered, in the end, bathetic. Where the speaker in *The Emigrants* could at least provide some access to the female exile's thoughts and fears, this speaker reads only surface: "the multiplied miseries that wait on mankind" in a time of war are, for her, reducible to financial need (l. 24).[30] As the speaker privileges her own need to provide succor, she also demonstrates the continued pull of the real. The poem's poeticizing is diminished but its enthrallment to the material is enforced.

Smith's use of voice allows *The Emigrants* a force that compensates in many ways for the poem's almost tidal fluctuations. Her translation and self-quotation in "The Female Exile" indicate an examination of the effects of revoicing. In both poems, a mismatch between voice and art prevents the full establishment of a consistent symbolism. In *Salisbury Plain*, Wordsworth uses voice both overtly, through the embedded narrative spoken by the Female Vagrant, and more subtly, in the ghostly voice heard by the Traveller as he stands gazing, "astonished," on the "wild," "forlorn," and "vacant" plain (ll. 74, 61, 62). Liu argues that, in *Salisbury Plain*, "everything we have read points toward the writing of some tragic tale able to explicate the historical necessity of pain. But the 'herculean' struggle of the poem is not therefore to unfold that tale. Rather, the poem denies explication by suspending narrative in ever more obscure replications."[31] For Liu, Wordsworth attempts to transcend the conditions of his poem by, in essence, underwriting it: deliberate obscurity creates the fuzzy edges that encourage readers to see emblem and symbol rather than exposition. However, it is exactly by reading *everything* that we can see the poem's vacillation between the symbolic and the real, which hinges, here, on the tale-telling ghostly voice. The "voice as from a tomb in hollow accents" warns against "that mountain-pile," identified in the previous stanza as "an antique castle spreading wide," not unlike the "Gothic battlements/ [That] frown on the plain beneath" to which Smith's "feudal Chief" returns, only to find his children slaughtered (*Salisbury Plain*, ll. 82, 78; *Emigrants*, p. 143, II: 292–3). In two stanzas, this voice characterizes the plain as a Gothic scene of magic, human sacrifice, hell-fire, and blood; the "voice was from beneath but face or form/ He saw not, mocked as by a hideous dream" (ll. 100–101). Wordsworth brings this voice directly into the narrative; as heard speech it takes on an author-proxy role. Its words paint the plain as a mythic space, devoted to replaying past scenes of violence, rather than as a mere geographic space, albeit a physically challenging one. The Traveller is thus primed to "read" his surroundings as symbolic of the fear and bewilderment he duly feels; when the speaker of the poem compares the solidity of the "dark and waste" plain to "ocean's shipless flood" (l. 109), we can see how determined the poem is to emblematize, and terrorize, the scene. Hence the Traveller, as "agonized" as the landscape, to use Liu's term (pp. 165–6), reaches the "lonely Spital," enters it, and hears another voice he is primed to identify as otherworldly:

> Here shall he rest til Morn her eye unclose.
> Ah me! that last of hopes is fled apace;
> For, entering in, his hair in horror rose
> To hear a *voice* that seemed to mourn in sorrow's throes.
> 16
> It was the *voice* of one that sleeping mourned,
> A *human voice*! and soon his terrors fled ... (ll. 132–7, emphasis added)

It is only at the third mention that this voice is humanized. The Traveller, then, is led from voice to voice and from the symbolic to the imagined, back to the real, and to the eventual "realistic account of distress" told by the Female Vagrant (*SP*, p. 6).

The poem, however, prevents us from accepting this trajectory. With the entry of the Female Vagrant, the poem subsumes much of its voice to hers, and from her we learn of her encounter with an "old man" who, "beckoning from the naked steep/ Came tottering sidelong down" to her "hollow deep" to "ask the hour" (ll. 165–6, 163). The mundanity of his request belies any turn to the symbolic, as does the matter-of-fact style in which he tells his own tale to the Vagrant: "He spoke ... of a swain who far astray/ Reached unawares a height and saw beneath/ Gigantic beings ranged in dread array ..." (ll. 173–5). Strikingly, the old man tells the Vagrant of the same terrors as those intoned mysteriously to the Traveller; and in fact, it is the same voice:

> 11
> "For oft at dead of night, when dreadful fire
> Reveals that powerful circle's reddening stones,
> Mid priests and spectres grim and idols dire,
> Far heard the great flame utters human moans,
> Then all is hushed: again the desert groans,
> A dismal light its farthest bounds illumes,
> While warrior spectres of gigantic bones,
> Forth-issuing from a thousand rifted tombs,
> Wheel on their fiery steeds amid the infernal glooms."
>
> 21
> And oft a night-fire mounting to the clouds
> Reveals the desert and with dismal red
> Clothes the black bodies of encircling crowds.
> It is the sacrificial altar fed
> With living men. How deep it groans – the dead
> Thrilled in their yawning tombs their helms uprear;
> The sword that slept beneath the warriour's head
> Thunders in fiery air: red arms appear
> Uplifted thro' the gloom and shake the rattling spear.

Spoken directly in stanza 11, paraphrased by the Vagrant in stanza 21, the parallel stanza numbers confirm the repetition: rather than Liu's suspension of narrative, the poem offers a reiteration of narrative, a version of an historian's documentary proof, that effectively undoes the ghostly, symbolic aura of stanzas 10–11. The old man brings what had been terrible and mysterious into a real world where it is necessary to know the time, and where one's physical placement can determine what, and who, one hears. The Traveller on his "mound," the Vagrant in her "hollow," both listen to the same voice. The tale it tells inspires terror within the poem, but outside its boundaries it disables terror, undoes the attempted turn to the symbolic realm, and threatens to collapse the narrative. The poem presents this at the transcendent level – the elevated historian's point of view – but its strength of effect allows the ghostly explanation to override the mundane.

While *The Ruined Cottage* is more straightforward as to voice (we know who narrates at all times, for instance), in its movements from speaker to Pedlar to Margaret and back again it betrays an inability to create a *fully* functioning symbolic domain. *The Ruined Cottage* has been discussed as the first poem in which Wordsworth found his mature voice, moving away from the vexed politics of something like *Salisbury Plain* and toward a devotion to the imaginatively symbolic.[32] "The theme of the completed poem is the humanized imagination," of which Margaret is entirely emblematic (Gill, *Wordsworth's Poetry*, p. 140). It is one of Wordsworth's "simplest statements of one of the momentous arguments of Romanticism: that when Beauty comes to us now, it comes disguised, veiled, or disfigured."[33] The poem "transcends the concerns of politics and philosophy, and settles on the thing that had always fascinated Wordsworth, and which would provide his central subject for the rest of his career: emotional and psychological truth."[34] Margaret "is the very principle of enduring coherence that the poem also names the 'bond of brotherhood' or 'humanity' ... [S]he is the origin of the need for imagery" (Liu, *Wordsworth*, pp. 311, 315). But she is also – like the Female Vagrant, the Female Exile, the terrorized mother, and Smith's narrator in *The Emigrants* – a bereft woman, and pulls the poem back from the symbolic to the real in the details of her own tale. The poem allots to the Pedlar and the speaker the task of emblematizing her (as Bromwich notes, "the sadness of human beings is assigned a *general* cause" [p. 153]). Margaret, unlike the Female Vagrant, is not permitted to accompany her husband to war; instead, like Smith's Phoebe in "The Forest Boy," she is abandoned. Again unlike the Vagrant, she is unvoiced: where the Vagrant tells her own story to the Traveller, Margaret's is filtered through the Pedlar's and presented by the speaker. And we see signs that the speaker and the Pedlar somehow need Margaret's story to transcend itself, to mean more than just the tale of one woman's sorrow. As Gill notes, Margaret "let[s] her child and her garden die" (*Wordsworth's Poetry*, p. 138); his easy conflation of the human and the natural derives from the Pedlar's own association of the two: "Her infant babe/ Had from its mother caught the trick of grief/ And sighed among its plaything. Once again/ I turned towards the garden-gate and saw/ ..../ ... the earth was hard,/ With weeds defaced and knots of withered grass ..." (ll. 409–11, 414–15). Constantly moving from the real to the symbolic, the Pedlar situates Margaret as somehow outside the human economy; although at least eighteen months pass from the time of Robert's desertion of the family to the "Autumn" when we learn that Margaret's youngest child has died, the child is still a "little babe," and well before this Margaret has voiced her conviction that "my body [is] not such/ As others are ... I could never die" (ll. 436, 356–7).

The Pedlar wants the tale of Margaret to mean something more than itself, and so he rebukes the speaker at the beginning of the Second Part: "vain dalliance with the misery/ Even of the dead" is "wantonness," but Margaret's "common tale" can be elevated to "power" for those who "think" (ll. 223–4, 231, 229, 236). Hence "it would have grieved/ Your very heart to see her" is rendered more meaningful a few lines later: "it would have grieved/ Your very soul to see her" (ll. 361–2, 375–6). The transformation of heart (feeling) to soul (being) signals the emblematizing of Margaret and her story; "the Pedlar presents Margaret's suffering as a part of a larger pattern" (he historicizes it), leading the speaker to an understanding of the "persuasion of consolation" in the final "tranquil" images of Nature.[35] In Duncan Wu's words, "Margaret's torment acquires purpose" (p. 36). Hence Margaret and her story are subsumed, and, confronted with the transcendent image of Margaret "sleeping" in the "calm earth" (rather than dead), the Pedlar is inspired to "meditation" and "happiness" (ll. 512, 524, 525). Peter Thorslev notes that not all readers accept this symbolization; Thomas de Quincy "complained that the Pedlar ought simply to have written a letter to the War Office on Margaret's behalf" (p. 94).[36] Under the spell of the Pedlar's voicing of the tale, this seems an unimaginative reaction to the poem, and yet it also speaks to the unsteady transcendentalizing of the poem, to the pull of the real on the effort to find a speakable narrative. Margaret, like the terrorized mother, defects from her maternal duties so that she may become a symbol; the poem forces her to suffer unnecessarily so that her story may transcend its material basis. Yet the inescapable effect of this is to deprive her story both of meaning and of sense. No matter how the Pedlar dresses it up, in treating her as a symbol the poem makes her a senseless one. Her suffering is so extreme, so denaturing, that it must mean something, and yet as soon as she is made to suffer so extremely in order that she may become meaningful, her suffering becomes mere event. The real, then, wars in this poem with the symbolic, and the poem seems to recognize this; we all just walk away and go to the pub ("the rustic inn, our evening resting-place" [l. 538]). This tale signifies nothing once it is made to signify more than itself.

Theatres of War, Figures, and Role-Playing

Salisbury Plain plays with voice, and it also, like *The Emigrants* before it, creates a perhaps unintentionally theatrical tone as it sets the scene in its opening stanzas. As I noted above, *The Emigrants*'s overt scene-setting creates a conflict about what is real and what is imaginary. As we alight, with the speaker, "on the Cliffs" and "on an Eminence," we are confronted not only with a place but also the representation of a place, the capital letters invoking the figurative as well as the literal. Smith uses the language of theatrics to open her poem, which picks up on the image with which she closes her Dedication to Cowper: a moment of political theater "when, in the Parliament of England, the greatest Orator of our time quoted the sublimest of our Poets – when the eloquence of Fox did justice to the genius of Cowper" (*Poetry*, p. 122). She in turn uses a theatrical declamation to end the poem; her repeated imperatives as she addresses God lend the last lines not only an oratorical, but a dramatic tone: "cause thy creatures cease," "restrain that rage for power," "teach the hard hearts," "drive/ From the ensanguin'd earth," and allow the return of "Reason, Liberty, and Peace!" (pp. 146–7, II: 422, 424, 426, 432–3, 444). *Salisbury Plain* not only ends with similar declamations – "pursue your march," "uptear th'Oppressor's dungeon," "rear ... the herculean mace/ of Reason," "pursue your toils" (ll. 541, 542, 543–5, 547) – it opens with an image drawn from *The Emigrants*. The image of the hungry savage whose sufferings are nonetheless lightened by being all he has ever known, as opposed to those who break down under "memory of pleasures flown" (l. 21), echoes Smith's speaker: "the exil'd Nobles .../...must feel/ More poignant anguish, than the lowest poor/ Who, born to indigence, have learn'd to brave/ Rigid Adversity's depressing breath!" (p. 132, I: 310–14). The allusion offers readers a figure who is also a Figure, standing not only for *Salisbury Plain*'s but also for *The Emigrants*' philosophy of relative suffering.[37] The two poems create an almost filmic downward swoop in their opening lines, moving readers from the general to the particular with the effect of a theatrical prologue. We enter the tales of war, then, through a dramatic mise-en-scène, which then leads to the introduction of, among other things, the stock figures discussed above (for instance, the distressed Mother in *The Emigrants* who is both a figure in the poem and a Figure of emotive significance).

Both poems, however, also create a plethora of emblems, stand-ins for their counterparts in actuality.[38] *The Emigrants*, in particular, is loaded with figures and the figured: not only the emigrants themselves, each, as discussed above, representative of a group or class as well as of their own individuality, but also a wide variety of embodied abstracts. Freedom, Anarchy, Bigotry, War, and Vengeance alone occupy one eight-line passage (p. 127, I: 99–107); Order, Anarchy, Freedom, Confusion,

Virtue, Vengeance, Avarice, Envy, and Liberty another of ten lines (p. 133, II: 340–49). Sprinkled liberally through the rest of the poem we find Society, War, Desolation, Hope, Power, Care, Chivalry, Discord, Fraud, Reason, Want, Woe, Insult, Loyalty, Victory, Adversity, Venality, Nature, Humanity, Equality, Murder, Fear, Romance, Content, Disease, Poverty, Peace, Death, Fancy, Law, Pestilence, Piety, Superstition, Ambition, Licence, Pride, Oppression, and Revenge. The sheer numbers create a theatrical feel, as the figures cross and recross the pages like a Greek chorus. It is not, of course, unusual in a polemic to find such figuring: it lends force and gravitas to the piece, and shows a facility with rhetoric. Smith peoples the poem with non-people in order to make her point about the near-apocalyptic danger humanity is flirting with in its move toward total war. While it may not have the effect of transcendence, such figuring can nonetheless shift the poem from the material world of the real.

This is why it is so significant that Smith indiscriminately figures non-abstracts as well. A Cottage, Hills, trees like the "Beach [sic]" and the Ash, the emigrants themselves ("Sad Heralds of distress" [p. 127, I: 96]), Heretics, Monarchs, Men, the City, the Theatre, Courts, the Ocean, Heroes, Parasites, Exiles, Compatriots, the Moon, Freemen, a Mother, a Woman, an Infant, a Chief, a Porter, a Castle, Maniac, the Widow, the Orphan, Politicians. Smith takes what could well be "real" and resolutely Figures them, makes them exemplary of their group, and transforms them into emblems.[39] But she does so across the board: people, places, and things all take on a Figured theatricality that takes them away from the real but also, in the end, does not allow for a full enrollment in the figurative. There are simply too many figures in the poem, too many exemplars. It is as if the war has not only affected the emigrants, exiling them from their homeland, it has also exiled the poetry from its lexical field. This makes the occasions when the poem does not indulge in figuring all the more pointed: "they became/ The prey of dark suspicion and regret," or "The fearful spectres of chicane and fraud" (pp. 142, 145; II: 244–5, 355). How can the real be figured if the Figures are doing all they can to escape the real? On the other hand, how can a viable symbolism be achieved if using the figurative is simultaneously overindulged and inconsistent? In this theater, we seem to be asked to applaud the remarkable dance undertaken by the poetry, as it slips from one register to another.

Salisbury Plain is more restrained in its use of figures, but nonetheless follows *The Emigrants* in using the device as a sign of the real as inflected by the rhetorical. Hence, in stanza 3 "Refinement," "Love" and

"Friendship" are figured so as to enhance the suffering felt by the newly victimized: "how many thousands weep/ Beset with foes more fierce than e'er assail/ The savage without home in winter's keenest gale" (ll. 34–6). Figuring these tropes of civilized life elevates them – they become abstracts – but it also creates a contrast that poses the disabling question: Is their loss *really* a "foe" more "fierce" than homelessness in the face of winter's blast? Both *The Emigrants* and *Salisbury Plain* require hinds and savages to be foils for their suffering figures; figuring the "refinements" they have lost does not, however, fully allow them to overwrite the real suffering caused by physical exposure. Instead, this figuring creates a space in the poem analogous to what Liu has called Wordsworth's "final saving fiction," which is "his faith that transcendental imagination can at the last recollect history" (*Wordsworth*, p. 456). For Liu, this offers the "possibility that Wordsworth was his own critic" (p. 456).[40] In *Salisbury Plain*, as Wordsworth plots transcendence onto reality via presentation and re-presentation, dramatic doublings and significant figurings, he may not yet have established a self-critical capacity, but his poem shows an imbalance in its rhetoric that enables social criticism while also composing its own vision of unquestioned social inequalities. The Female Vagrant, then, is introduced in the poem as the unpointed "female wanderer" but within four stanzas has become "the Woman," slotted into a figured space so that her tale may become emblematic of those "foes more fierce" than "winter's keenest gale" (ll. 138, 163, 36). And her narration is duly mythic: she contends with Silence, Fear (twice), Misery, careless "proud Fortune," Disease, Famine (twice), Agony, Despair, and Death. As noted above, Liu has called her a "passive register of hurt" (*Wordsworth*, p. 188), but this is to underplay her facility with language and its impact. She does not merely suffer, she Suffers, and her Sufferings are themselves given a dramatic heft such that the poem begins to totter.

Correspondingly, the Traveller sheds "Pity's tear," itself a rhetorical response that embues him with something more than sympathetic fellow feeling (l. 400). The somewhat surprising mellow and bucolic final scene given to the pair results from the Figuring that has removed them from the real rather than reiterating the universal nature of their suffering. As morning breaks, the two

> ... now from a hill summit down they look
> Where through a narrow valley's pleasant scene
> A wreath of vapour tracked a winding brook
> Babbling through groves and lawns and meads of green.

A smoking cottage peeped the trees between,
The woods resound the linnet's amorous lays,
And melancholy lowings intervene
Of scattered herds that in the meadows graze,
While through the furrowed grass the merry milkmaid strays.
(ll. 406–14)

The poem invites the two to a feast: "for you yon milkmaid bears her brimming load,/ For you the board is piled with homely bread" (ll. 419–20).[41] The horrors of the night disperse as they enter a small personal Eden which in its perfection is both theatricalized (that is, staged) and unreal; not transcendent, but unbelievable. Wordsworth dispenses with his by now fabulous couple and turns to a conclusion figured in precisely the same tones as the ending of *The Emigrants*.

It is this combination of figured abstracts and tonal figuring that places both *Salisbury Plain* and *The Emigrants* in limbo at their conclusions. Both are infused with an anger and defiance at a cultural dysfunction that embed injustice in the social fabric. Smith's speaker inveighs against false Piety, Superstition, Ambition, Licence, Confusion, Pride, Oppression, Avarice, and Revenge, and calls on God to empower Liberty, Freedom, Reason, and Peace. Wordsworth likewise denounces Treachery, Misery, Oppression, Injury, Strife, Death, Avarice, Superstition, Exile, Terror, Bonds, Force, and Error, and seeks instead Justice, Peace, Truth, and Reason. Both, as noted above, makes lavish use of imperatives in the last lines; both march onto the stage of their poems and declaim, anchoring their rhetoric in figures that have, by now, overtaken both the real and the transcendent. There is an actorly quality to the voices that conclude these two poems, as if the last lines in both function as kinds of Epilogues, and this, while it is forceful, is also indeterminate. Are we meant to applaud, or feel inspired to undertake direct action? Is it entertainment, or instruction?

A problem seems to be that in trying to make real-life horrors even more vehemently real, both poets entangle their most overt anti-war poems in rhetorical knots. The more they load them with figures to enhance the power of the real suffering they describe, the more the poems depart from the world of the real. And yet, because of the indiscriminate figuring that characterizes both poems, nor can either achieve a transcendent historian's representativeness through figuring. We are left with poems that hover between the two states. As if Smith recognizes that there is a link between sustained social protest and the theatrical, however, in "Written for the Benefit of a Distressed Player" she relies entirely on a staged war poem. The distressed player is not a soldier, nor is he, like the Female Exile or the Female Vagrant, directly victimized by war. He is, instead, a casualty of a warring society, a reflection of conditions in the same way that, for instance, "the oppression of one female vagrant [could be] seen to have intimate links with the reasons why ... the country was plunging into an unjust war" (*SP*, p. 5). Dated to November 1792, published in 1797, this poem, like "The Dead Beggar," occupies a dual temporality: the country is both in a pre-war state and well into the lengthy engagement that lasted for, more or less, another twenty years. Key to the poem is its entirely dramatic nature: the speaker is an actor, although this does not become clear until the third stanza; as he recites his lines for the "benefit" of the reader, the poem itself acts for his "benefit." The images of poverty he presents are refracted through the theatre, "mingling – with real distresses – mimic pains" (l. 28). Actors make a speciality of inhabiting different personae – "an Hero now, and now a *Sans Culotte*!" – and Smith's figuring makes plain the theatrically emblematic nature of the rhetorical strategy (l. 26). But Smith pushes her conceit until it threatens to overtake the poem and call into question every figure it offers:

> See in our group, a pale, lank Falstaff stare!
> Much needs he stuffing: – while young Ammon there
> Rehearses – in a garret – ten feet square!
> And as his soft *Statira* sighs consent,
> Roxana comes not – but a dun for rent! (ll. 29–33)

The theatrical and the real merge, as do the parts of the actor's speech: stuffing standing for costumed padding and the food the actor goes without; jealous Roxana replaced by the even more imperious bailiff. As the distressed player turns to the ostensibly more "blest" Fisher and Peasant, however, the uncertainty underlying the Figure in a poem that is completely dramatic comes to the fore. The player presents these figures as real, living lives more stable than that of an actor. However, his Fisher catches, not fish, but smuggled goods; his "fishwife" ("*Poissarde*") calls to mind the women who marched on Versailles; his Peasant lives the life that in *The Emigrants* led to disease and waste; the Peasant's "rude, yet tranquil hut" seems as pastorally unlikely as the "smoking cottage" in *Salisbury Plain* (l. 55; l. 410). Even the Peasant's imagined "lisping children [that] hail their sire's return" are derived from poetry, in a misquoted passage from Gray's "Elegy" that actually reads "No children run to lisp their sire's return."[42]

The poem gives voice to a figure who asks for "timely bounty" and reminds his audience that "where means are given,/ To aid the wretched is – to merit Heaven" (ll. 70–71). In modern terms, the player is a busker, who performs his piece and then hands round the hat. His moral tag draws attention to the social value of charity, and to the benefit, this time, the action confers on the giver (which the poem glosses with reference to Shakespeare). But this quiescent ending calls to mind the similarly enervated conclusion to "The Dead Beggar," where social suffering is allowable because of the potential moral good it can do to the onlooker. As the distressed player enacts his playlet to activate our benevolence, the poem itself ratchets up the drama and the playacting. It depicts suffering and need, but it does so rhetorically. The clever layers of its device result in a poem about an oppressed and needy member of society who acts the part rather than enacting it. He is indeed a Figure in need, abandoned by his poem which, in confronting directly the Figurative, finds only impasse.

Art for Art's Sake

Bruns notes that "knowing as becoming what you know has its mortal risks"; if one depends on knowing the other in order to access or come to know some version of the self, "what if the other [is] a monster?" (p. 405). Similarly, what if the other is so abjected by the poetry that she dissolves into it? Margaret's status as object in *The Ruined Cottage* is what allows her to stand for Wordsworth's outrage at the victimization caused by war, and the Pedlar's narrative brings the poem's story into history. And yet Margaret herself never transcends the poem's plot; she merely symbolizes her own loss. Her "apathetic loss of emotion"[43] manifests as an apathetic loss of self *to* emotion, as she stands, first, for rural contentment (*pace* the distressed player's Peasant) and then for emotional devastation. What she never attains is an identity as a human being within a poem that assigns thought and reflection to the Pedlar only, it seems, so that he may give meaning to Margaret's death.[44] Since it would have had meaning anyway, one must ask why the poem needs to make Margaret into art? As a narrative strategy it does not work; as I have suggested above, the poem finds it impossible to remain in the rarified air of Margaret's abjectness. She is reduced to a forsaken, bereft, and not very sane woman, oblivious to her child's needs, a bad gardener, and a monomaniac. Throughout the poem she inhabits roles, or more pertinently provides snapshots of emotional states in reaction to her surrounding conditions: loving everyone while she felt loved ("no one went away/ But it seemed she loved him," ll. 102–103), abandoning everything when she felt abandoned. Her sole purpose is to illuminate and emblematize. She is a piece of art composed so that the poem *means something*; she is art for art's sake.[45]

Why, then, is she so feeble? Why is her function so in need of the Pedlar to point it out? Why is she so hard to read, to the point that, as the reader is told at the start of the Second Part, the Pedlar can finish glossing the suffering she endures at her husband's sense of his own redundancy with a look of "easy chearfulness" and the speaker can allow her "simple tale/ [To] pas[s] from my mind like a forgotten sound" (ll. 201, 203–204)?[46] At least, this seems to be the speaker's desire; instead, he finds himself in Bruns' dilemma, faced with a monster whom he nonetheless must come to know so that he may know himself.[47] So, with a "heartfelt chillness" in his veins, he "begged of the old man that for [his] sake/ He would resume his story" (ll. 213, 219–20). However, this merely serves to underline Margaret's insubstantial position in the poem, since it is her *story* rather than her identity as a character that attracts the speaker. In other words, she has long since been transformed into an emblem; before the Pedlar even introduces her he has created her as a piece of art: "I see around me here/ Things which you cannot see" (ll. 67–8). The problem is that in a poem about how war and its oppressive effects creates victims, Art is not sufficient. "Margaret" is as much as figure as Joy, Tyranny, or Liberty; the difference is that she is supposed to be a "human tenant" of the poem. And the difficulty with Margaret as art is that she and her story leave the Pedlar in a state of "happiness." This is a far cry from "the misery/ ... of the dead" he mentions as he resumes Margaret's story at the speaker's urging, and it emphasizes the gulf between art and the real, the transcendent and the material (ll. 223–4). The one thing the poem *cannot* represent through emblematizing Margaret is the suffering caused by war. James Butler notes that, in "style and content, *The Ruined Cottage* ... looks forward to *Lyrical Ballads* and *Michael*, rather than back to *Adventures on Salisbury Plain* ... [It] is not a work of social protest." On the other hand, he then spends a substantial paragraph charting the ways in which the poem "does accurately reflect social conditions" (*RC*, p. 4). The poem is a war poem that picks up and then dispenses with social protest and the accurate reflections of social conditions; like "Dead Beggar" and "Distressed Player," it turns away from critique. Unlike those poems, however, it is not quiescent; it is, instead, complacent. "She is in her grave and oh! the difference to *me*"; for the victims of war, the difference it makes is to themselves. As soon as such a figure becomes the artistic representation of another's sense of self, her artifice collapses under the weight of the poem.[48] And this is why, I think, that readers react like De Quincy, wanting some redress for Margaret. Nicholas Roe has argued that in poems like *The Borderers, The Prelude*, and "Tintern Abbey," "Wordsworth's most transcendental claims reflect back upon the life out of which they emerged."[49] This seems to be, however, what he cannot fully work through in his 1790s war poems: the transcendent and the real clash continually, now one, now the other dominating, but neither claiming control over the poems.

History, in the making in the 1790s, provides an impetus and subjects for Wordsworth and Smith, both deeply invested in pictures of revolutionary Liberty and social justice, both nonetheless writing war poetry in the 1790s in which the war seems itself to destabilize the poetics. As they attempt to write suffering, the better to right suffering, both find that the poetic collision with the real collapses the symbolic. The historian's transcendence is only restored – or, more accurately, pictured – when their poems return to the safety of the Self; hence the sonnets and their explorations of the darker states of mourning in the second volume, or the new forms of personalized (even if only tangentially autobiographical) subjectivity followed by Wordsworth in the *Lyrical Ballads*. In poetry that engages with war and its effects, Smith and Wordsworth demonstrate the impossibility of achieving full symbolic transcendence, and hence resolution. They poeticize a failed project of recuperation: they attempt to inscribe individual, even individuated, suffering, only for the poems to fold in on themselves. In *The Ruined Cottage*, especially, but in all the poems under discussion in this chapter, the move to transcendence is, arguably, a kind of coping strategy on the part of the speaker who also reads the situations thus presented: "What can this mean? It must mean something more than itself." From here it is a short step to what Michael Scrivener sees as John Stuart Mill's "explicitly Romantic notion of the literary: the belief that the most subjectively inward is the most poetic subject matter."[50] In their war poetry of the 1790s, however, Smith and Wordsworth illustrate the pull of the outward, the politics of liberty versus oppression, and the failed experiment of a poetics of flawed and constricted transcendence.

3
Subject to Place, Subjected by Poetry

> But near one ancient tree, whose wreathed roots
> Form'd a rude couch, love-songs and scatter'd rhymes,
> Unfinished sentences, or half erased,
> And rhapsodies ... were sometimes found –
>
> Smith, "Beachy Head," 1807

> – Nay, Traveller! rest.
>
> Wordsworth, "Yew-Tree," 1798

Both Smith and Wordsworth are identified with specific landscapes: the South Downs in Sussex, the Lake District in Cumbria. While Wordsworth has had the advantage of more than a century's worth of embedding and iconicizing, Smith is on the verge of becoming a more visible feature in her home landscape, and of course her sonnets set in and around her childhood home, as well as "Beachy Head," perform the function of creating landscapes, inspiring and enabling the speaker's verse, among other things.[1] Within Romanticism, place often functions as the originary home, the childhood setting, the progenitor of memory which itself informs Romantic poetry; it underpins critical understanding of much of Wordsworth. For both poets, place offers the creation of locality, which in turn leads to a kind of anchoring within the landscape, so that self (or perhaps selves) can be derived *from* landscape, and hence naturalized: Wordsworth *in* the Lakes, Smith *on* the Downs. A kind of place-identity, or place-identification, can be attached to both poets, encouraged by the frequent return to place(s) in their poetry, and their memorializing of rivers, stones, flowers, animals, and diverse locations. This immersion in locale, however, is not without its problems, and both Smith and Wordsworth write into some of their locale poetry a distinct unease, which often corresponds to a speaker's inability to see *past* place, or to recognize the relation of *this* place to *that* one. Their deep concern with how poetry and the creative, poetic imagination might be placed within or drawn from locale, in other words, is complex; it is about what is written, about what is not written, and significantly it is about the process of making the written artefact itself.

This chapter explores what I variously call locality poems, locale poems, and topographical poems. The last is the simplest to define: poems that arise from, or are set within, a specific landscape. They rest on the tradition of the loco-descriptive, but do more than describe a place: they also, in intangible ways, *make* place (occasionally through the simple act of naming and claiming: Emma's Dell, Joanna's Rock, Mary's Nook being familiar examples). Locality and locale poems are related: locality poems are associated with a place (Bignor Park in Sussex, for instance) that is recognizable and, in topographical terms, known. Locality draws on associations of local knowledge, particular features of the landscape, the scene of certain activities, even legal definitions of local limitations (see OED). Locale, by contrast, brings in event: according to the OED, it is "a place considered with reference to some particular event or circumstances connected with it; a quarter in which certain things are done, or which is chosen for particular operations." It is where something of significance has happened or will happen: not mere quotidian activities, but things of moment, things to be remembered. And it is highly place specific; indeed, the examples cited by the OED before 1816 omit the final "e," conflating the "here" (local) with the "right here, right now" (locale). In useful ways, the locale poem proceeds from, or emerges from, the locality poem, which in turn is immanent in the topographical. The South Downs and Lakes presented in Smith's and Wordsworth's poetry might be, but are not very often, simple setting (topography); they can be, and often are, particularized through the poem itself (locality); and they become locale when they enable or enliven poetic activity itself.

The interconnectedness of place and poetry for Smith and Wordsworth makes it harder to detach place from the poet for each. As with so many of their personalized poems, both poets establish another kind of "real" when they write about real places, either localized or *localed*. As the previous chapter demonstrated, the real – that is, the worldly, the documentable, the historical – impinges on poetry in specific ways: the relationship between reality, realism, and an avoidance or elision of such things via something as intangible as transcendence pulls a poem nearly to pieces. But the enquiry that underlies attempts to see if the real can exist within poetry is the same that wants to understand "what is a poem" and make it anew; an experimental ethos that informs poems ostensibly concerned merely to set down for the record the places at which a poet found inspiration, or poetic material. So the topography of a poem is important, but it is there to begin things; as both poets know, place, like the past, is another country, especially once it is imported to poetry. The places of the poems, then, derive from localities, and are at once re-imagined, re-mapped, re-placed: *localed*. And as the next section will illustrate, this begins at the earliest point, through titles that draw the reader's attention to the making of the poem as well as the placing of the poem.

Writing and Composing

We are trained to read the Romantic poet as one in tune with a Nature that is knowable through poetry. Alive to the history of poetics, he (for it is usually a "he," and he is usually Wordsworth) takes up the genre of the loco-descriptive but uses the poem not merely to explore topography; rather, he develops something new, what Geoffrey Hartman labels nature poetry. Focusing on the inscription poem, Hartman notes that Wordsworth moved it from a place-bound notation to an evocation of "the poet in the grip of what he feels and sees," "contain[ed] ... in the act of writing."[2] Thus, in knowing Nature, we know the poet, and vice versa. The poem *becomes* topography; the poet, in exercising his physical mobility, facilitates an imaginative peripatetics that institutes traveling and writing as a joined activity, and resting and reading as perhaps its necessary corollary.[3] The freedom of movement that characterizes Wordsworth's poetry, in contrast to, for instance, the anxious homeboundedness of so much of Coleridge's work, has for many readers established him as *the* poet of place, and also of pace. This chapter, however, will explore the consensus that Wordsworth inaugurates a Romantic condition that Jonathan Bate describes as being "always aware of himself in relation to the landscape, [and] conscious of his own acts of naming" by bringing Smith into the picture.[4] As they create a poetics of Nature, both poets also think about what it means to *write* such poetry, and what it means to do so in solitude. The result is a poetics of spatial and compositional geographies, where not only the poet's locale matters, but also who the poet purports to be and how the poet conveys or makes permanent the poem.

Smith and Wordsworth take the emphasis on describing place that is the point of the loco-descriptive and transfer it to the poet who inhabits the poem – a speaker who is written to suggest, strongly, an identification with the author her- or himself. This is achieved partly through the consistent, although not constant, use of the first person; settings that evoke the past, or a possible past, of the author; a titular suggestion that someone (the poet?) has physically inscribed the poem. But they also use place to explore the idea of "the poet": are there better and worse ways to "be" this figure? Can locale disable rather than enable the poetry of Nature? Smith and Wordsworth understand that geography can be internal as well as external: they use place to access what might be called inner space, meaning not simply the "imagination" or creativity but the topography of the poet. Geography can also be time dependent as well as place dependent, the "when" as significant as the "where." It is embodied as an actual place, and this very actualizing creates a further layer of imagined engagement with space and place. The poet *is* the locale; the poet is *in* the locale. Thus, place is concrete, a location where something happened, and a metaphor, where its realm is enlarged. For Smith and Wordsworth, locale becomes poetic even as poetry becomes localized. More than any other poets of their generation, Smith and Wordsworth attach their poetry to place and suggest that, somehow, the production of poetry is place dependent, and in so doing they raise questions of composition and supposition: what is it that is supposed to be composed? What Mark J. Bruhn calls "this sense of incommensurateness between our factual being and our fictional role-playing" provides a backdrop for the locale poems under discussion in this chapter.[5]

According to Bruhn, Wordsworth uses place to explore a new form of the bounded sublime; where earlier poets like Gray and Thomson allowed for "any number of orientations" in their representations of place, Wordsworth displays an "insistent proximity" which focuses his poems *right here* (pp. 413, 410). And it is from the "right here" that we are afforded "sublime transportation" (p. 417) as "Wordsworth stretches deictic pointing beyond the limits of space-time and into the imaginative sublime" (p. 420). Bruhn's examples are "Yew Tree" and "Tintern Abbey," and his point is important, especially if Smith's sonnet "Written in the Church-yard at Middleton in Sussex" is considered. Literally underpinned by an exact place deixis in the form of a note ("Middleton is a village on the margin of the sea, in Sussex ..."), the poem moves from life-in-death (waves tear bones from their graves) to death-in-life (the speaker is dead to peace), a transition from the "right here" to the imaginative sublime that suggests where Bruhn might have taken his argument if his examples had not jumped from Thomson straight to Wordsworth. Smith's poem also fuses the geographic with the compositional – it is, by title, *written* – which brings into focus the link within these poems between the speaker and the writer, the composed and the real, the abstracted and the embodied.

In presenting what Smith and Wordsworth do in their locality poems as a poetics of topo/geographies, this chapter takes as its starting point the emphasis on the "hereness" of place and space both poets convey. Smith's repeated use of "written" in her sonnets' titles finds its analogue in Wordsworth's contributions to the *Lyrical Ballads*. Wordsworth's subsequent turn to "composed" in many of his 1802 sonnets raises the question of the connotative difference of the terms.[6] For both poets, it is evidently important that they locate not only the action of their poems but also their physical creation, and this has to do with their explorations of the relationship between poet – more properly, speaker – and place. "Nature, solitude and the imagination are ... geographical concerns," notes Michael Wiley; they grow out of and because of place.[7] Smith and Wordsworth transform the description of place into a mapping of the act of poeticizing place. Nevertheless, as this chapter will show, they are not simply charting locales; they are also problematizing them. Solitude itself draws their attention; their locality poetry does not uncritically present solitude as a panacea, a space for personal regeneration or peace, or something to turn to after disillusion. It may present a space for composition, and a kind of private library for the storing of "lines." As both poets show, however, this is not without its limitations.

Franco Moretti has demonstrated to great effect that "geography is not an inert container, is not a box where cultural history 'happens', but an active force, that pervades the literary field and shapes it in depth ... [A] literary geography ... may indicate the study *of space in literature*; or else, *of literature in space*."[8] Moretti's concentration on the novel occludes the significant fact that, for Smith and Wordsworth, these are not "two very different things" (p. 3), but, rather, mutually dependent aspects of their locale poetry. The spaces they poeticize (geographic place and creative, imaginative space) are contingent on the poems that are written and composed specifically *here* and *now*. The temporal suspension is, perhaps, what links them; what Andrew Bennett calls "a unique impossibility" enables this fruitful paradox. As Bennett notes, "'written' or the equivalent in the title typically both asserts the contemporaneity of the act of writing and displaces that act to an historical past, to a prior moment of writing."[9] By locating the moment and place of the poem's beginning (or completion), Smith and Wordsworth merge place and space, creating a new geography that is always there and always already lost, thoroughly mapped and yet, in its poetic state, impossible to find. This is because this poetic geography is based on a simultaneously internal and external locale: mutually dependent states.

The titles of "written" and "composed" poems begin the mapping of place and space the poems undertake. Although Bennett distinguishes between Wordsworth's use of the words "written" and "composed" in his inscription poems, he does not explore their differing resultant landscapes.[10] But it is an important distinction, all the more so since Smith, in all her work, "composes" only one poem (Sonnet XLII, "Composed during a walk on the Downs, in November 1787"), while Wordsworth places most of his "written" poems in the *Lyrical Ballads*, turning to "composition" mainly post-1800. This suggests that "writing" and "composing" are not interchangeable for the poets; they fulfill different effective functions.[11] If a poem is "written," who does this? Does a "composed" poem have a necessarily physical shape; is it space more than place? If the act of writing is "supposed," has it actually happened? And how do such questions mesh with the undoubted production of poetry – the words on the page that we read? What, in other words, are Smith and Wordsworth doing when they "write" and/or "compose"? Where are they, and perhaps most importantly who are they?

As Bennett also notes, "writing" is an "act" (p. 80), which seems to require an agent as well as certain supplies: paper or some surface, a writing implement. The agent is probably still, even if only momentarily (writing while moving is inconvenient at best): sitting, reclining, standing. By contrast, "composing" can take place at any time and any place; it requires no materials and no advance preparation. It can be "spontaneous" (Bennett, p. 83) or at least have that appearance; it can be audible or purely internal. It does not presuppose the production of a concrete something, whereas "writing" leaves something behind, an object that has been inscribed. And yet, "composing" leads the reader to the process of putting or pulling something together; it implies an architecture, a system of planning, that belies its apparent spontaneity. Where "composing" is the process, "composed" implies completion: something now exists, something now takes up space, something can now be plotted. Shadowing composition's free style, then, is an expectation of finality: the "composed" is an object, a kind of embodied imaginary, a mapped internal landscape or geography. An aspect of the poet's mind and imagination has now been placed.[12]

There is a similar slipperiness to "written." Bennett argues that the "final impossibility" of the inscription poem is "the fact that the poem is not written when it is said to have been written" and that we, the readers, can't be there, in the place and space wherein the poem is asserted to have been written, in Geoffrey Hartman's words, "'before our eyes'" (pp. 89, 88).[13] But this seems predicated on a supposition that there is a real speaker called Wordsworth (for Bennett) who has really written a poem – or rather, cannot have, and thus the entire scene can only be a "fiction of inscription" (p. 88). However, as the immaterial act of composition yields a materialized *something*, so too the written maps an unexpected space. Its status as agent-led, tool-dependent, locale-bound opens possibilities rather than leading inexorably to the impossible; it creates a scene that maintains its own reality while being, at the same time, thoroughly artificial. In other words, who writes? The "written" gestures toward the plottable: a real space, a real place, an actual date, a mapped experience. In the case of the "written" as practiced by Smith and Wordsworth, this leads not to the impossible but to art: artifice, artfulness. Locale becomes location, or setting; inscription becomes the scripted. Writing as a creative, physical act, then, is also a feint: one does not need to be the, or indeed *a*, poet to *write*, although ultimately a poet is required to clarify the difference.

Both "composed" and "written," then, occupy more space than they seem to. The one is invisible yet noticeable; the other is physical yet corporeally indeterminate. When attached to locale, they map both place and space, allowing the emergence of a poetics of geography. When, where, what, and how: the locality poem creates a kind of nature preserve within its lines, writing and composing the two places Wiley calls the "unrealized world" and the "real one" (p. 16). Topographically precise and compositionally located, this kind of poem serves to enact its own origin. If we consider the scene that is suggested by a poem "supposed to be written," with its simultaneous "real" and "unrealized," then the act of imagination that produces a poem is itself plotted, made into a place where something has happened while also not happening. "Supposed to be written," in effect, describes both the "composed" and the "written": the clash between the concrete (or real) and the insubstantial (or imagined) finds play in "supposed." And this takes us back to the critical association between inscription poems and nature poetry, showing how "locale" operates more subtly than "inscription" by not merely reflecting, describing, or even inscribing nature, but rather interrogating the nature of Nature through examining the nature of the poetic process. The system of composing and writing, and its reliance on a place and time of creation, coordinates artifice and reality, with the poet acting as mapmaker. We should not be surprised, however, given the potential and even impetus for artifice that characterizes a poetics of geography, if the poet/mapmaker, in charting localities, also explores different landscapes of subjectivity.

At the Intersection of Artifice and Reality

By anchoring their poems in a version of reality with titles like "Lines composed..." or "Supposed to be written...," Smith and Wordsworth in the first instance link the imaginative process of composition with the mechanical process of writing: the "spontaneous overflow" so famously "recollected in tranquillity." The fiction of actuality thus created links the eighteenth-century loco-descriptive with a Romantic emphasis on the individual creative mind. But this familiar story fails to recognize the deeper artifice both poets explore. By insisting on the specificity of composition and dictation, they also promote the living nature of the poems' speakers; that is, if the lines are "written September 1791, during a remarkable thunder storm, in which the moon was perfectly clear, while the tempest gathered in various directions near the earth," then they are by inference the result of the speaker's experience.[14] The details offered in the title serve to ground both poem and poet, in this case Smith. And yet this poem, for instance, lacks the clearest sign of an actual speaker: there is no "I." Smith thus lingers at the intersection of artifice and reality: the speaker is both there in the storm and not-there in the poem. Similarly, when Wordsworth offers "lines written at a small distance from my house, and sent by my little boy to the person to whom they are addressed," the very mundanity of the title assures its readers of the poem's actuality, encouraging us to believe in "Edward," for instance. But Wordsworth's familiar manipulations of his past and present in his poetry mean that for him, as well, some of the poetry that is most seemingly "real" questions its own reality. In examining some of their poems in which the moment of writing is fixed by place, date, or both, we can see that for Smith and Wordsworth, locality performs multiple functions: literalized as in some ways responsible for the coming-into-being of the poem, but also figuring the move away from reality that so many of the poems reflect. And in turn reality itself fractures: is that what *really* happened "in Germany, on one of the coldest days of the century"? Was this *really* "written in Bristol in the summer of 1794"? What is gained by this geographic and temporal placement – why focus on the scene of writing or composition at all?

It is striking how many of Smith's poems are located by place and/or time in the title. Of course, what many consider her most mature poem, "Beachy Head," is entirely taken up by its locale, past and present, while *The Emigrants* sets its two Books precisely by date and location to meaningful effect: a morning that is neither bright nor a new dawn in Book I, but is rather a "Wintry Morn, [where] the struggling light/ Throws a faint gleam upon the troubled waves" (p. 125, I: 1–2); a spring afternoon where "the early leaves ... fear capricious winds" and the flowers are "timid" as the country settles into the "horrors [of] War" (p. 137, II: 23, 24; p. 138, II: 45). Fully one quarter of her *Elegiac Sonnets* (23 of 92), however, are also locality poems, while another four of the "other poems" of this collection are set by place and date, as are two of the "other poems" in the *Beachy Head* volume. Nine of the sonnets are set by both place and date, nine by place alone, and five by date alone. Altogether, eleven of her poems name their place and date of composition in the title, thirteen offer the place only, and five go by date. Of the dates used, Smith consistently settles on what might be seen as months of transition, spring or autumn; of the fourteen that provide a date, only four fall in different seasons (three summers, one winter). Predominantly, October and November, April and May locate these poems. Further, of the places noted, most are isolated: either uninhabited countryside, or churchyards, or seashores. The major exception is the group of poems written at Brighthelmstone in November 1792 (and discussed in Chapter 2), a specificity that also characterizes Book I of *The Emigrants*, although in that poem the town itself is merely a backdrop for its dramatic cliffs.

For Smith, writing rather than composition seems to be key. In her one "composed" poem, Sonnet XLII, she presents her poem in the title as having arisen from "a walk on the Downs, in November 1787." Specific to time and place, the poem is also specifically a composition in a way most of Smith's sonnets are not: it follows the Spenserian rhyme scheme, its imagery plotted onto a poetical map often characterized as the hardest to master.[15] The poem is heavily reliant on a poetic, rather than a topographical, locale; its Elizabethan structure is clothed with a Classical dress and invocations of the past that mirror the "ruins of the year" of line 2. "Falling leaves and wither'd fern" are complemented by the "shrieking night-jar" that, a note tells us, "is supposed by the peasants to portend misfortune" (ll. 4, 8; *Poetry*, p. 42). The poem's ending references to "Syren Hope" and a promethean "vulture Care – that feeds upon the heart" belie the token mention of the "revolving seasons" and "propitious Spring" (ll. 13, 14, 11, 9). Predicated upon the past, in both structure and imagery, this poem is thoroughly composed: it adheres to its system with the finality of a completed thought. And, being composed rather than written, it seems to exist in the realm of thought until read, until it becomes a poem in a book. Smith plays with notions of composition's ephemerality when she appends her note to the poem, which not only functions as a kind of anchor, but also introduces a tone of scientific pragmatism that is at odds with the literary character of the sonnet; the "shrieking night-jar" which acts in the poem as a portent transforms in the note to a thing: "As I have never seen [this bird] dead, I know not to what species it belongs" (*Poetry*, p. 42). The poet who can walk and compose, lost in poetical musings on death and pain, maintains as well a scientific detachment that separates the portent bird from its real-life equivalent. The poem, then, is as composed as is possible, tied to its literary landmarks, with a speaker who paradoxically signals her lack of interest in flights of fancy.

Every other locality poem is either "written" or "supposed to be written." And they are intensely local, by which I mean that Smith uses as her settings places that seemingly function as versions of home. It is not always rural: for every Farm Wood and Arun riverbank there is a Brighton, a Bristol, a Weymouth, and an Exmouth – real locations in which Smith has lived. But instead of conveying a sense of belonging and security, they poeticize the dissolution of home: Farm Wood belongs to lost "dear days" (Sonnet XXXI, l. 13), Bristol's healing waters have no effect on the "palsied Fancy" (Sonnet LXIV, l. 10), "balmy" Exmouth is the site for "the vigil of the wretched" (Sonnet LXVIII, l. 6), the resort of Weymouth is "black and gloomy" in winter (Sonnet LXXI, l. 3). Every place that is written, and that sees the poet writing, serves only to signal its own impossibility as a location available to the poet; either imagination, or hope, or joy, or life is stymied. The most desirable location of all, Smith's childhood home of Bignor Park, features in her final sonnet, Sonnet XCII, but its presence only reaffirms that for the speaker, there is "no happy home" (Sonnet LXII, l. 12[16]). One of the few summer poems, this sonnet reflects the inability of the "written" poems to capture the expected nuances of their locations: although set in summer, the poem is invaded by the same "leaden vapours," "dark shadows," and "gathering clouds" of the sonnets' autumn (ll. 3, 5, 6). The "Bignor Park in Sussex" that so markedly announced Smith's provenance on the title page of the first editions of the sonnets now finally proves to be out of reach: "nor for me/ Return those rosy hours which here I used to see!" (ll. 13–14). In being "written at," these poems use the local and the known as springboards for a journey into locations wherein the permanence of writing is used to suggest transience, ephemerality, and loss.

As noted above, the dates are almost all transitional: months marking seasonal turns, creating a liminal aesthetics and a border tonality to the geographies she specifies. So, for instance, the three sonnets specifically set in October (XII, XXXII, and LXXXVII) and the one that could be (XLVI: Autumn 1788) poeticize kinds of edges or liminalities: a "solitary seat" "on some rude fragment of the rocky shore" (XII, ll. 3, 1), "the banks of the Arun" (XXXII, title), the "walks obscured" by decay (XLVI, l. 6), or a "faded," "dejected," "blast[ed]," stalled autumn of life without hope of returning spring. In writing these poems, the poet writes states of mind that arise directly from setting; the pathetic fallacy operates in reverse, since instead of Nature reflecting human moods, it seems that the mood of the poem, and the act of writing it down, proceed from atmosphere and location. And although this group of October poems includes a body, a somebody to write them, that figure is not always an "I," easily associated with the poet. Hence Sonnet XII links its speaking I with a shipwrecked, drowning mariner. Sonnet XXXII pairs its "I" with a "shadowy phantom pale" (l. 5). Sonnet XLVI substitutes "the musing wanderer" for an "I" (l. 3). The late Sonnet LXXXVII allows itself a writer, but it is one of the few dated poems to lack a year: "Written in October," it could be any October. It functions as a tone poem, encapsulating the waste of an autumn that brings not harvest and plenty but "stubble sere" and a "half-leafless wood" (ll. 4, 8). Writing a poem, then, does not lead to the production of an artefact so much as the enactment of a selfhood who is in the process of, essentially, decomposing. The permanence of the written artfully overturns itself and creates something always on the point of fading away.

Where the autumn poems emphasize decay and dissolution rather than fruition and completion, the two poems "written" in spring (XXXI and LIV) allow for the returning vitality and life of the season, even if neither, unsurprisingly, can be felt or internalized by the speaker: "Ah! what to me can those dear days restore,/ When scenes could charm that now I taste no more!" (XXXI, ll. 13–14). However, the poems share a writerly image that indicates a function of the written arising entirely from its scribal condition: a "thoughtless," "unthinking" hind, whose taxing springtime labor directly signifies his existence as a body rather than a mind (XXXI, l. 9; LIV, l. 11). The speaker, of course, is *all* mind, envious of the "respite" enjoyed by the sleeping woodman (LIV) and the shepherd (XXXI). And yet sleep carries with it a condition of mindlessness, and for the speaker, writing these two poems engages the self who is a *writer*, for whom the mind and the imagination demonstrate new shoots of life. Remembering how Smith's "composed" sonnet conveyed a fully formed sense of itself as a composition, these two springtime writings take the speaker-writer in unexpected directions. Sonnet XXXI features one of Smith's irregular rhyme schemes – *abab baab cdcdee* – mapped onto a stanzaic structure that entirely departs from a sonnet's: sestet/ sestet/couplet. Sonnet LIV is laid out as a quatrain/quatrain/sestet, with a rhyme scheme that invokes both the Petrarchan and Shakespearian forms: *abab cddc dedeff*. Using poetic convention as a seedbed, the writer of these sonnets works carefully through form, which suggests a kind of new growth more appropriate to springtime than the poems' tone and imagery allow, but which also emphasizes their status as written down, worked out, pieces of poetry.[17] Location in time – the temporal geography of the sonnets – creates a locale wherein the written is concretized and enlarged. As is so common in her sonnets, Smith uses form to query the limits of form, but when she does this in poems that also announce their status as written (down), she moves from merely setting scenes to mapping a new geography of poetry.

The state of writing in these sonnets encourages a sense of the reach of the imaginary, which extends beyond the locale poems to embed a physicality of place as fundamental to the poetry. Indeed, occasionally a poem creates a specificity entirely to anchor its narrative in reality, as when the titular note[18] to the non-specific "Elegy" literalizes its locale of a graveyard:

> This elegy is written on the supposition that an indigent young woman had been addressed by the son of a wealthy yeoman, who resenting his attachment, had driven him from home, and compelled him to have recourse for subsistence to the occupation of a pilot, in which, in attempting to save a vessel in distress, he perished.
>
> The father dying, a tomb is supposed to be erected to his memory in the churchyard mentioned in Sonnet the 44th ["Written in the church-yard at Middleton in Sussex"]. And while a tempest is gathering, the unfortunate young woman comes thither; and courting the same death as had robbed her of her lover, she awaits its violence, and is at length overwhelmed by the waves. (*Poetry*, p. 52)

Sonnet the 44th, a gloomy, gothicized poem, in turn has *its* actuality reinforced by a note:

> Middleton is a village on the margin of the sea, in Sussex, containing only two or three houses. There were formerly several acres of ground between its small church and the sea, which now, by its continual encroachments, approaches within a few feet of this half-ruined and humble edifice. The wall, which once surrounded the church-yard, is entirely swept away, many of the graves broken up, and the remains of bodies interred washed into the sea; whence human bones are found among the sand and shingles on the shore. (*Poetry*, p. 43)

So we know where we are, but we also see how close we are to dissolution: in "Elegy" the protagonist allows herself to be swept away by the waves, and in Sonnet XLIV the location itself is being claimed by the sea. The decomposition exemplified by the uncovered bones in the sonnet enacts the undermining of the poem's desire to place itself, for if we turn to the real landscape written of by Smith, the village of Middleton-on-sea, we learn that despite the apocalyptic tone of the poem, the place itself still survives, although the glebe (the area of land belonging to the ecclesiastical living granted to the parish) has been steadily eaten away by the waves. The location, in other words, is there and not-there, just as the poem is fixed – "written" – and in flux, or "shrinking" as it succumbs to the waves. In this light, it is significant that this poem locates itself by place only, and lacks a date; thus the graveyard is suspended at the point of disappearance, but never quite goes.

Do these poems fix a sense of place, or destabilize their own actualities? Certainly the churchyard at Middleton seems to function as simultaneously actual and imaginary. The factual tone of the note is complemented by the melodrama of a poem which "breaks the silent Sabbath of the grave!" where "with shells and sea-weed mingled, on the shore/ Lo! their bones whiten in the frequent wave," and whose speaker is "doom'd – by life's long storm opprest,/ To gaze with envy on their gloomy rest" (ll. 8, 9–10, 13–14). The speaker's quickstep into metaphor substantiates the poem's theatricality while also functioning as another form of dissolution. Similarly, one of the most specific of the sonnets, Sonnet LIX, "Written September 1791, during a remarkable thunder storm, in which the moon was perfectly clear, while the tempest gathered in various directions near the earth," rejects its own physicality by failing to include an agent to do the writing; as noted above, this poem functions without an "I." The closest it gets is the mention of a "spirit conscious of superior worth" (l. 10), who only enters after eight lines of disembodied observation of the storm. The poem seemingly thus writes itself, morphing into being almost as a consequence of the storm, while the "spirit" does battle with another metaphorical tempest, "the tumult of the troubled earth." It seems that, for Smith, locality can encourage both an absorption of place and a turn toward disintegration, but if we return briefly to the two poems most close to home, literally, an interesting reversal occurs. In Sonnet XXXI, "Written in Farm Wood, South Downs, in May 1784," the corporeal figure of the "thoughtless" hind is also rendered as an "unconscious *spirit*" – that is, insubstantial – while the speaker laments the loss of "those dear days ... when scenes could charm that now I *taste* no more!" (ll. 5, 9, 11, 13–14, emphasis added); only a body with a tongue can "taste." And in Sonnet XCII, "Written at Bignor Park in Sussex, in August, 1799," the speaker describes how "visions bright and warm/ With which even here my sanguine youth begun,/ ... are obscured for ever!" (ll. 5, 7–8). Obscured visions imply eyes with which to see. As much as the speaker represents "mind" to the laborer's "body," s/he is still a writer with a physique: ears and eyes and a working brain. Smith's locality poems do more than simply place a speaker or date a composition. They also encourage an exploration of what it means to insert geographic locality into a work of the imagination; they create a landscape wherein poetry is actualized even if the idea of a speaker is not. Locality poems emphasize a sense of a real person writing about real feelings, ideas, or things. Smith, however, seems to find it more interesting or fruitful to flirt with the autobiographical as a feint, to set a "real" scene only to decompose it, and to see how far the "actual" can be stretched before it becomes unrealized.

Wordsworth's use of place and time has received extended critical attention, from "Tintern Abbey" (or the lack of it) through the "Poems on the Naming of Places" through London, Calais, and Yarrows both visited and unvisited. Likewise, his use of the autobiographical and his sometimes significant departures from fact have been well documented. So observing that Wordsworth makes extensive use of localities of place and date is not in itself new. However, in conjunction with Smith certain interesting congruences arise, especially within the date parameters of this study. In poems up to 1807, just after Smith's death, Wordsworth also sets most of his dated poems in spring or autumn: other than the famous sonnets dated August 1802 we see March, September, October, and November. Second, Wordsworth often uses a secluded locale to explore the effects of isolation, and even the London and Calais sonnets are often as much about being solitary as they are about community. Like Smith, Wordsworth uses specificity to explore the idea of a selfhood rendered subordinate to a place or a date, or a speaker overtaken by the contents of his own poem. His geographies, like hers, are temporal as well as locational. Wordsworth, too, both "writes" and "composes" poems, but he demonstrates an interest in the composed that suggests that, for him, composition is a distinctly different act from writing. Almost all of his "written" poems appear in *Lyrical Ballads*, while most of his "composed" poems come later, in the burst of writing leading up to 1807.[19] If "composition" lends itself more to a sense of the imaginative and the "spontaneous," as Bennett describes it (p. 83), then by shifting from the "written" – ostensibly physical, tool bound, and *placed* – to the "composed" signals as well a shift in the imaginative process, a move toward a kind of creative unmooring; a map without beacons, in effect. And yet, when Wordsworth appends a specific date, August or September 1802 for instance, it is almost always to a "composed" poem; the "written" poems may emphasize something on which they have been inscribed (a slate tablet, a stone), but they are almost always vague in terms of time and place. Wordsworth, then, complicates both styles of recording poetry as much as Smith does.

One of the most fully charted temporal geographies is, of course, the late summer of 1802, which is sometimes "composed" and sometimes allowed simply to *be* (e.g., "September 1802"). These are also, of course, among the most clearly autobiographical of Wordsworth's short poems. If the act of composing is to put something together, then we might see one such composition to be the poet himself, arranging and mapping his response to and understanding of his belated return to France. Wordsworth composes these poems only to unsettle them; the uncertainty and anxiety they express mirror Smith's, as does Wordsworth's use of rhyme scheme and internal structure to suggest discomposure. In "Composed by the Sea-Side, near Calais, August 1802," the declamatory style and patriotic tone imply a need to compose the poem's voice through the poem itself. The marginalized position – "by the Sea-side" – and the distracting not-thereness of the poet recall Smith, yet someone inhabits the poem and claims the evening star as "my Country's emblem" (l. 7). The poem works to unsettle its speaker from its location, first through its concentration on a distant, sinking star, then through its awkward detachment of the pronoun "I" in line twelve from its physical place in line fourteen: "I, with many a fear/ For my dear Country, many heartfelt sighs,/ Among Men who do not love her linger here" (ll. 12–14). The poem's rhyme scheme unfolds serenely enough, only to jump modes in line nine: *abba abba cdcede*. Two tercets (*cdc ede*) *might* combine to a sestet, allowing the poem to be mostly Petrarchan, but punctuation and the flow of ideas create a 6/5/4 declension, the apparent extra line gained by a caesura in line six. The poem's artfulness overlays its artifice, since for all its apparent candor the poem leaves out the most necessary of autobiographical questions: why? "Why" Wordsworth is in France emerges from factual knowledge of the man; why the speaker is there is occluded by the poem's bombast. Locality, here, blocks our access to the poem – we remain on the periphery.

The temporal specificity of "To a Friend, Composed near Calais, On the Road Leading to Ardres, August 7th, 1802" and "Composed Upon Westminster Bridge, Sept. 2, 1802" follow the unmapping of the seaside near Calais at similar compositional levels. "To a Friend" mixes reminiscence of past happiness with evocations of present trauma, but departs radically from its Smithian setup in the last two lines. The poem is steadily composed: a Petrarchan opening is reflected by two quatrains that blend easily to an octave, while the sestet is only slightly broken, by punctuation, into tercets. Although the speaker labels "citizen" "a hollow word,/ As if a dead Man spake it!," he then leaps from "despair" to the statement that "I feel [it] not: happy am I as a Bird:/ Fair seasons yet will come, and hopes as fair" (ll. 11–12, 13–14). The poem hangs between joy and sorrow, life and death, then and now, even as its composition takes place en route from Calais, "on the road leading to Ardres." In "Westminster Bridge," the speaker creates stasis through composition: the city he presents exists only in its poetically depopulated state. It is resolutely unreal, despite its mappable setting; it posits a naturalized urban topography where "ships, towers, domes, theatres, and temples lie/ Open unto the fields, and to the sky" (ll. 6–7). Unlike "Calais" and "To a Friend," this poem regularizes its outlandish content through rhyme scheme and structure: *abba abba cdcdcd* is upheld by a clear octave-sestet. And yet the place of composition, a bridge, implies a suspension between two points, which here could be read as reality and fiction (artifice):

> Never did sun more beautifully steep
> In his first splendour valley, rock, or hill;
> Ne'er saw I, never felt, a calm so deep!
> The river glideth at his own sweet will:
> Dear God! the very houses seem asleep;
> And all that mighty heart is lying still! (ll. 9–14)

The enjambment of line six, quoted above, suggest that ships and so on *lie*; the affirmation of line eleven ("Ne'er saw I") as easily refers to what has *not* happened, what has *not* been seen or felt. This poem, so securely composed, plots, like Smith's Sonnet XLII, a geography of poetic destabilization through composition. If we compare the contemporaneous "Written in London," one of the few post-*Lyrical Ballads* "written" poems, what is striking is that the *act* of writing, here, involves an over-writing: the poem is too full of punctuation, with every sentence broken down into multiple subclauses. Its final sentence, in lines nine to fourteen, is practically impossible to parse:

> ....Rapine, avarice, expence,
> This is idolatry; and these we adore:

> Plain living and high thinking are no more:
> The homely beauty of the good old cause
> Is gone; our peace, our fearful innocence,
> And pure religion breathing household laws. (ll. 9–14)

The poem may be "written," but it does not appear to have been *read*.

The "composed" does not guarantee a purity of imaginative expression, then, and the "written" may unwrite itself. Wordsworth follows Smith in this complex poetic terrain, with the real and the artificial, the placed and the unplaced, in fruitful competition. For instance, in "Written in GERMANY, on one of the coldest days of the Century," the poem hints at Gothic excess while also, in its subtitle, settling itself thoroughly within the realm of the real: "I must apprize the Reader that the stoves in North Germany generally have the impression of a galloping Horse upon them, this being part of the Brunswick Arms" (*LB*, p. 225). Not only is this poem "written," it also expects a "Reader"; and the movement from the sublime cold of the temperature to the ordinariness of the heat source suggests a speaker for whom hyperbole is a familiar form of expression. The conversational opening – "A fig for your languages, German and Norse,/ Let me have the song of the kettle" – draws the speaker away from the foreign and unfamiliar to the known and comforting, while the poem's concentration on a freezing fly who, in its disorientation ("like a traveller bemaz'd," l. 21), stands in for, albeit temporarily, the speaker particularizes the poem even further. The poem draws from its locality a sense of actuality compromised, as noted, by the Gothic tinge, but more than that it undermines its own reality by the contrast it draws between the lonely and isolated fly and the speaker's opportunity to "draw warmth from the cheek of my Love[,]/ As blest and as glad in this desolate gloom,/ As if green summer grass were the floor of my room,/ And woodbines were hanging above" (ll. 32–5). This turn toward the romantic pastoral is also a turn toward the rurally isolated, a shift in genre from Gothic sublime to the beautifully familiar. The poem plays a variety of tricks with its presentation of the actual, not the least of which is autobiographical misdirection: although in Germany with his beloved sister, the poem's gesture is toward a romantic love, and its association of love with green summer grass and hanging woodbines places it firmly in the realm of the imagined, if not the clichéd. I would suggest that this indicates Wordsworth's development, in this poem, of a speaker for whom locality functions merely as fodder for a display of creative limitation; the poem's actuality is overtaken by nods toward an imaginary alternative reality – the world of the fly, "the cheek of my Love" (l. 32) – that breaks down both generically and autobiographically.

Since geographic specificity does not guarantee accuracy, it is not surprising that poeticizing place, for Wordsworth as for Smith before him, does not guarantee an agent. "Written in March, while resting on the Bridge at the Foot of Brother's Water," despite the geographic and temporal specificity of the title, lacks a speaker either to write or to rest. Proceeding as a series of impressions or observations – "The cock is crowing,/ The stream is flowing,/ The small birds twitter,/ The lake doth glitter,/ The green field sleeps in the sun" (ll. 1–5) – the poem, like Sonnet LIX, seems to compose itself, to arise from the landscape it processes. Without an "I" to substantiate a speaker, but written from the point of view of some kind of entity, the poem's reality relies on an absent presence. Where the presence in Sonnet LIX could be said to be spectral, given the darkness of the poem, here we seem to have a fantasy speaker, a playful spirit or sprite of the new Spring. The acts of writing and resting, contingent on an actual human presence, are incongruous in a poem that does little more than list not what *it sees*, but what *is seen*. For Wordsworth, this seems to be a way to give prominence to the setting, to allow it, rather than the viewer, to dominate the poem, but if this is the case in "Written in March" then the question arises of the force of the title. *Someone* has both written and rested. As with Smith, the actuality of the poem both fixes it as permanent while the poem itself destabilizes the topography thus offered.

The Dangers of Composing

Both Smith and Wordsworth, whether writing or composing, use locality to explore poetry, creating a geography inflected by place, time, the real, and the not-real. Theirs are singularly lonely locales, however; with the exception of the lover in "Written in Germany" and Smith's thoughtless hinds, almost all of their locale poems are populated only by the poem's speaker (and occasionally, as we have seen, not even by that figure). This means that another characteristic of the locale poem is solitude, which prompts some questions: is solitude necessary for the making of such poetry? Do composition and writing rely on isolation – at least in the world invoked by the poem? Does a poetics of geography imply an empty space, save for the Poet, and does it rejoice in its emptiness? It is a critical and poetic commonplace that Romantic poets privilege Nature as the ideal space for contemplation leading to self-knowledge. The natural landscape, nurturing, empowering, and enlivening, contrasts with the corruption and crowds of urban life. The Poet in Nature can thus achieve the highest creative potential, can access a deeper imagination, "something far more deeply interfused." In this formulation, "Nature never did betray the heart that loved her," and the Poet proves his (or her) fitness by recognizing this fundamental truth. It is usually accepted, as well, that Romanticism itself privileges the idea of solitude and isolation as especially suited to the needs of the poetic genius, whose gifts resonate like echoes in mountainous terrain or murmur like streams infiltrating the literary landscape. This idea, or call it an ideology, reifies an understanding that, for instance, urban culture corrupts while the countryside purifies (drawing from Wordsworth's Luke who "began/ To slacken in his duty, and at length/ He in the dissolute city gave himself/ to evil courses," or Radcliffe's Valancourt who "has never been to Paris," or Coleridge's "gentle-hearted Charles" who "hast pined/ And hungered after nature many a year/ In the great city pent"). It also gives critics a position to argue against as they uncover new areas for fruitful study such as sociability. What has as yet not been fully considered, however, are the differing types and moral impacts and implications of solitude itself. And here it becomes urgent to push past the hinterlands of locality poetry, because both Smith and Wordsworth highlight a flaw in the idealization of Nature as a refuge for privileged creative minds. What happens when the Poet's self-belief is not borne out? What happens when creative Genius is a delusion? Both Smith and Wordsworth explore the ramifications of retreating to Nature and isolation for, essentially, the wrong reasons, and in doing so both poets shadow narratives of naturalized poetic genius with a disillusion that leads to misanthropy, on the part of the "genius" inhabiting the poem and the writer whose belief in Nature's restorative powers is undermined by the poetry nature inspires.

The idea that the Romantic Poet depends on solitude is nicely captured by John Woolford, who, in an essay on Tennyson, describes the "post-Romantic poet" as striving to "overcome the isolation, at once social and metaphysical" of the preceding generation.[20] Similarly, Christopher Rovee settles on Wordsworth "as the iconic figure of a Romanticism defined by solitude and introspection," while Beth Lau makes the more general remark that "Romantic poetry celebrates solitude and individualism."[21] For Clara Tuite and Gillian Russell, "Romanticism's traditional identification [is] with the lone poet, withdrawn into productive introspection, with individualism rather than collective activity, and with the cultivation of the authentic rather than the performative self."[22] Jeffrey Cox sums it up expertly: "Creation in isolation, with only nature's song for company, with 'poetic feeling' as the lyric's content, and with no concern about an audience for these scraps thrust behind some books – this is the model of Romantic creativity as exploration of unique subjectivity."[23] For all of these critics, the Solitary Poet functions as a foil for the burdened poetic descendant, the "unexpectedly social 'Wordsworth'" (Rovee), a new understanding of Jane Austen as invested in the solitary rather than the social, a new understanding of Romanticism as invested in the social rather than the solitary, and an invitation to engage in "contingent, communal creative exchange" (Cox, p. 333). In other words, Romantic poetic solitude is an accepted construct, established through successive discussions of organicism, for instance, and the textual scenarios hinted at already. Writing and composition are, says Zachary Leader,

> associated with the organic (by which is partly meant the whole or complete) and with process (which implies incompletion). The organic view conceives of writing as occurring in a single, seamless moment, the moment of inspiration, without superadded or "inorganic" refinements ... When writing is conceived of as process, the notion of a finished work – "finished" in all its senses – is slighted.[24]

The Solitary Poet depends on both operating, although Leader opposes them as "seemingly contradictory" (p. 2), in a standard formulation that also, in Leader's argument, serves to disable the possibility of revision and rewriting. Leader's insight opens a chink in the wall of received wisdom about Romantic isolation, but even he seems to rely on a uniform solitude, what Mark Philp calls "the isolationism of the Romantics," a blanket characterization that interrogates neither term.[25] Even, then, as they replace the Solitary Poet with another construct, such approaches also rely on its familiarity; or, if they seek not to replace it but rather to extend the opportunity to experience it, they likewise assume a common understanding of its meaning.

Solitude thus acts as a kind of *monoimage*, derived from generations of reading poems that seem to enact a shared vision of the value of isolation to creativity. This in turn has relied on an understanding of Romantic poetry as sincere and authentic, especially when spoken in the first person.[26] If, however, not all retreats to nature and solitude carry the same weight – if the Solitary Poet is not unitary but as capable of dissimulation as any other public speaker – then such poems become vehicles for the poets' own testing of scenarios of isolation. In other words, if we replace the commonplace of the Solitary Poet with the specific examples offered by Smith and Wordsworth, and probe their representations of creativity in seclusion, then an interesting additional dimension to the written and the composed opens: we can begin to discern the *dangers* of solitude. In the terms of this chapter, solitude threatens to disable the transformation of topographical *place* into poetic *locale*.

Although it is increasingly true that work on Smith's *Elegiac Sonnets* recognizes that some are translations and adaptations of, among others, Petrarch and Goethe, most commentators still conclude that, nonetheless, they represent expressions of a personalized female experience endorsed by the poet Smith herself. Thus, even those poems not spoken by a recognizable Smith, for instance the translations, are in the end spoke by a Smith who ventriloquizes true sentiments via muted stand-ins. While I would not want to argue that none of Smith's sonnets carry a personal tone – clearly, those about her daughter's death do – nonetheless a close examination shows that Smith embeds in her sonnets a different attitude toward sorrow and woe in solitude. Isolation and solitude shut down, rather than enliven, creative capacity. In Sonnet XXXVI, the speaker suggests that Poesy has made some recompense for life's calamities. Using the image of the Wanderer – an exemplary Solitary – the speaker links the refreshment he gains from "weaving gay wreaths beneath some sheltering tree" with that allowed by the "flowers" of poetry (ll. 5, 7). But the speaker associates "Friendship and the Muse" (l. 8); this comforting poetry has not been composed in isolation but rather in a creative confluence of society and solitude. It is only when life darkens, when the speaker anticipates "new clouds of evil yet to come," that both are lost: "her pencil sickening Fancy throws away,/ And weary Hope reclines upon the tomb" (ll. 10, 11–12). It is important that Fancy sickens not from actual, but from expected, "evil"; it is important, too, that Smith places "sickening" so that it can modify both "pencil" and "Fancy." Fancy sickens – creativity ceases – and the pencil sickens – composition ends. In the accompanying plate the pen lies discarded on the ground, and Fancy's parchment is blank. Smith creates a speaker whose expectation of woe results in the inability to compose further; the poem ends with a gesture toward a death desired but unobtainable. This speaker has exchanged the flowers of poetry for a stock image of comfort; the speaker has abjured Friendship and the Muse on the basis of unspecified future evils. The result is creative and imaginative blankness: the lone poet experiences creativity's nemesis, empty imagery.

In Sonnet LXII, "Written on passing by moonlight through a village, while the ground was covered with snow," which originally appeared in *The Old Manor House*, the speaker is again a wanderer, whose self-characterization as "cheerless and unblest" figure him as a pariah, an outcast, lacking in spirit and life (l. 1). Whereas the speaker of Sonnet XXXVI is effectively ungendered, though leaning toward the masculine, this speaker carries for the knowing reader a residual maleness: the poem is spoken by Orlando Somerive, just returned from a spectacularly unsuccessful sojourn as a soldier in the American Revolutionary War, who wanders the countryside like a revenant.[27] Rejected by his society, the speaker creates a scenario that sees him rejecting society in turn: rather than seeking shelter, the speaker casts the "village labourers" as almost of another species, "tast[ing] that quiet I pursue in vain!" (ll. 3, 4). The speaker places himself as different in every particular from the sleeping villagers, wandering without purpose or destination; his poem, then, takes him nowhere: "I only fly from doubt – to meet despair!" (l. 14), a movement from uncertainty to hopelessness that trades a solid refuge for abstract concepts, even as the speaker chooses solitary wandering over social integration. The novel provides a context that emphasizes this: Orlando has met only suspicion and distrust from those to whom he has applied for help, and hence he creates a narrative wherein the wanderer debars himself from human contact. But nature, instead of rewarding the solitary poet with solace and inspiration, is a "cold waste," while the moon "leads to no happy home." In essence, the poem only allows the speaker to recycle his situation in verse: another version of creative stagnation. The poem effectively undercuts the locale-making its titular "written" implies.

Wordsworth, seen as the "icon" of Romantic solitude and introspection by Rovee, follows Smith's lead in complicating the attractions of solitude and the parameters of poetic genius. Although poems like *The Prelude* and "Tintern Abbey" famously endow nature with the facility to enliven and nurture the creative imagination, in "Lines Left Upon a Seat in a Yew-Tree" (where the written is subsumed to the artefact left behind) Wordsworth also explores the results of a misguided and self-promoting retreat to nature; there, as well as endorsing the notion of creative genius, he makes plain the limitations of arrogance and self-aggrandizement. The moral of the poem is clear: "pride,/ Howe'er disguised in its own majesty,/ Is littleness," and the subject of the poem, having met with indifference rather than the admiration he expected for his talents, is pitied by a speaker for whom "true knowledge" and "true dignity" are defined by "lowliness of heart" (ll. 46–8, 56, 57, 60).

What is interesting, however, is that the outcast shares with the speaker and with the Wordsworthian subject a reverence for nature and the landscape that, were it not for the overt moralizing, would otherwise identify the poem's subject as exactly Wordsworthian: "these gloomy boughs/ Had charms for him ..../ .../ ...he would gaze/ On the more distant scene; how lovely 'tis/ Thou seest, and he would gaze til it became/ Far lovelier, and his heart could not sustain/ The beauty still more beauteous" (ll. 21–2, 30–34).[28] But instead of solitude and nature leading to a rebirth for the subject, not even the "beautiful prospect" of the title can lift him from himself; hence, "he would sigh/ With mournful joy, to think that others felt/ What he must never feel" (ll. 38–40). The subject's solipsism is not condoned by the speaker, who calls him a "lost man" (l. 40); the subject's position as a kind of pastoral elegist figure shades the typical function of solitude and nature – to nurture the creative imagination – with a strange dysfunction, for "on visionary views would fancy feed,/ Til his eye streamed with tears" (ll. 41–2). The subject somehow cannot translate vision to insight, and so his heart cannot sustain – maintain, nourish, suffer – nature's beauty, and his eye cannot see past his own tears. It is clear that the poem's subject provides a "how not to experience solitude" lesson.

But what of the poem's speaker? And who, or what, is that speaker? The poem opens with an exhortation to a "Traveller" to "rest"; the orality of the opening anticipates that of "Michael" ("If from the public way you turn your steps") and implies an embodied speaker and a companion traveler. But the title of the poem is "Lines left upon a Seat in a Yew-Tree," and although we learn in the poem that the "seat" is the subject's "only monument," there is no mention that he himself wrote "lines" (l. 43). If the poem is itself the "lines," then the speaker does not so much speak as write, his words somehow drawing the attention of passing travelers in order to enlighten them about the dangers and limitations of solitary solipsism. And yet, much of the poem simply judges the solipsist, placing him within a natural scene he is unable fully to comprehend, and making sure the reader understands this – which means that the writer of the lines makes sure any reader understands his own superior abilities. There is something uncomfortable about a poem that exists merely to critique another, and that trumpets its own moralizing. It is as if, by leaving his lines on the seat, the writer of them implies that nature itself endorses his point of view: poetry has become an object, a document that presents itself as truth-telling. Shifting the perspective from the subject of the poem to its speaker/writer shifts, as well, the misanthropic impulse; as much as the subject was unable to "sustain/ The beauty" of nature (ll. 33–4), so too the writer of the lines cannot even see nature in his concentration on the failures of the subject. There is a double feint here: invited to learn from the object lesson of the subject, the lines' writer in turn comes under scrutiny, and we realize that the figure the poem presents as deluded in his self-belief may well be not the subject of the poem, but its inscriber. In simply leaving his lines on the yew tree's seat and expecting passing travelers to heed them, the writer of the poem displays his own "rash disdain" and "pride" (ll. 19, 20).[29] The result is a kind of false locale.

In the concluding sections of "Beachy Head," Smith presents a figure whose chosen state of isolation and solitude resonates strongly with that in "Yew-Tree," but she textures her presentation by incorporating aspects of the writer of "Yew-Tree" as well. The "stranger" who makes his home in a derelict "mansion" and spends his days and nights "wander[ing] forth" both sings and writes his "plaintive" songs (p. 170, ll. 507, 506; p. 171, ll. 512, 529). The oral songs are repeated by "peasant girls," and the written are left, significantly, "near one ancient tree, whose wreathed roots/ Form'd a rude couch"; more than simply "lines," there are "love-songs and scatter'd rhymes,/ Unfinished sentences, or half erased,/ And rhapsodies" (p. 172, ll. 528, 573–4, 574–6). The stranger, "of Solitude ... enamour'd," "to the murmuring wind, of cold neglect/ And baffled hope ... told" (p. 172, ll. 559; p. 171, ll. 527–8), linking his experience of the world to that of Wordsworth's poem: "against all enemies prepared,/ All but neglect" ("Yew-Tree," ll. 17–18). Where Wordsworth's figure is silenced, however, requiring the presence of the "lines" to tell his story, Smith's leaves hints through his own scattered lines.[30] His lines, or rhapsodies, invoke a nature drawn from the world of the *Lyrical Ballads*, even as he recalls the speakers and solitaries of those poems. Smith interweaves the stagnated wanderers of her sonnets with the self-important solitaries composed by Wordsworth, and produces a figure whose immediate trauma, being crossed in love, blends with a more generalized rejection of the world and its "cold policy" ("Beachy Head," p. 174, l. 661). Pointedly, where Wordsworth's misanthropic lines-writer disallows his subject the solace of vision, Smith describes her "visionary, nursing dreams ... [as] not indeed unhappy. Summer woods/ Wave over him, and whisper as they wave,/ Some future blessing he may yet enjoy./ And as above him sail the silver clouds,/ He follows them in thought ..." (p. 174, ll. 655–60). With the addition of "a host of golden daffodils," the stranger's "ideal bliss" (Smith) would clearly be "the bliss of solitude" (Wordsworth). It would not, however, be a scene of creative energy, since the stranger, like the subject of "Yew-Tree," melts into the text, "gliding like a ghost" through his own "unfinished sentences" (p. 172, ll. 571, 575).

If solitude is meant to facilitate the highest and most meaningful poetics, it must somehow find a match with a poetic genius itself outward-looking and elevated, if one follows the standard Romantic formulation. But, as Smith and Wordsworth show, if solitude is sought because the poet is "flying from something that he dreads, [rather] than [seeking] the thing he loved" ("Tintern Abbey"), or regards an isolated space as all the better to be seen in, or finds himself unable to move beyond past disappointment, neglect, or rejection, then the poetry itself will collapse, stagnate, and decay. Vision will diminish and art will become artificial. It is because both Smith and Wordsworth can also create solitaries for whom isolation enables creativity that their portrayals of a false poetics of solitude are so meaningful. They are not simply undermining the usefulness of solitude, but rather differentiating: Smith's "upland solitudes/ .../ Scenes of fond day-dreams" ("Beachy Head") and Wordsworth's "wild secluded scene [which impresses] thoughts of more deep seclusion" ("Tintern Abbey") lead directly, in both "Beachy Head" and "Tintern Abbey," to clarity and new visions of selfhood and enlightenment. Their other speakers, although still first person, betray their limitations through the nature of their verse: blocked, empty, morally bankrupt, in which even nature is underwritten. For Smith and Wordsworth, solitude is, and must be, more than a "sequester'd vale" (Sonnet XXII) or a "dear nook unvisited" ("Nutting").

The trans-text

Not even poetry, then, can overcome the dangers of a self-indulgent rejection of community. Isolation and solitude effectively dislocate poetry – its locales become mirages of solipsism rather than landscapes inviting exploration. Composing and writing may well take place *in* isolation, but if the poem itself can only imagine static solitude, then it suffers poetic loss – it shrinks its own space, becomes mere topography. Poetry requires, in the end, a specific form of community: readers, and figures who merely "compose" or "write" lines represent, in these poems, automatons whose verse leads "to no happy home." Smith and Wordsworth show, in their manipulations of form and their reinvigorations of the acts of composing and writing, that poetry can become, itself, a place; locality poems intensify the interrelations between temporal and spatial geographies, art, and the imaginative or poetic process. The sterile poetry produced by the solipsist contrasts strongly with the creative cycle that results when poetry is read and subsequently remapped. A rigid poetics of geography complicates the imaginary, and destabilizes a trusting reader; but compositions of locality that are not subject to place can open a new level of the written.

Probably Wordsworth's most well-known and most thoroughly studied "written" poem is "Lines written a few miles above Tintern Abbey, On Revisiting the Banks of the Wye During a Tour, July 13, 1798."[31] Its titular locality has been analyzed extensively, most usefully by Marjorie Levinson, who unpicked its vexed and veiled references to political and historical events. There is also the matter of the critical shorthand that has mistitled the poem and reinserted an Abbey where for Wordsworth there was none – or at least not at this particular location on the banks of the Wye. Nonetheless, the poem is almost always read as dealing with the true, real, or actual: Wordsworth really had visited the valley in 1793; he really did revisit it in 1798; he really did compose extempore; and he really did find in the poem an expression of poetic creativity and maturation that satisfied him enough that he never revised it – almost unique for this poet. The locality of the title, and its use of "written," reinforces the physicality of the title: someone is writing (just as someone wrote in March). The poem relies on this physicality: the "I" dominates the narrative, straight through to the end, when the turn to the "dearest Friend" allows for an ever more deeply inscribed treatment of the self. The layers of personal history offered by the poem further its status as autobiographical, as real. There is a someone in this poem, whose self-referentiality and scene-setting are easily read as autobiographical; the actual and the poetic seem, for once, to coincide. A poem is written; a figure hears, beholds, reposes, views, and sees, all within the first fifteen lines. Its originating event, following Levinson, occurs in July 1793, coyly deflected to the day before Bastille Day, and months into a new war with France.[32] But the specificity of the title is made less resonant by the emphasis on the passage of *years* in the poem's opening lines – and if five summers as well as five long winters have passed, then readers are tacitly directed not precisely to July 1793, but to the summer of 1793.

Some time in June or July of 1793, Smith publishes *The Emigrants*, signed "Brighthelmstone, May 10, 1793." Although neither "written" nor "composed," the poem is minutely located in its "Scenes" which set each Book in time and space. Using locality as a backdrop for the exploration of politics, inhumanity, and exile, Smith creates a well-peopled solitude; the speaker is in isolation but surrounded by figurative and literal others. Book II is set "on an Eminence," and from the vantage point the poem explores, among other things, the speaker's childhood "on my native hills, [where] I learn'd to gaze/ On these delightful landscapes" and her journey from "unconscious" "play" to "never-ending toil,/...terror and ... tears!" (p. 138, II: 37–8; p. 144, II: 334; p. 145, II: 350–51). The poem ends with a turn to the Divine worshipped not through "regulated sanctity" in "domes of human architecture, fill'd with crowds,/ But on these hills ...":

> [Where] I might breathe the air perfum'd with flowers,
> Or the fresh odours of the mountain turf;
> And gaze on clouds above me, as they sail'd
> Majestic; or remark the reddening north,
> When bickering arrows of electric fire
> Flash on the evening sky – I made my prayer
> In unison with murmuring waves that now
> Swell with dark tempests, now are mild and blue,
> As the bright arch above; for all to me
> Declare omniscient goodness ... (p. 145, II: 387; p. 145–6, II: 390–91, 396–405)

The geography charted by the poem is the development of the Poet in Nature, who is only able to see the Emigrants and recognize their plight because of her apprenticeship on her "native hills" (p. 138, II: 37).

Book II opens with resonant lines:

> Long wintry months are past; the Moon that now
> Lights her pale crescent even at noon, has made
> Four times her revolution: since with step,
> Mournful and slow, along the wave-worn cliff,
> Pensive I took my solitary way ... (p. 137, II: 1–5)

And now the trail leads back to "Tintern Abbey," with its opening emphasis on the passage of time[33]:

> Five years have passed; five summers, with the length
> Of five long winters! and again I hear
> These waters, rolling, from their mountain-springs
> With a sweet inland murmur. – Once again
> Do I behold these steep and lofty cliffs,
> Which on a wild secluded scene impress
> Thoughts of more deep seclusion ... (ll. 1–7)

Smith's eminence and Wordsworth's "few miles above" locate the two poems in a similar topography, but *The Emigrants'* temporal placement, summer 1793, opens a new locality for Wordsworth's 1793 reference. As much as he revisits the banks of the Wye, he also revisits the scene of inspiration and influence: those "waters, rolling from their mountain springs" (l. 3) evoke the "dim cold sea,/ That melancholy rolls its refluent tides" in Book I of *The Emigrants* (p. 128, I: 158–9). With this history providing an alternative backdrop, a different kind of locale emerges for Wordsworth's poem. It suggests that the writer of "Tintern Abbey" is also a reader of *The Emigrants*, and that the moment that inspires "Tintern Abbey" arises from poetry rather than history. "Tintern Abbey" is a trans-text; it acts as a rider to *The Emigrants* while also mapping its own terrain. Wordsworth locates its moment of genesis in both time and place: the summer of 1793 in which upbringing, location, memory, and poetry are so enduringly intertwined; the panoramic eminence from which the natural landscape and the landscape of the poet's imagination are most visible. *The Emigrants* is not "written," but it composes key elements of the emergent Romantic poet. The gesture of "Tintern Abbey" toward the consuming importance of a moment located five years past places Wordsworth, in this respect, as Smith's composition.

4
Modeling the Romantic Poet

Chapter 3 discussed how place informs constructions of the poet. This chapter explores a form more usually associated with the post-Romantic period, the dramatic monologue, to suggest that the egoistic personae developed by Wordsworth and Smith in effect deconstruct a particular kind of poet. Read by many as establishing the use-value of the autobiographical within Romanticism, much of Wordsworth's poetry is discussed as arising from a particular function of self-reliance; in the same way, Smith has emerged as a prime user of biographical details to underpin her expressions of unhappiness. I want to trouble this conclusion, and will do so first by projecting the dramatic monologue back to, initially, the 1790s as *dramatized* monologues, a fine distinction that is meant to acknowledge how Smith and Wordsworth write performances of selfhood. They model several versions of Poet through an emphasis on revealing, discretely, how speakers perform questionable identities, in the process undoing their own poetry; Smith and Wordsworth concentrate on establishing the parameters of the Poet, filtered through an exploration of the artfully constructed Self. In some of the most composed of the *Elegiac Sonnets*, in "Beachy Head," in *Lyrical Ballads*, and in *The Prelude*, the "theatrical," to use Judith Pascoe's term, underpins and indeed creates the personalized narrators of the poems.[1] Often read as thinly disguised autobiographies, their presentations of sincerity and authenticity are, this chapter contends, dramatized, the position of Poet itself a role. Anticipating (or perhaps providing the template for) the Victorian dramatic monologue, the personalities speaking the poems reveal aspects of themselves despite their best efforts at concealment; Wordsworth and Smith write Selves that are simultaneously Self and Other. The Keatsian egotistical sublime, instead of functioning as an unconscious revelation of solipsism, becomes a tool by which the poets can act out fantasies of unified subjectivity. For the late eighteenth century, fascinated with an emerging culture of celebrity and individuality, Smith's and Wordsworth's poetry helped to form an expectation that the poetic was personal. It also undermined such expectations and created a space within poetry that critiqued these narrow parameters. In this way, the Romantic dramatized monologue, like its later version, relies on the power of the artful to expose the limitations of the personal.[2]

Keats is so very matter-of-fact in his identification of the "wordsworthian or egotistical sublime" and its contradistinction from his own version of the "poetical Character" as chameleonic and without identity that his definition goes by and large unchallenged.[3] With its lower-case "w," "wordworthian" becomes an adjective, detached from the person Wordsworth although derived from how Keats read him: as overwhelmingly inhabiting his poetry, and as a Self defined by an excessive writing of the Self. It is not difficult to see that for Keats, Smith's poetry would occupy the same space: writing wherein the "nature" and "identity" of the poet, far from being "annihilated," take center stage and claim full readerly attention (Keats, pp. 279, 280). Smith, of course, encourages this response with her increasingly detailed and personalized Prefaces and Dedications; Wordsworth may be more retiring but the force of the poetry remains the same.[4] However, to describe the autobiographical – perhaps more accurately called the meta-autobiographical – poetry of the two as dramatic or dramatized allows us to interrogate the certainty of Keats' formulation. As far back as 1957, Stephen Maxfield Parrish described "The Thorn" as Wordsworth's dramatic monologue; his work established the feasibility of moving the development of the genre back a poetic generation.[5] Even for Parrish, however, "The Thorn" was proto-Victorian in its enactment of the monologue: Wordsworth wrote a poem not about a mother or a tree, but about a speaker whose nature was revealed through his own first-person narrative (p. 101 *passim*). Turning to the meta-autobiographical poems of both Smith and Wordsworth allows for a more specifically Romantic version of the dramatic monologue to emerge: one in which the egotistical sublime is the *pose* rather than the drawback, and in which the writing of the Self is achieved through deliberately literary inscription and blissfully unaware elocution.

In many ways this is also about how the "Romantic" is read back into the poetry. The Wordsworth and Smith of the 1790s, in their experimental mode, use poetry as a conduit to different models of knowledge and understanding. Their continual explorations of form, content, and the ideas derived from each supports their rendering of a poetry that, in effect, quests for rather than settles on certainties. Up to this point, however, this has kept the process distinct from the poet. Experiments with form, engagements with event, interrogations of place and space have highlighted the *writing*, but in this chapter I want to look at the *writer* – or, rather, I want to consider how Smith and Wordsworth write about themselves writing about "themselves." The layers are necessary, since presentations of self – whether through displays of autobiography or of ego – define a central understanding of Romanticism that, as I outlined in the Introduction, blossomed in the nineteenth-century readings of, and decisions about, Wordsworth. The Wordsworth that emerged, by consensus, was the sincere people's poet whose authentic voicing of a rapidly disappearing, equally authentic countryside took precedence over a contrasting version that emphasized his conflicted portraits of self and other. This in turn came under scrutiny in the late twentieth century, first in critical moves to restore autonomous voices to the silenced figures ventriloquized by Wordsworth (in the work of, for instance, John Barrell or Marjorie Levinson) and then by increasingly subtle versions of a Wordsworth for whom the voicing process was itself a form of ethical conflict (here one could cite Don Bialotosky, David Simpson, or David Bromwich).

When Wordsworth writes (of) himself, however, he is balancing these, and other, approaches. The sincerity that readers, as this chapter will show, still find attractive and plausible coincides, frequently, with a destabilizing of its values. The cult of personality that values, even mandates, a known and knowable poet-speaker has persisted, precisely because Wordsworth's presentation of the speaking self is so powerfully personalized. The place-identity discussed in Chapter 3, with its evocative realizing of the localities written and composed into permanence, is mirrored by the person-specific moves Wordsworth makes in the *Lyrical Ballads* and *The Prelude*. As with place, however, this enables a doubled awareness: poetry *might* uncover the real person, but it probably, or usually, doesn't (and shouldn't). Sincere self-presentation, this chapter argues, is immediately called into question at the point of composition. In other words, as well as grappling with the ramifications of portraying, and voicing, others, Wordsworth pointedly engages with the drama of doing so to, and with, himself.[6] Thus, his *Lyrical Ballads* present a number of moments of pure self-exploration; that is, capitalizing on the idea that Self can be adequately and suitably present in poetry.

This style – perhaps more accurately labeled a genre – informs Smith from the start. Her earliest published poems, all of which were reprinted in the first edition of *Elegiac Sonnets*, appeared in the *European Magazine* and other periodicals from the early 1780s.[7] Although they are the same elegiac sonnets she names and claims in 1784, all written (and read) as if emanating from the same sorrowful and coherent speaker, these early versions are published piecemeal and anonymously or pseudonymously. Her common pseudonym, "S.C.," in its simple reversal of initials, is an impenetrable disguise once coupled with the change in sex she enacts in a note attached to the version of Sonnet I first published in the *European Magazine* in September 1782: "The last line ... is very like the last lines of Pope's Epistle from Eloisa to Abelard; the author is sensible that *he* is something of a plagiarist..." (*Poetry*, p. 218, n. 17, emphasis added).[8] This play with identity dissembles the autobiographical slant so heavily promoted in the *Elegiac Sonnets*. Anonymous or otherwise secret publication in periodicals was not uncommon; writers often tested poems in this way, or otherwise used pseudonyms to preserve their privacy or their reputation.[9] The notable issue here, however, is the pains with which readers of Smith assign her poems to her personal, selfed voice, from contemporary readers who wept over her sorrows (or conversely scolded her for publicizing them) to twentieth-century critics like myself who have read them as emblematic of (a) woman's experience. It is as hard to uncouple the "real" Smith from her putatively autobiographical verse as it is with Wordsworth. Both write the Self so finely that delineation overcomes discrimination. Readers want them to be sincere expressions, authentic voicings of the poet.

This chapter suggests, however, that in writing Self both Smith and Wordsworth continue the experimentation that informs their investigations of poetry itself. In other words, the question "What is a Poem?" underlying their hybridizing is matched by two correlaries: "What is a Poet?" and "Who is the Poet?" Smith and Wordsworth undertake, in the poems under discussion in this chapter, an investigation into the depth and breadth of the Poet via reference to Life – their lives, but refracted through art and its twin, artifice. Once Life is poeticized, what has it become? If Self is written, is it possible to retain authenticity? The poetry invites inquiry exactly because its autobiographies are such feints; as I will discuss below, the feint is a key aspect of the Victorian dramatic monologue, and Smith's and Wordsworth's poetry demonstrates clearly how much of that genre is indebted to the poetry its Victorian practitioners read as sincere (because they wanted to). Approaching Smith and Wordsworth as Romantic dramatized monologists, however, provides a structure for their poetry. This is not meant to be monolithic – indeed, some of their autobiographical poetry is just that – but it opens the space needed to query the consistent association of poet and speaker, of Self with selfhood. As poetry provides the building blocks, so too poetry enables the inspection of the resulting construction. Neither Smith nor Wordsworth is content with reproduction; as Chapter 1 showed, querying existing models is key to their 1790s output. This chapter demonstrates how much further they take the experiment when the subject is the Poet.

The Sincerity Topos

Interestingly, most critics who explore the sincere and authentic in Romantic poetry focus on Wordsworth, and most acknowledge, at least in passing, the contructed nature of Wordsworthian sincerity, despite its self-conscious appearance as unmediated. Robert Langbaum, writing in 1957, notes that "whether the romanticist projects himself into the past, nature, or another person, he never forgets that he is playing a role," and that sincerity is an "effect" to be achieved.[10] David Perkins refers to "the drama of sincerity" and "the impression of spontaneity," arguing that poetic form "compromises the ideal of sincerity."[11] Even Lionel Trilling calls poetic sincerity "a congruence between avowal and actual feeling."[12] However, they agree in presenting Wordsworth as somehow innocent, a kind of dupe of sincerity's propensity to expose its own falsity in representation. He is a poet who strives for authenticity: "he writes as though he were talking to close friends or to domestic companions" (Perkins, p. 143); he "wr[ites] of a self in whose authenticity he utterly believed."[13] Leon Guilhamet probably takes this furthest when he writes that, for Wordsworth, "the language of sincerity, drawing sustenance from truth, leads men to understand truth."[14] None of these critics, writing between 1957 and 1974, would have admitted Smith to the same plateau on which they placed Wordsworth, but her tone is equally intimate, whether crying out for succor in the *Sonnets* or recounting conversations with friends in the Prefaces. When she calls herself "an early worshipper at Nature's shrine"[15] she offers the same "autobiographical illusion" and follows the same strategy of giving "facts from within" that Langbaum finds in Wordsworth (pp. 52, 78). For both poets, sincerity and authenticity operate much of the poetry; the question is not whether this is true, but whether the two poets are at the mercy of sincerity's inherent insincerity, or whether they play with this, and consequently with the picture of the Poet as authentic, emotionally open, transparently Selfed.

A critical investment in the idea of the Romantic writers as moving against the mainstream of their culture, derived from understandings of their poetry as by definition experimental, innovative, and anti-cultural, coupled with an understanding of authenticity as a poetic goal, even if a compromised one, informs characterizations of the sincere Wordsworth. However, even as the Romantic poetry written by Wordsworth builds on its literary past, representing continuity as well as innovation, so too the poetic Self written into his and Smith's poetry develops in a culture highly interested in public displays of personality and subjectivity. Studies subsequent to Guilhamet began to note a more conscious and self-aware poetic stance. Frances Ferguson, in 1977, countered the isolationist egotistical sublime by simply, and vitally, noting the "various provisions for an audience" even in Wordsworth's seemingly most private poetry, which immediately introduces the idea of performance, even though Ferguson did not name this as such.[16] William Galperin extends Ferguson's insight so that the audience becomes the guarantor of Wordsworth's sincerity: the Authentic Self "was written as, and was the product of, an interchange with a hypothetical reader" (p. 66); the poet is compelled to create poetry in which his sincerity is maintained and verified. If the Romantic poet – Wordsworth or Smith – writes poetry that implies its own audience, however, then a performance has begun and authenticity itself is replaced by its dramatized understudy. Therefore, according to Sheila Kearns, writing about the self "involves ... the performance of a reading of the self in and through the construction of the autobiographical text"; for Elizabeth Fay, "romantic sincerity is also an aestheticization of the self ... [A]cting and being (acting the role of the self) are the same"; for Pascoe, "Wordsworth was drawn to dramatic realizations of the self" (p. 219).[17] Even Deborah Forbes, who attempts intriguingly to fuse the sincere with the performative, says that Wordsworth "is a sincere poet *because* he makes his sincerity questionable"; in other words, he unpicks that of which he was previously understood to lack awareness.[18]

Curiously, even as they formulate a new critical understanding of Wordsworth as decidedly performative, and of the autobiographical poem as more dramatic than authentic, none of these critics explores the place of the dramatic monologue in Romantic autobiographical poetry – or rather, as I called it above, the meta-autobiographical. Indeed, Forbes rejects the idea fully, explaining that while a poem like "Tintern Abbey" *could* be a dramatic monologue, the readerly need to believe in a "speaker-poet" overrides this possibility. Otherwise the speaker's "imprecision" and "mysticism" become "laughable": "it is truer to the poem, and to everything we know of Wordsworth, to believe that we are supposed to share the speaker-poet's sense of awe in the face of things he cannot explain" (p. 85). This reading, of course, re-engages with the sincere, since what seems to underlie Forbes' comments is a desire to read the poem as truthful in the Guilhamet sense. Without "truth," without a speaker-poet whose ego creates the sublimity of the incomprehensible, then the poem fails. Forbes' stance is very close to Langbaum's, who judges that "Wordsworth never consciously discovered the dramatic monologue, though he is always hovering on the edge of the form," writing instead dialogic "dramatic lyrics" where the subject is the Self rather than the exploration of another created Self (p. 53). This frequent critical return to an evocation of Wordsworth's Self suggests more the constancy of Keats than of Wordsworth; it seems precisely the discomfort Wordsworth's technique arouses – the suspicion that his persona is not nearly as coherent as it pretends to be – that prompts so many readers to realign Speaker and Poet. As Fay points out, "Wordsworthian scholars do not like to regard William Wordsworth as invested in roles beyond that of seer and sage because the concept of role playing seems deliberately at odds with Wordsworth's insistent sincerity" (p. 18).[19] For the purposes of my argument, it is exactly this insistence that allows the coherence of Wordsworth's speaker to be questioned. Similarly, Smith's insistence on sorrow and personal need, and its primacy for her readers both then and now, hints at its own artifice. For both poets, the poetry of the Self coupled with the exploitation of an expectation of sincerity – an expectation that each encourages – results in the Romantic dramatized monologue.

If we question not only sincerity but also autobiography, however, we create a space for the dramatized monologue. The key elements of the Victorian form are that the dramatic monologue is spoken by a "speaker indicated not to be the poet" in "the presence of an auditor" with a "high degree of naturalistic presentation"; "the poet must convince us of the actuality of the character in order to secure a full emotional engagement."[20] For Victorian writers, speaker-proxies like the Duke of Ferrara or murderous madmen maintained a difference from the poet. Smith and Wordsworth anticipate the form, but they explore exactly the figure of the selfed Poet, dwelling on his/her tendency toward self-aggrandizement, intense introspection, self-conscious literariness. Critics have tended to read these poetic attributes as derived from the autobiographical self presented in the poetry, the unconscious self-exposure of the egotist. But in a culture saturated with spectacle – theatrical, political, journalistic, even poetic (think the Della Cruscans, for instance) – and increasingly fascinated by celebrity, then attempts by a poet to ascertain "What is a Poet?" are at least hinting toward a drama of self-representation, especially when the answer is that "He is a man speaking to men": a man declaiming, performing, delivering a monologue.[21] Or, in the case of Smith, a woman whose private sorrows are publicly pronounced: "toujours des Chansons tristes" (Preface to the Sixth Edition of the *Elegiac Sonnets*). In other words, the Author writes a Self (Persona) who, within the poetry, enacts a sincere and authentic selfhood. In so doing, the Persona inadvertently exposes his/her limitations as a self-obsessed Subject through a self-reflexive poetics. Crucially, this is done in the presence of some kind of auditor: a Friend, a Sister, a reader who is implicitly (sometimes explicitly) invoked. Poetry, then, is the vehicle by which the exemplary Romantic poet, Wordsworth or Smith, at once writes Romantic ego into being, and calls its value into question.[22] As auditors, we are simultaneously seduced and repulsed by the display of selfhood. Do we rescue Smith, or dismiss her as a pest? Do we admire Wordsworth, or accuse him of solipsism?

Viewing the meta-autobiographical as a dramatic feint, to use Sinfield's term, means re-viewing the egotistical sublime as Keats' misreading. By the time he makes his judgment, in 1818, the figure of the Romantic poet is well established, in many ways derived from the personae explored by Smith and Wordsworth. The general applicability of Keats' pronouncement to a certain style of writing probably accounts for his lower-case "w," while the fall from favor Smith's poetry had already undergone, combined with the young poet's unease with identifying a female poet's influence as central, justifies "wordsworthian" over "smithian." For both older poets, poetry affords a space wherein experimentation with different forms of subjectivity is possible, and to insist on the reliability, the *authenticity*, of the autobiographical misses, I think, the fundamental innovation of both poets: seeing that poetry itself creates subjectivity, that sincere expression is always mediated in some way by the artistic process, and that even the most autobiographical verse flirts, at the least, with artifice. Reading the autobiographical as meta-autobiographical, then, means that we can interpret the "I" of the *Elegiac Sonnets*, "Beachy Head," the *Lyrical Ballads*, and *The Prelude* as a *characterization* of selfhood by Smith and Wordsworth, their attempts at understanding the nature and character of the Poet, and their identifications of the encompassing Poet's drawbacks.[23] The subsequent evaluation of Wordsworth as a supreme monologist and Smith as a tiresome moaner suggests, however, a certain failure of the project. Whether over- or under-reading, such reactions to the coherence of the speakers each poet writes, so attractively embellished with autobiography, point toward what always lurks just behind experimentation: the risk of over-reaching.

The *Elegiac Sonnets* and the Depths of a Poet's Sorrow

It is a critical commonplace that Smith uses her *Sonnets* to explore – some would say indulge – her sorrows, ranging from her unhappy marriage to her unsettled lawsuit and poverty to her worries and griefs over her children. As her letters show, however, Smith could suit her tone to her genre; while the letters are frequently angry and distressed, they are seldom woeful or self-pitying.[24] The problems that led to her unhappiness are well documented by Smith in an almost legalistic way: she frequently backs up her complaints with facts, figures, and papers to prove her point. The straightforward determination evinced by the letters functions as a competing form of autobiography to that written into the *Sonnets*, which themselves offer a variety of Selves from which to seek the "real" Charlotte Smith.[25] And readers duly seek; as Pascoe notes, the *Sonnets* created a "cult of the beleaguered and self-dramatizing female, a poetic identity that brought Smith considerable success" (p. 16) as her readers responded with a sympathetic consumerism to the need expressed in the poetry. As Pascoe's use of the term "self-dramatizing" suggests, however, the sincerity of the *Sonnets* is compromised by what Pascoe defines as the "performative" but what I see as *performance*, not Smith acting out her sorrows for an appreciative audience, but Smith composing a speaker who is determined by the expression of sorrow. This speaker exposes her personal limitations inadvertently, through the act of composition itself; the poet critiques a speaker who laments ceaselessly but who does nothing to improve her situation.[26]

Because of the intensity of the Prefaces to her *Sonnets*, in which Smith the author constructs a Poet at the mercy of "the Honourable Men" who control the lawsuit over her father-in-law's will, the sonnets, whether transplanted from her novels, translated from Goethe or Petrarch, or transparently spoken by an autobiographical Charlotte Smith, appear as the collective woes of the author.[27] But Smith is as diligent in undercutting this appearance once in the body of the work as she is in cementing it in the paratexts. There are a variety of sorrowing stances that Smith's speakers take up, and she varies also her endorsements of their styles. The speaker of Sonnets XII, XLIV, and LXXX, for instance, does little more than sit and lament her fate. In each, Smith vocalizes a passive victim, one who longs for the release of death but who does nothing to forward this. In Sonnet XII, "Written on the Sea Shore. – October, 1794," the speaker is not specifically gendered in the poem but the accompanying plate, showing a female figure, suggests a female speaker – not, however, Smith, given the youth and physical vulnerability of the woman.[28] The speaker occupies, then, a space associated with the woes of Charlotte Smith, but is dissociated from her via the plate. Further, the "mournful temper" of the speaker's "soul" is linked by pathetic fallacy with the "wild gloomy scene" (pp. 8, 7), while the poem's tone is overdetermined by the storm-tossed imagery; in other words, this speaker writes a poem whose very compositional seamlessness invites investigation.[29] As I argued in Chapter 1, the *Elegiac Sonnets* as a text are engaged in experiment, in finding ways in which form can evolve. And, remembering Daniel Robinson's persuasive ideas that Smith's use of the term "essays" in the title of the first editions of the *Sonnets* (*Elegiac Sonnets, and Other Essays*) points to the inherent experimentation of the collection, it is significant if a poem declines the chance to innovate. As Robinson notes, "the 'elegiac sonnet' is for Smith very much an experiment, an 'essay,' that is, an attempt," and the *Sonnets* as a whole engage in "the deliberate yoking of seemingly disparate forms."[30] Given this, it is significant that Sonnet XII, the first to feature the passive speaker, is written so very correctly. The imagery is unimpeachable, the tone wholly consistent, and the rhyme scheme unadventurous, even if also "illegitimate": *abba cddc effe gg*.[31] Smith's rhyme schemes often furnish clues to the meaning of her sonnets, and here the very regularity of the rhyme suggests that for Smith, this speaker is lacking a fundamental spark.

Sonnet XLIV, "Written in the church-yard in Middleton in Sussex," also demonstrates a poetic perfection that regularizes its macabre content. Often discussed as an example of Smith's "striking" morbidity (Robinson, p. 193), it features the passive speaker whose strength of imagery is not matched by strength of character. The speaker subsumes herself to the scene she witnesses: invisible in the poem until line 13, even her sex is unclear, intimated only by the poem's similarity of scene to Sonnet XII. Again, a speaker watches an external tumult and wishes for, but does not seek, the "gloomy rest" of the dead (l. 14). The poem updates the graveyard school, its details of decomposed bodies more conventional than is usually acknowledged.[32] Its strong imagery in this context is less innovative than thoroughly poetical, and its rhyme scheme is again regular: *abba cddc ecce ff*. The slight disruption to the full regulation of Sonnet XII suggests the critical intervention of the poet in the construction of the sonnet's self-regarding speaker. As if impressed by the potency of her imagery, the speaker suffers a lapse in the rigor of her rhymes. The speaker-as-poet, defined by her sorrows, paralyzed by their evocation, grasps for rhyme but can only repeat herself. Smith shows the effect on poetry of an overriding concern, a monomania the expression of which requires compositional convention but which also corrupts this convention from within.[33]

Sonnet LXXX, "To the invisible moon," sees the speaker attempt a more vigorous style, only to fall back into a dramatized passivity. The sonnet opens by invoking Sonnet IV, "To the Moon," in such a way as to differentiate this speaker from that of the earlier sonnet. Where the "I" in Sonnet IV "delight[s] to stray" "by [the moon's] pale beam" (ll. 2, 1), this speaker emphatically negates the comfort the "soft Evening's Queen" offers to those who feel "mild Sorrow, such as Hope has not forsook" (ll. 1, 5). Once again passive and still, the speaker states that "*I* prefer from some steep rock to look/ On the obscure and fluctuating main" (ll. 7–8). Like the speaker of Sonnet XII, this Poet prefers the "troubled deep" (l. 10) to the "mild and placid light" of the moon (Sonnet IV, l. 5). And like that speaker, this one does little more than compose herself. Constructing a parallel series of fiery images ("the martial star with lurid glare," "the red comet shakes his blazing hair," "the fire-ting'd waves" [ll. 9, 11, 12]), and the by-now familiar regular rhyme scheme (*abab cdcd efef gg*), the speaker takes refuge in full poetic correctness. Further, even as this correctness was undercut by repetition in Sonnet LXIV, here Smith utilizes near-rhyme to suggest her speaker's incapacity: Queen/serene and reign/main (ll. 1, 3, 6, 8). Suffused by a generalized woe, compelled to write and rewrite her sorrow, the passive speaker takes refuge in poetic perfection, displaying for her readers her ability to compose, to be an expressive Poet. But the more she writes, the more her expression is overcome by its own constructedness: correctness increasingly gives way to mere convention. This is the poet who wears out her welcome; what Fay calls Smith's "'naturally' melancholic pose" (p. 22) characterizes a Poet-figure who cannot see beyond her own sorrow, and cannot write anything else.

The dramatizing of the passive speaker allows Smith to explore the ways in which poetry enables subjectivity. By writing a speaker whose personality she on the one hand seems to claim, and on the other simply declaims, Smith demonstrates what E. Warwick Slinn views as the unique performativity of poetry: poetry is "a cultural event which participates in cultural reality, reconstituting or reshaping that reality in the very act of reiterating its norms; and its capacity for referential aberration, pointing in both directions, both inside and outside itself, draws attention to the double action."[34] As dramatized monologues, these sonnets enact sorrow and also undermine its influence. It is because not all the sonnets feature a passive speaker whose griefs are unspeakable that we can unpick the reality shaped by these, following the hints that

Smith embeds in the composition of such seamless poetry. Unimpressed with poetic posturing, Smith allows her passive speaker to expose her own limitations as a poet and as a persona through the very medium that lends her a kind of reality. But these poems do not plumb the depths of the poet's sorrow; Smith gives more credence to the speaker of the sonnets she transplants from her various novels, whose sorrows are less generalized but whose compositional pedigree is more complex. This is achieved in two main ways: she creates clear links between the novel-sonnets' tropes and those of other, more clearly autobiographical sonnets; and she allows the speakers of the novel-sonnets to compose more innovative poetry. This is especially clear in the five sonnets she includes from her novel *Celestina*, all spoken originally by Celestina, and thus doubly feminized in the *Sonnets*. Moreover, since most editions of the *Sonnets* signal the novel as source in the sonnets' titles, readers approach them as they do the Werther sonnets, aware of an existing backstory. Indeed, just as the five Werther sonnets enact a kind of playlet, so too the five Celestina sonnets can be seen as five acts in a drama. The dramatic element of the Celestina sonnets is thus both more and less obvious: more because the knowing reader recognizes the "I" as someone other than Smith, less because the sentiments uttered by Celestina are also those associated with the autobiographical Smith-poet.

As the sequence opens, Smith hints at the constructed nature of the poems by using "supposed" in the title: "Supposed to have been written in a church-yard, over the grave of a young woman of nineteen" (Sonnet XLIX).[35] Robinson notes that this is one of the few sonnets to mourn a specific death (p. 190), but he does not elaborate on the double feint the poem offers: the specific death is here only "supposed," and the mourning figure is both "From the novel of Celestina" and the general *Sonnets* speaker.[36] Despite eventually banishing the poems' novelistic origin to the notes, then, Smith does not eliminate the information altogether; the poems' speaker, therefore, becomes indeterminate: is she Smith, Celestina, or some combination of the two? Sonnet XLIX, featuring the speaker lamenting "over the grave of a young woman," reverses expectations by congratulating the dead "virgin" on her escape from "human ills" and her achievement of the constancy of the love of her "youth": "still for him shall faithful Memory save/ Thy form and virtues from the silent grave" (ll. 9, 5, 11, 13–14). Whereas in the novel Celestina composes this poem to mark her "despondency over having lost, as she thinks, the love of George Willoughby" (Curran, *Poems*, p. 45, n. to Sonnet 49), in the *Sonnets* this poem resonates most clearly with Sonnet XXIV, "By the same [Werter]," in which Werter imagines the effect his death will have on Lotte/Charlotte: "Yes – CHARLOTTE o'er the mournful spot shall weep,/ Where her poor WERTER – and his sorrows sleep!" (ll. 13–14). The speaker of Sonnet XLIX substitutes an existing corpse for her own projected one, but the scenario is the same: the bereft lover lingers over the grave of the deceased, remembering. The auditor in this poem, the dead woman, is enlivened by aware readers, who knows *Sonnets*-style despair when they see it. The familiarity of the scene begins to undercut its pathos – this is, after all, Sonnet XLIX, but little has changed in the 26 sonnets since Sonnet XXIV. The stagnation of sentiment is slightly relieved by a more adventurous poetic structure than that managed by the passive speaker discussed above – *abab baab bcbc dd* – which goes beyond simple repetition to suggest an inwardness and self-obsession expressed through rhyme. The structure is also provocative, simultaneously arranged in three quatrains and a couplet by rhyme, and in two quatrains and a sestet by punctuation, as if the speaker-poet is using poetry to explore competing articulations of selfhood.

In fact, all the Celestina sonnets exhibit structural innovations except Sonnet LIII: "The Laplander." Sonnet L, with its sorrowful "Farewel, ye lawns! – by fond remembrance blest,/ As witnesses of gay unclouded hours" (ll. L. 1–2), reflects the nostalgia of many of Smith's more clearly autobiographical sonnets to the river Arun and the South Downs, where she contrasts the happy "dear days" "when thoughtless joy, and infant hope were mine" with the "sense of pain" and "breaking heart" she now feels (Sonnet XXXI, l.13; Sonnet XLV, l. 3; Sonnet V, ll. 7, 8). Sonnet L's speaker, too, sets her past happiness in a specific landscape (glossed as "Alvestone, Willoughby's country seat" by Curran [*Poems,* p. 46, note]) and uses her departure to signal her emotional loss. Her rhyme scheme, *abab bcbc dede ff,* falls back on the repetition of the passive speaker, but her structure utilizes the combination practiced in the previous sonnet. Sonnet LI: "Supposed to have been written in the Hebrides," recalls Smith's sonnets of longing addressed to or about her dead daughter Augusta: "I could with *thee* for months and years be blest;/ And of thy tenderness and love possest,/ Find all *my* world in this wild solitude" (ll. 6–8).[37] Its rhyme scheme reflects the speaker's increasing torment – *abba caac dede ff* – and its structure innovates on that of the previous two sonnets by substituting an octave/sestet for the quatrain/quatrain/sestet arrangement.

The speaker thus continues to perform her anguish poetically, while Smith continues to exploit what Slinn calls poetry's "referential aberration" and its ability to "foreground constitutive language through intensive poetic devices" (pp. 66, 69). Smith's deployment of rhyme and structure in the Celestina sonnets provides the key whereby we can interpret the drama the speaker performs. The speaker, having begun by declaiming over a grave and moved through scenes of farewell and longing, in Sonnet LII initiates a subjective split, imagining an "unhappy Pilgrim.../ .../ Divided far from all he fondly loves,/ [Who] Journeys alone, along the giddy height/ Of these steep cliffs" (ll. 1, 3–5). The Pilgrim's situation anticipates that of the speakers of two later sonnets, an exception to the backward-looking of the other sonnets but one which demonstrates Smith's interest in creating contrasting speakers who perform similar emotional states. Sonnet LII presents a figure imagined by the speaker who wanders alone through a December night and whose situation prompts the speaker to call herself "unblest" (l. 11), revisited in Sonnet LXII: "Written in passing by moonlight through a village, while the ground was covered with snow," whose speaker is also "unblest" (l. 1).[38] The figure, on the "giddy height," "hears, with ear appall'd, the impetuous surge/ Beneath him thunder!" (ll. 4, 8–9), even as the lunatic of the much-studied Sonnet LXX: "On being cautioned against walking on an headland overlooking the sea, because it was frequented by a lunatic" "views with wild and hollow eyes/ Its distance from the waves that chide below" while the speaker positions herself "on the giddy brink" (ll. 3–4, 9).[39] Although the rhyme scheme of Sonnet LII is fairly regular, it veers off toward the end (*abab cdcd efefef*). More importantly, in this poem the speaker-poet loses control over structure. The sonnet is excessively punctuated, divided by clauses into a nine-line segment, a four-line segment, and a two-line segment (line 9 ends and begins a segment). Further, lines 1, 8, 11, and 14 contain twelve, twelve, eleven, and twelve syllables respectively. This moves beyond poetic innovation to poetic breakdown. Order is only restored, in Sonnet LIII: "The Laplander," through a complete loss of the speaker's subjectivity. Describing the Laplander, the poem recalls both Sonnet XLIII ("The unhappy exile") and Sonnet LIV: "The sleeping woodman. Written in April 1790,"[40] but unlike them it subsumes the speaker entirely to the figure: the "I" does not appear. Written *abab cdcd efef gg* in an octave/quatrain/couplet structure, the poem is mechanical, "perfect" like those of the passive speaker, but here Smith seems to be allowing the speaker to perform absence rather than presence. The speaker-poet thus dramatizes the ultimate despair, a complete loss of self, in a kind of poetic suicide. Smith does not forgo the "I" very often, and to do so here indicates her compositional distance from the poem's voice, and its limitations.

The *Lyrical Ballads*: Curious William

The enduring association between Wordsworth and his poetic voice is based on the idea that he is a poet who speaks truth, by which I mean both an emotional veracity and a historical one.[41] Once the "I" is introduced, it is an autobiographical "I," and although certain aspects of his personal past may be exaggerated, revisited, or otherwise retold, readers have often felt that to read, say, "Tintern Abbey" or "Nutting" or the shorter lyrics of the *Lyrical Ballads* was to gain insight into the true nature of the poet. In the 1790s, however, Wordsworth is himself still working out the parameters of the selfhood he writes into his poetry. As the Advertisement intimates, the (amalgamated) author of the *Lyrical Ballads* views the collection as a series of experiments, not as a coherent outpouring of personal reflections. Smith uses her paratexts to write a sorrowing, beleaguered Poet into the public perception – a figure who for many years proved marketable, until she didn't – and uses the poems themselves to cast doubt on the integrity of this characterization. Her voicing of sorrow and her embodiment of its limitations through form provides a further example of the experimental thrust of *Elegiac Sonnets*. Wordsworth, however, unknown and obscure until the first decade of the nineteenth century, does not in the 1790s have the visible public person that Smith does, and, further, in his Advertisement does not publicize a defined Self whom readers could associate with the writing poet. Although by 1800 this becomes a part of the project, when the *Lyrical Ballads* are reissued as by "W. Wordsworth," the 1798 poems occupy an as yet murky space, where the speaker projects a personalized selfhood, and yet the reader does not know who that is.[42] Even as Smith maintains a consistent tone in sonnets written and published over a number of years, so too the Wordsworth who publishes in 1798 and 1800 utilizes an autobiographical tone and suggestively autobiographical content attractive to readers who duly sign up to this reading once the biographical self "W. Wordsworth" is revealed. As this section discusses, this is itself a kind of feint. If we approach these poems as dramatized monologues, then a new layer emerges, one of implicit critique and discomfort. We see this in the way that the speaker of "We are Seven" (1798), "Anecdote for Fathers" (1798), and "Song" (1800)[43] revels in his curiosity about things, and in the way the speakers of "Tintern Abbey" (1798), "Lines left upon a seat in a Yew-Tree" (1798), and "Nutting" (1800) are, quite simply, curious, which is to say odd, peculiar, and strange. The poems, studies in forms of alienation, push and pull their readers, their speakers undermined by the narratives they tell.[44]

Curiosity, for the speakers of "Anecdote for Fathers," "We are Seven," and "Song," is inextricably linked to violence and loss. In each, the speaker's need to know what he sees as "truth" results in damage: to the interlocutor, to the poem's subject, to the speaker himself. The inner life or psychological state of being that the poems explore is only that of the poet Wordsworth (as he comes to be known) if we accept that Wordsworth displays obsessive, possessive, and deranged behavior. Instead, the poems allow Wordsworth to create speakers whose limitations reveal themselves both narratively and poetically. By this I mean that Wordsworth, like Smith before him, makes use of poetic technique to signal his speakers' unsatisfactory personalities. Wordsworth grants his speakers a personalized tone that works meta-autobiographically; the reality that he creates is based on but separated from his autobiographical reality through the poetic process. Kearns has noted that "the production of the autobiographical text makes the author subject to the reading of others" (p. 25); when Wordsworth writes the meta-autobiographical, he becomes both poet and reader by building into the poems a frustration with the speakers and their motivations. The "independent fictional world" (Sinfield, p. 55) of the speakers depends on their psychological coherence, so that Wordsworth can construct a figure of the Poet who is not, in the end, poetic enough to overcome his own propensities.

In "Anecdote for Fathers," the speaker creates expectations of a moral with the subtitle "shewing how the art of lying may be taught." The speaker's disengaged and amoral stance, however, is discernible in his use of "art"; for him, "lying" maintains an aesthetic appeal.[45] Wordsworth's later insistences on the poem's purpose indicate his creative discomfort with the poetic picture he draws, for as much as he emphasizes in letters "the injurious [mental] effects of putting inconsiderate questions to Children,"[46] the poem dwells more on the potential physical injuries with which the speaker threatens the child. The speaker's fragile mental state is hinted at in stanza 4: "A day it was when I could bear/ To think, and think, and think again;/ With so much happiness to spare,/ I could not feel a pain" (ll. 13–16). The repetition and ellipses in the stanza suggest the speaker's inability to poeticize adequately his emotional loss; indeed, "I could not feel a pain" is problematic precisely because of the emotional stasis it implies. Wordsworth thus uses poetic simplicity – or, more properly, a lack of poetic complexity – to suggest the speaker's own inabilities to access depth.

When the speaker consequently turns to the "slim and graceful" boy "by [his] side," his disjunctions, both emotional and poetic, become more plain in the unsignaled shift from lambs and sun to a comparison between Kilve and Liswyn (ll. 17, 18). At this point, as the reader begins to suspect a certain instability in the speaker, the speaker obligingly indulges both his curiosity and his propensity to violence: "'My little boy, which like you more,'/ I said and took him by the arm –/ 'Our home by Kilve's delightful shore,/ Or here at Liswyn farm?'" (ll. 25–8). We note the speaker's loaded question; as the protagonist in a dramatized monologue the speaker's obvious rhetorical positioning exposes his obsession with the past and with enforcing the present through his curious probing of Edward. The menace of "took him by the arm"/ "held him by the arm"/ "still I held him by the arm" (ll. 26, 30, 34) acts as the physical manifestation of the obsessive speaker's haranguing: "tell me," "say why so," "tell me why," "And five times did I say to him,/ 'Why? Edward, tell me why?'" (ll. 29, 37, 38, 47–8). There is nothing gentle about what is, actually, an interrogation, a pathological curiosity that forces a confidence and then, relieved (spent?), can afford to pity the victim (the repeated "dearest" of l. 57). The poem's tone overturns, by the end, the "happiness" the speaker has invoked in stanza 3; instead, the speaker's compulsive curiosity darkens the poem and infuses it with violence and hostility. Simplicity, in this poem, masks a dedication to uncovering "truth" by any means necessary.

Similarly, in "We are Seven," the speaker appears more benevolent, but nonetheless devoted to an ideal of "truth" that belies his mildness. The "simple child" of this poem shares with Edward a "rustic, woodland air" (ll. 1, 9); the speaker's imagery links the children with nature, but also with simplicity and naïveté. His diction represents a desire to control his interlocutor through language, a desire frustrated in both poems. As in "Anecdote," the speaker carries a weight of implied loss and emotional stagnation; his opening emphasis on death, and his statement that "Her beauty made me glad," indicate an unsatisfied need that lurks somewhere in the dash preceding "Her beauty": an ellipsis gesturing toward something left unspoken. As the speaker questions the girl, he becomes increasingly desperate for a "truth" that matches his understanding; curiosity here indicates the speaker's powerlessness rather than his (desire for) omniscience. As the poem progresses, the girl's obliviousness to the speaker's increasing bafflement transforms his questioning into badgering, a verbal violence that is ultimately as unproductive as the physical violence in "Anecdote." The speaker's curiosity about the girl's siblings masks his need to dominate and control her answers. When she does not provide the answer that matches his understanding of truth, he displays the same obsessive need to find it as we saw in "Anecdote," only here he becomes his own victim. "'But they are dead; those two are dead!/ Their spirits are in heaven!'" (ll. 65–6), he exclaims wildly, losing control both verbally and poetically.

The speaker in "We are Seven" differs from that in "Anecdote" in his disorientation. Logical questioning has not resulted in logical answers, and "truth" has been revealed to be subjective. The death that infuses the poem is more about the speaker's metaphorical death – he, as Smith's speakers do under similar duress, disappears from his own poem, allowing the "little maid" the last word – than the physical death of her brother and sister. And again, the poetic personality exposed in the poem obsesses over truth, using curiosity to bolster a lack of emotional depth. As with "Anecdote," Wordsworth much later contextualized the poem, characterizing it as "illustrat[ing] the perplexity and obscurity which in childhood attend our notion of death" (Brett and Jones, p. 286). However, it is plain that in the poem only the speaker is perplexed and obscured. As a dramatized monologue, the poem serves to further Wordsworth's exploration of an unsatisfactory poet-figure, one who is consumed by curiosity and only too prone to violence. He consistently does not reward this speaker with satisfactory outcomes to his persistent questioning, but rather allows him to undermine his own notions of truth and understanding, and he shadows the poems with a darkness borne of loss, violence, and death.

"Song" punctuates this by linking the speaker's curiosity with the devastating loss of both the poem's object and the speaker's equilibrium. Returning to Slinn's formulation of the performativity of the poetic, "Song" uses brevity and ellipses to enable the full destructive effect of curiosity: its "combination of lyric expressiveness and dramatic mimicry" (Slinn, p. 69) means that we follow the speaker's gradual revelations as if we experience the poem with the speaker. Here, curiosity is implicit: the repeated questions and disruptive violence of "Anecdote" and "We are Seven" are exchanged for a muted, internalized form of loss. The speaker's curiosity manifests itself in the metaphors he enlists and then declaims, a poetic device *par excellence* that recalls Pascoe's description of Wordsworth as a kind of strolling minstrel (p. 196 *passim*). Here, he composes a speaker who in turns composes Lucy through a series of images notable for their elusiveness: "untrodden ways," "half-hidden," the single "shining [star] in the sky," "she *liv'd* unknown" (ll. 1, 6, 8, 9), building an overall image – Lucy – herself to become notorious for her mystery. The speaker knows (of) Lucy because he has ferreted her out, much as he ferreted out answers from Edward and the maid (or at least tried mightily to). But as he has discerned her, as he has satisfied his curiosity by unearthing the curiosity that is Lucy, he also decomposes her, and the end of the poem switches the focus from Lucy to the speaker: "But she is in her Grave, and oh!/ The difference to me" (ll. 11–12). The reader realizes that the poem's first line – "She dwelt among th'untrodden ways" – is not so much a standard narrative opening as a statement of loss in itself, the past tense of "dwelt" literalized. The speaker's self-congratulation in having prised Lucy from her hidden spaces, and in having found just the right form of words to embody her, turns in the last line to a despair communicated as elliptically as "A day it was when I could bear/ To think, and think, and think again" ("Anecdote") or "Her eyes were fair, and very fair,/ – Her beauty made me glad" ("We are Seven").

Although the speaker of "Song" is perhaps less culpable than that of "Anecdote" or "We are Seven," he is nonetheless the most destructive. His desire to see, know, and uncover Lucy, to try to determine her essence – her truth – through metaphor, enacts her loss repeatedly, as each metaphor itself is about something on the edge of vanishing. Therefore, while the speaker of "Song" is perhaps a better poet than that of the other two poems, he is more of a threat than either of them. Left hanging by Wordsworth, his expressiveness is, in the end, *in*expressive; his monologue undoes Lucy, himself, and language. In part this is "the process by which both [Wordsworth] and his audience are forced to recognize the limits of their comprehension" (Ferguson, p. xiv); that is, this and the other Lucy poems are about the unsayable. But it is also a dramatizing of the poetically incomprehensible, an engagement with mystery for the benefit of an auditor/reader who, in this poem, is kept mystified by the poetry itself. Our curiosity is whetted and endlessly stymied. In "Song," Wordsworth writes a speaker whose language is evocative but patently meaningless, by which I mean not that it has no meaning but that its meaning is hampered and disabled by a speaker whose curiosity has got the better of him. "Oh! The difference to me": unable to express his meaning, the speaker takes refuge in obscurity.

Wordsworth flips the trope of curiosity in his highly personalized poems "Yew-Tree," "Nutting," and "Tintern Abbey." Here, the meta-autobiographical illustrates the pitfalls of a concentration on Self and its development. Clearly, Wordsworth was exercised by the idea of poetic evolution, but as "Yew-Tree" shows, he was also cautious about the pitfalls associated with such a concentration on Self. As Smith does in "Beachy Head," in these poems Wordsworth develops a persona whose self-interest overrides the poetry to the point of estrangement, from sense, clarity, and, especially, the reader, who is both appealed to and sealed off from the poetry. Curiosity thus morphs from a stance taken *by* the speaker to an inherent aspect *of* the speaker: the "stranger" addressed by the speaker is thus less alien to the poem than the putatively autobiographical speaker. As Wordsworth noted when speaking of Robert Burns, the poet may "avail himself of his own character and situation in society, to construct out of them a poetic self – introduced as a dramatic personage – for the purpose of inspiriting his incidents, diversifying his pictures ... and giving point to his sentiments."[47] To read these poems, then, as "meditation[s] upon the live tissue of the poet's own, genuine experience" is to miss that composing moments wherein a poet "gives birth to his sublime ego, his self as a poet" is as much a pose, a feint, in Sinfield's terms, as it is a "fact."[48] Wordsworth gives a semblance of familiarity to the voice so that even in 1798 readers can see the poems as originating in the autobiographical, but he does so to explore what it means to be self-conscious to the point of oddity, where landscape, friends, poetry itself become merely outshoots of the poetic imagination.

Wordsworth tries out his persona of the self-obsessed speaker in "Lines left upon a Seat in a Yew-Tree." Here, he distances his speaker from the poem's subject, but as many critics have pointed out, the poem pushes the idea of a resemblance between subject and speaker: "the speaker becomes that subject of whom he speaks ... The speaker and his subject are one divided self."[49] This is the secret as recognized by the reader and as exposed inadvertently by the speaker. Reinstating the autobiographical, such approaches find meaning by projecting Wordsworth into his portrait of collapsed subjectivity. However, Wordsworth uses a displacement of subjectivity to achieve a combination of the subjective and the objective in this poem. The slippage that encourages the identification of speaker with subject allows him to dramatize estrangement; the repeated appeals to a "Stranger" further this, since the Stranger is both an auditor (the reader's stand-in) and an aspect of the speaker himself, an internalized audience of one witnessing the speaker's attempt to overcome his own attraction to isolation. Galperin sees this as part of Wordsworth's mythic self-creation: "the creation of a 'Poet' by creation of an Other in whose image the poetical self ... is simultaneously fashioned" (p. 67). The poetical self in "Yew-Tree" is less than ideal, though certainly mythic. In true dramatic monologue fashion, the poem begins in mid-speech: "– Nay, Traveller! rest" (l. 1).[50] Compelled to stop, the auditor's curiosity is assumed by the speaker, whose tale of "one who owned/ No common soul" (ll. 12–13) so anticipates Smith's picture of the clearly Wordsworthian figure in "Beachy Head."[51] Smith's response to Wordsworth's myth-making points to the self-reflexive nature of the poem, but it also demonstrates its dramatic tone. As he unfolds the story of the solipsist whose "unfruitful life" (l. 29) is spent in resentment of an unappreciative world, he also composes a natural setting redolent of what comes to be accepted as a Wordsworthian ethos: "he then would gaze/ On the more distant scene; how lovely 'tis/ Thou seest, and he would gaze till it became/ Far lovelier, and his heart could not sustain/ The beauty still more beauteous" (ll. 30–34). Images like these recur, more forcefully, in both "Tintern Abbey" and "Nutting," and it is in the confluence of the poems that its self-referentiality emerges.[52] This speaker rehearses obsessions that Wordsworth then assigns to a personalized speaker in the other two poems: the recluse has special gifts "by genius nursed" (l. 13); he intends to benefit the world with their dissemination, but meeting "jealousy and hate" (l. 16) he turns inward, retreats to nature, and ends his days looking only and "ever on himself" (l. 52).

On its own this poem is simply narrative, a moral tale cautioning against solipsism. Read in the context of the other two, however, its status as a tonic against the self-obsessions of "Tintern Abbey" and "Nutting" become apparent. When the speaker in "Tintern Abbey" recalls "evil tongues,/ Rash judgments ... the sneers of selfish men,/ ... greetings where no kindness is, [and] all/ The dreary intercourse of daily life" (ll. 129–32), we are back in the world of "Yew-Tree": "the taint/ Of dissolute tongues ... jealousy, and hate,/ And scorn .../ [And] neglect" (ll. 15–18). Although more expansive and detailed, the nature that attracted and nurtured the speaker of "Tintern" is the same as that which nourishes and compensates the speaker of "Yew-Tree." Indeed, the poetic sensibility that the speaker unfolds in "Yew-Tree" *is* "Wordsworthian," barring the "rash disdain" (l. 19) that the more securely personalized speaker carefully avoids indulging in. "Yew-Tree" acts as a kind of "note to Self," where the Self addressed is the dramatized Poet whose obsessions with recognition and appreciation overcome his more attractive traits of skilled natural observation and sharp poetic style. As with Smith, this is partly revealed at the level of structure; when the speaker writes "what if here/ No sparkling rivulet spread the verdant herb" ("Yew-Tree," ll. 2–3) we are reminded of all the waters that "murmur" elsewhere in Wordsworth's poetry, and when the speaker ponders "What if these barren boughs the bee not loves" (l. 4) we balk at the awkward phrasing of the line. By displacing his potential for total isolation onto the recluse in "Yew-Tree," but simultaneously revealing his sympathy for and identification with his döppelganger, the speaker inadvertently dramatizes his alliance with, rather than difference from, the recluse. The reproach of the poem's last stanza as self-directed is clarified if we turn briefly to "Lines written in early spring," where the speaker's refrain "Have I not reason to lament/ What man has made of man?" (ll. 23–4) and the poem's overall tone of despairing contempt suggest that the speaker of this "Lines" and the recluse of "Yew-Tree" are the same – and hence the speaker of "Yew-Tree" is also one with them.

The self-estrangement of "Yew-Tree," and its picture of the Poet as a curiosity to be observed, reverberates in "Tintern Abbey." Here, the coherence and conviction of the Poet's self-representation mask what is, in effect, an enactment of the estrangement infecting "Yew-Tree." Despite the many and varied ways in which the poem has been associated with Wordsworth's own personal and poetic development, it nonetheless figures as one of the most perfectly formed of Wordsworth's dramatized monologues, especially if one reads something like "Yew-Tree" as an entr'acte. Forbes' need to discount "Tintern" as a dramatic monologue and reinstate the sincere in order to avoid reducing the poem to the "laughable" (p. 85) ironically enough points to the deep significance of the poem's dramatizing of poetic sensibility. Similarly, Richard J. Onorato's insistence that, "despite the seemingly dramatic utterance of ["Tintern Abbey"], the poet [plainly] does not pretend to know more than his 'character' says" illustrates the strength of the character inhabiting the poem.[53] Whereas the speaker in a Victorian dramatic monologue is, mainly, separate from and unlike the author (*In Memoriam* would serve as a notable exception), Wordsworth's version constructs a speaker who is, vitally, both Self and Other: an Other dependent on aspects of the Self who writes the poem, but who is estranged from the sincere and authentic. In "Tintern," the Romantic dramatized monologue is uttered by a speaker who functions as a dramatized Self; who is, therefore, not Wordsworth but the Poet, pulled back from the despair of "Yew-Tree" by the presence of a distinct auditor, the Sister.

Wordsworth's contention that he composed the poem extempore during a walking tour and that "not a line of it was altered, and not any part written down til I reached Bristol" (Gill, p. 692) is frequently quoted as evidence of the poem's authenticity; as Gill says, despite some qualifications this account is "clearly essentially correct" (p. 692).[54] As with the other Fenwick notes quoted above, the belated nature of Wordsworth's assertion invites query, but just as important, Wordsworth's statement of the poem's composition history is no more than that. Setting the desire to read the poem autobiographically aside, its use of autobiography to underpin the drama infuses the poem with performative import. As the poem opens, the scene is set in the first 23 lines: the famous "steep and lofty cliffs," the spreading prospect, the deliberately pastoral vista. As the second verse-paragraph begins, the speaker shifts to the drama of the Self: his visceral connection to scenes of natural beauty, his reliance on "feelings .../ Of unremembered pleasure" and "that serene and blessed mood" in which he "become[s] a living soul" (ll. 31–2, 42, 47). By the third verse-paragraph, the speaker begins to declaim, voicing a soliloquy derived from "the picture of the mind" (l. 62); a theatrical phrase by which Wordsworth indicates the speaker's pose. The conversational tone of "I cannot paint/ What then I was" (ll. 76–7) and the self-delusion that allows the speaker to convince himself that "other gifts/ Have followed" the loss of "aching joys" and "dizzy raptures" (ll. 87–8, 85, 86) further contribute to the poem's presentation of a dramatized speaker. The poet who here constructs a world in which the present is always better than the past, and for whom obscurity – both in phrasing and in his own self-conception – is always preferable to plain speaking, is as peculiar as the recluse in "Yew-Tree."[55] Further, his auditor is completely subsumed to the picture the speaker paints of himself as idealized poet. This speaker-poet cannot see beyond his own conception of the world of psychological growth, and therefore his auditor becomes merely a representation of his former self. Self-obsession means that the poet sees only himself, and by locating, in the final verse-paragraph, his disturbed past and possible unpleasant future in his sister, he is able to recast what had been "hours of weariness" (l. 28) as "[un]disturb[ed] ... chearful faith" (ll. 133–4).

The "impression of spontaneity" (Perkins, p. 210) that the poem creates, and that Wordsworth encourages in the Fenwick note, is not borne out by the "abstract, polysyllabic, orotund, and, in short, successfully dignified and emphatic" diction Perkins also sees (p. 206). Dignified and emphatic as it is, the diction of the poem, its deliberately obscure and mysterious phrases, its uncertain tone, and its unaware theatricalisms are the product of a speaker whose need to be poetic by being a Poet overwhelms his ability to "speak to men" using their language. Instead, we get a picture of the Romantic Poet as self-obsessed Curiosity, the subject of the strolling minstrel described by Pascoe (p. 196 *passim*). Where the speaker of "Yew-Tree" enacts despair, that of "Tintern" exults, having been supplied with an auditor whose vulnerability supplies what "Yew-Tree" lacks: a sympathetic audience. And where "Tintern Abbey" provides the drama of the self-obsessed Poet, "Nutting" supplies his backstory. By installing both a present and a past

"Self" in the poem, Wordsworth emphasizes the speaker's concentration on his own needs and desires. "Nutting" uses memory to suggest that the self-obsessed speaker feels curiosity only about his own poetic development; the philosophy of the last few lines shows not insight, but blindness. The theatricality of the poem almost disguises its import as a dramatic monologue; Wordsworth grants the speaker a kind of self-awareness but disables it almost immediately in the pride and complacency with which the speaker reviews his past: "a Figure quaint," "my frugal Dame," "more ragged than need was," "I forc'd my way" (ll. 6, 9, 12, 13). The sensual scene that excites the man lost in memory, his "voluptuous" enjoyment of its luxuries, and the inevitable violence of his destruction of the bower contribute to the making of a Poet for whom everything, especially pliant Nature, exists to forward his own poetic project. Wordsworth embeds in the poem allusions to his other key dramatized monologues: the "temper known to those, who, after long/ And weary expectation, have been bless'd/ With sudden happiness beyond all hope" (25–7) which reverses the gloom of the recluse in "Yew-Tree"; "the violets of five seasons" and "fairy water-breaks [that] do murmur" (ll. 29, 31) which recall the opening lines of "Tintern Abbey" (and, incidentally, key lines of "Song"); the conflation of "my present feelings with the past," the "sense of pain," and the "Spirit in the woods," which also invoke "Tintern" (ll. 47, 50, 54).

The poems are linked via allusion, the speaker revealed to be the same, and the concerns identical: how does the Poet justify his ways to men? Ferguson describes "the perceptions and the language which repeatedly construct narrative roles for Wordsworth," and calls "Nutting" a "drama, a rewritten romance" with a "script" that Wordsworth "self-consciously follow[s] ... until experience no longer matches" (p. 75). But this seems to be exactly what needs to happen: the speaker must follow a script until thrown off-guard, and then must expose his inability to submit to his experience, and instead must attempt to conquer it. To suggest that *Wordsworth* both writes the poem and is unable to master its deviations from a "script" is to say that he is at the mercy of his poetry, that *it* writes *him*. Rather, the speaker of this dramatized monologue fails to appreciate the ramifications of his concentration on Self, and so his closing turn to the hitherto invisible auditor resonates with self-absorption and shallow mystification: "Then, dearest Maiden! move along these shades/ In gentleness of heart; with gentle hand/ Touch, – for there is a Spirit in the woods." (ll. 52–4). Curiosity satisfied, the speaker unsurprisingly puts a halt to the Maiden's progress and abruptly concludes the poem. As with "Yew-Tree" and "Tintern,"

Wordsworth writes "Nutting" obscurely, using a diction reliant on metaphor and repetition; while such a style is effective individually – that is, critics can make much of "a sense sublime/ Of something far more deeply interfused" ("Tintern," l. 96–7) or "a sense of pain" ("Nutting," l. 51) or "his heart could not sustain/ The beauty still more beauteous" ("Yew-Tree," ll. 34–5) – when read as a group the images begin to lose their potency. They begin to sound like the images a poet would use who is trying to display his poetic talents, who is asserting, through diction, his artistic depth. They transform the individually autobiographical to the meta-autobiographical, and they suggest that for Wordsworth, as for Smith, poetry is performative because it is poetry that allows for the construction, and consequent undermining, of inadequate types of poetic subjectivity.

"Beachy Head": The Poet Makes History

In the 1790s, Smith suggests the inadequacy of passive sorrow by writing speakers as limited poets. In the first years of the next decade she begins a new form of experiment that has to do with manipulating voice within individual poems, populating them, unexpectedly, with diverse figures not always in agreement with each other. What she calls, in letters, her "local poem" explores a variety of personalized viewpoints and landscapes, and utilizes what John Anderson has called a "mosaic" of stances.[56] Where the sonnets provide snapshots of grieving, and aggrieved, speakers, "Beachy Head" explores a palette characterized by mutability and held together by an overriding interest in (re)writing narratives. Specifically, "Beachy Head" is concerned in a number of ways with narratives of history: the personal history that has fueled two decades of poetry; the scientific history that has created the geography, botany, and anthropology of Beachy Head; the literary history that informs the creative structure of the poem; and the political and social history that anchors the identity of the speaker(s). The poem contains a number of voices whose characteristics flavor its different sections; it is less *a* dramatized monologue than a collection of them, with the occasional descriptive monologue thrown in for variety.[57] Like Wordsworth, Smith "repeatedly emphasizes the truthfulness of [her] poems' images by reference to the places and people they describe" (Pascoe, p. 226), creating a matrix of facts to support the speakers' shifts of person. But as he does in the *Lyrical Ballads*, Smith bypasses sincerity in "Beachy Head," writing instead a dramatic reconstruction that involves memory and history but reveals the specifically constructed nature of each when utilized in poetry. As Ferguson says of Wordsworth, but which is just as applicable to Smith, "out of the discontinuities of both language and life, [the poet] wrests a poetry of memory which enacts and re-enacts the impossibility of constructing one individual self which would be 'there' for language to imitate" (p. xvi). Smith uses the intricacies of language, memory, and history to devise a series of speaking selves, which suggests that if a poet can speak convincingly in different and competing voices, then the plausibility of coherent poetic subjectivity is problematized. "Beachy Head," as Smith's final work, may or may not be complete; like so many Romantic fragments, its coherence and vision call into question its denomination as unfinished. But even if it was "not completed according to the original design" (*Poetry*, p. 153), it nonetheless offers a consistent unraveling of the rapidly establishing Romantically subjective speaker. It dramatizes, in other words, both wholeness and disunity, and it does this most forcefully through its delvings into varieties of history.[58]

According to Theresa Kelley, in *The Prelude* Wordsworth's speaker "hides" his sources so that he may appear "original" in his genius, "yet this sleight-of-hand is only a disguise, and a half-hearted one at that, for an inventional strategy that multiplies its effects as [it] proceeds."[59] Kelley is describing Book 5, famously informed by Cervantes, the story of Scheherazade, and the Bible. In "Beachy Head," Smith pursues a strategy that dispenses altogether with the hidden, using her footnotes to clarify and expand on the (hi)stories she poeticizes. As I have discussed elsewhere, Smith is adept at suiting her voice to her genre, and hence the tone of the notes is factual and narrative-based, whereas the tone of the poem is colorful and image-based. In terms of the dramatized monologue, however, this goes beyond tone: we see that the speaker of the notes is aware of the poem, and reacts to its content, although the speaker of the poem seems oblivious to this competition, at least at first. The note speaker, a well-read historian, provides a running commentary on the scenes devised by the self-consciously poetic Poet who speaks the poem.[60] As Wordsworth will do in *The Prelude*, Smith writes a speaker in "Beachy Head" whose concern is to establish her (for want of a neutral pronoun) credentials as Poet. As I discuss in the final section of this chapter, Wordsworth will use elements of composition to critique this figure; Smith uses, as she did to such effect in *Elegiac Sonnets*, structure: thus one part of the poem subtly evaluates another via differing understandings of the place and value of history.

This is most strikingly apparent when the poem's speaker, using the trope of the prospect view claimed in the first 117 lines of the poem, turns from sketching the progress of a day to a more ambitious topic: "bid[ding] recording Memory unfold/ Her scroll voluminous" (p. 158, ll. 119–20). The speaker-poet here reveals her slippery diction: Memory refers not to personal memory, the history of the poet, but to a kind of public memory, History itself, beginning with the Norman invasion of Saxon England. Or, as the Poet has it, "when from Neustria's hostile shore/ The Norman launch'd his galleys, and the bay/ O'er which that mass of ruin frowns even now/ In vain and sullen menace, then received the new invaders" (pp. 158–9, ll. 121–5). The Poet, grandiose and obscure, here institutes a policy of deliberate erudition: not Normandy but Neustria, and within the next few lines, not Sicily but Trinacria, not Naples but Parthenope (p. 159, ll. 128, 130). The Poet devotes herself to a specifically poetic diction; the Historian of the notes quickly shows her impatience with such ornate elegance. Interjecting "Pevensey Castle" when the Poet mentions "that mass of ruin," yet doing so only within her own note (*Poetry*, p. 158), she then anticipates the Poet's following vignette of only 5½ lines with a massive flow of information. Well before the speaker even mentions "Scandinavia," the Historian interrupts with four paragraphs of material that quickly move on from Scandinavian invaders to those from "the coasts of Provence and Sicily" who in 844 "penetrated even to Paris: and the unfortunate Charles the Bald, king of France, purchased at a high price, the retreat of the banditti he had no other means of repelling" (*Poetry*, p. 158). There follows a very full paragraph that moves from "Rollo, otherwise Raoul" and his enlightened rule of "Neustria, since called Normandy" and Brittany; to the Crusades and the Norman rescue of Salerno from the "bas[e] and coward[ly]" "Mahometans" in 983; to the movement of "other bodies of Normans ... into Sicily (anciently called Trinacria)"; to the conquest of "the fertile island of Sicily" by "three brothers of Coutance, the sons of Tancred de Hauteville, Guillaume Fier-a-bras, Drogon, and Humfroi" and the subsequent possession by the Normans of "Naples (Parthenope)" (pp. 158–9). The Historian cannot resist the attractions of plain history; despite announcing that "How William, the natural son of Robert, duke of Normandy, possessed himself of England, is too well known to be repeated here," she tells the tale anyway, and finishes in the present day: "In a marsh not far from Hastings, the skeletons of an armed man and horse were found a few years since, which are believed to have belonged to the Normans ..." (p. 159). The Historian then pauses for breath, having comprehensively countered the Poet's worrying tendency to skip the details in favor of the abstract vista encouraged by the prospect view.

The Historian's own "scroll voluminous" (l. 120) ensures that the Poet's offhand mention of "Dogon, Fier-a-bras, and Humfroi" – "Trinacria to their power/ Yielded her wheaten garland; and ... thou,/ Parthenope! within thy fertile bay/ Receiv'd the victors" (ll. 127, 128–31) – is corrected and elaborated on before it even happens. The Poet's casual and inaccurate naming ("Dogon" for "Drogon"), for instance, is shown up by the conscientious Historian, who also makes sure we all know to what Trinacria and the other place names refer in modern usage.[61] The Historian even corrects herself, deciding that, after all, the story of William the Conqueror was not "too well known to be repeated here." At this point, it is the Historian who is the most intelligible, recognizing the obscurities the Poet will fall into even before the Poet has done so (the Historian begins at the first mention of "the period" of the Norman conquest). Smith seems to grant the Historian an awareness that the Poet lacks; after the long note has gone over history so thoroughly, it seems superfluous to do so again, but in lines 131–42 the Poet moves on to Taillefer's song of Roland as if the Historian has never spoken. This means the oft-repeated story of William is repeated yet again. True to her genre, the Poet does not stop to identify details, but sweeps through history rapidly, leaving the Historian once again to identify the "holy pile" of line 138 as "Battle Abbey ... raised by the Conqueror, and endowed with an ample revenue, that masses might be said night and day for the souls of those who perished in battle" (p. 159). As competing speakers, the Historian seems to have the edge over the Poet, relying on facts rather than fanciful imagery.

However, it appears that the long note does more than simply allow the Historian to provide a full history. It also hints at the personal autonomy of the Historian as a speaker separate from, and not fully in sympathy with, the Poet. The Poet names William obliquely as "the conqueror" and moves directly from her description of the Battle of Hastings to a warning to "modern Gallia" that "the imperial mistress of the obedient sea" will never again fall to a conqueror (p. 159, ll. 143, 151). The Historian, on the other hand, calls William "the Conqueror" in her note on Battle Abbey, but in the previous note has made clear his descent from the admired Roland, and even in this note emphasizes his generosity rather than his status as violent invader. In the next note, the Historian again maps out the events the Poet sees as France's "one day of triumph" (l. 159), recounting the 1690 sea battle between British and Dutch ships on the one side, and French ships on the other, wherein the "French, from ignorance of the coast, and misunderstanding among each other, failed to take all the advantage they might have done of [their] victory" (p. 160). Once again, the Historian interrupts the flow of the Poet's language, beginning her explanation at the word "Batavian" rather than "triumph" ("Thou, leagued with the Batavian,* gavest to France/ One day of triumph" [p. 160, ll. 158–9]). The Historian chooses when she will gloss the poem, and she also adds her personal interpretations to the history she provides: so the French both win and lose their battle.[62] The Historian makes a point of veiled and outright disagreement; the Poet does not seem to notice.

With these two speakers alone, Smith "tell[s] and retell[s] tales ... transform[ing] fixed categories by unfixing them" (Kelley, p. 134).[63] The Historian increasingly reveals her personal take on the facts she relays; the Poet, meanwhile, begins to gain authority simply by declining to notice the Historian. Both speak in distinct and distinctive voices, and each dramatizes a subjectivity indebted to Smith's long experience in writing voices. And crucially, neither is privileged, since the foreknowledge that the Historian displays at the poem's start comes more and more to bolster rather than undermine the Poet's endeavors. For instance, the Historian cedes her descriptive abilities entirely to the Poet in her note to line 481: "how wide the view!" Stating baldly that "So extensive are some of the views from these hills, that only the want of power in the human eye to travel so far, prevents London itself from being discerned," she then gives up: "Description falls so infinitely short of the reality, that only here and there, distinct features can be given" (p. 169). The Historian falls back on a kind of factual exhaustion. Meanwhile, the Poet is undaunted:

> But if the eye could reach so far, the mart
> Of England's capital, its domes and spires
> Might be perceived – Yet hence the distant range
> Of Kentish hills,* appear in purple haze;
> And nearer, undulate the wooded heights,
> And airy summits, that above the mole
> Rise in green beauty; and the beacon'd ridge
> shagg'd with heath, and swelling rude
>
> Of Black-down
> Like a dark island from the vale ... (pp. 169–70, ll. 484–92)

Despite the Historian's dismissive tone, the Poet shows exactly what poetry is capable of; by now, the value of imagery, and of imagination ("*if* the eye ..."), has overtaken its earlier historical vagueness. The Historian even finds herself following the Poet: "the distant range/ Of Kentish hills" is reiterated as "A scar of chalk in a hill beyond Sevenoaks in Kent, is very distinctly seen of a clear day"; "the beacon'd ridge/ Of Black-down" becomes "This is an high ridge, extending between Sussex and Surry. It is covered with heath, and has almost always a dark appearance. On it is a telegraph" (pp. 169, 170). In both these cases, the Historian repeats the Poet's image, rather than vice versa.

By the poem's end, although the Poet has not taken precedence, she has achieved parity with the Historian; the final account of the man the Poet calls "the Hermit" and the Historian, factual as ever, names as "Parson Darby" is, it is true, narrated first by the Historian glossing the Poet's introductory lines "Within a cavern mined by wintry tides/ Dwelt one" (p. 175, ll. 673–4). But the Historian seems to have lost her certainty, for after briefly sketching the man's story, she ends on a note of anxiety: "As it is above thirty years since I heard this tradition of Parson Darby (for so I think he was called): it may now perhaps be forgotten" (p. 175). "So I think"; "it may now perhaps be forgotten" – what is merely "thought" is not evidence of fact, and what good is history if no one remembers it? Meanwhile the Poet fleshes out the story of Parson Darby, using her creative abilities to paint the picture of a figure who offers a curious riposte to the recluse in Wordsworth's "Yew-Tree": "his heart/ Was feelingly alive to all that breath'd;/ And outraged as he was, in sanguine youth,/ By human crimes, he still acutely felt/ For human misery" (p. 175, ll. 687–91). History and Poetry have played off each other throughout the poem; Smith has used the two to comment on both style and substance. By privileging first one and then the other, she has avoided a final judgment; rather, the poem has explored the potential of each viewpoint, giving to each a singular voice which resonates with an autobiographical authority. And this is key: as alternate identities, the two counter expectations of a highly personal and self-based poetry; memory is as much about history as it is about the individual, and the individual embodies more than simply her own personal subjectivity. Smith explores, in "Beachy Head," the landscape of a poetry that culminates both a literary career and a historical era. And by isolating her voices, by writing subjectivities distinct from her own, she requires her readers to recognize the mutual value and necessity of Poetry and History by vocalizing the limitations of the two when divided.

Throughout her career Smith plays with voice and stance, channeling male precursors like Goethe or Petrarch; ventriloquizing her own characters, both male and female, in her novel-sonnets; reprising her own plots as she moves from poetry to fiction to drama. Her poetical role-playing is readily apparent in a poem such as "Written for the benefit of a distressed player, detained at Brighthelmstone for debt, November 1792," spoken as if by the player himself ("so we, the buskin and the sock who wear ..." [l. 13]) and thereby, as I noted in Chapter 2, introducing the double meaning of "benefit": both "for" his pecuniary *assistance* and "for" his benefit *night* (when all proceeds go to the author). Here, the poet is both player and author, male and female, genuinely concerned and playacting. But even in poems where the autobiographical seems to be most searingly present, as in the sonnets memorializing Smith's daughter Augusta, identity is not fixed, and so the same poem can present the bereaved as *mother* (for readers who know of the autobiographical event) and *lover* (for readers dependent on the poem's evocative imagery alone). The doubling of voice in "Beachy Head," therefore, literalizes the multiples inherent in Smith's poetic project. While she never verbalizes the question "What is a Poet?" her poetry shows that this is one of her primary concerns. The "I" is "not-I" at one and the same time.

The Prelude: Composition and Literary Metaphor

In turning to *The Prelude* I mean to close my discussion of the Romantic dramatized monologue by showing how, even as he writes his most convincing version of the autobiographical self, Wordsworth, like Smith before him, peppers his epic of the self with a self-conscious use of compositional imagery that suggests the ultimate futility of achieving a fully authentic selfhood through the act of writing. Even as Smith's miniature epic "Beachy Head" writes the Self through writing the Other, and explores subjectivity through its inherent drama, so too Wordsworth in *The Prelude* shows that the most dramatic of monologues is that of the Man who, finally, tries to speak to men. But the poem is also inherently artificial, "staged" in Michael O'Neill's terms, stocked with rhetorical devices in Theresa Kelley's reading, "dialogic" according to Brooke Hopkins; even Abbie Findlay Potts tries to reconcile its "autobiography" with "its pre-Christian myth," a script that effectively undoes its sincerity.[64] Potts' account is representative of readings that want to view Wordsworth as sincerely authentic even as they advance viewpoints that undermine this: for Potts, *The Prelude* "relates the Poet of Wordsworth with the Great Teacher, with Christ Himself" (p. 345), since the speaker of the poem grows into the shape and character of the Poet via biblical imagery. However, unless Wordsworth's sense of his own talent masked a deeper sense of his own divinity, Potts' account serves mainly to underscore the essential drama of the poem: it is poetic for poetry's sake, to reify and authorize the speaker as Poet, which also means revealing or exposing his self-preoccupation – his preoccupation with Self. Even as this allows the Poet to establish himself poetically, it also means that sometimes Wordsworth builds into the poem a kind of discomfort with such single-mindedness. With such self-aggrandizement, can this poet be a "true" Poet? Is there a danger that the growth of the poet's mind will overcome and disable the poetry itself? The anxiety that inhabits the poem is both of the author and of the Poet: the author writes a subject who, often, writes only of writing, and in this way Wordsworth encodes a dissatisfaction with an ego-bound "Poet, gentle creature as he is" (*The Prelude* I: 145).

The 1805 *Prelude*, as the first complete version of the poem, offers Wordsworth the opportunity to trace events and experiences from his past, poeticized and dramatized for his domestic readership. The limited number of readers, and their familiarity, suggests the instability of the poem's project; in exploring the birth of the poetic soul or genius, Wordsworth was as yet unwilling to display his creation to a wider audience. Viewed as a constant work-in-progress, the poem "refers to Wordsworth's own experiences, to historical events, to aesthetic and philosophic concepts, to other literature."[65] Despite the well-documented changes and manipulations to its autobiographical content, Gill and most others privilege, of the poem's many directions, the single track of Wordsworth's life. And of course he does reference many personal events, although he leaves out or disguises many others. The transformation of his love affair with Annette Vallon into the doomed romance of Vaudracour and Julia offers a broad hint to the poem's basic artifice, however. By representing a key life event as a key poetic drama, Wordsworth indicates the prime place the dramatic and the newly composed holds in this poem of his life. Hopkins, in noting Wordsworth's self-quotation, extends this to self-impersonation, noting that by Book 9 "the narrative begins to represent the discourse of another," another who is still Wordsworth but also no longer Wordsworth (p. 287). Hopkins explains this using Bahktin's theory of "double-voiced discourse" and argues that "the poem's central rhetorical interest and source of pleasure is the relationship between the voices *within* the poem itself, particularly as the narrator impersonates and sometimes even parodies his earlier self" (pp. 281, 289).[66] He emphasizes that in *The Prelude*, the auditor is the poet himself; in this way, the drama is played out both *by* and *for* the author. By keeping his readership small, Wordsworth can use the poem to explore and establish the identity of the Poet, to enact and voice his subjectivity, to dispute and debate his limitations.

Most of the thirteen books of the 1805 *Prelude* are concerned with role-playing, story-telling, and a metaphorics of composition that suggest the speaker's attempts to discover his poetic credentials by writing them into existence. To cover the poem thoroughly would require a separate study entirely devoted to *The Prelude*; here, I will concentrate on aspects of Books 1, 7, 8, 9, and 12. Book 1 immediately engages with an auditor/reader by assuming a sympathy with a speaker newly "free, enfranchised, and at large" (1: 9). Indeed, did we not know we are reading *The Prelude*, the speaker's mention of "bondage," "captiv[ity]," and "prison" would hardly be reassuring; that he speaks in metaphor is not readily apparent, and only gradually unfolds itself. Given generic convention – the conventions of the written – the opening lines might be spoken by a madman or a criminal, rather than a poet. By line 54, we are reasonably sure that we have not stumbled across one or the other, assuming that "the holy life of music and of verse" would hold little appeal for either. But the mystery of the opening lines characterizes the Book as a whole; the speaker presents himself as divided, unmanageable, blocked, and cloaked. The self-conscious role-playing means that each time the speaker calls himself a Poet, or invokes the name, the poem seems to call attention to his need to use poetry to cement his identity. When, for instance, he laments that he has "been discouraged," unable to capture "those phantoms of conceit" peopling his imagination (1: 134, 130), he describes his creative impairment in lines of fluent poetry:

> ... gleams of light
> Flash often from the East, then disappear
> And mock me with a sky that ripens not
> Into a steady morning: if my mind,
> Remembering the sweet promise of the past,
> Would gladly grapple with some noble theme,
> Vain is her wish; where'er she turns she finds
> Impediments from day to day renewed. (1: 135–41)

The speaker seems not so much blocked as in full stream; his subsequent rehearsal of chivalric and epic themes (1: 172–271) leads to the suspicion that the figure of the Poet is thematic rather than corporeal, more a fit subject for poetry than the figure who speaks. The speaker's reference to "variegated stor[ies]" (1: 223) hints at his own multiple nature. And because he is able to poeticize his anxieties about writing so elegantly, this multiplicity seems both known to him, and hidden.

Throughout the Book, the speaker tries to convince himself and his auditor that he is the Poet that he wants to be, moving from theme to theme and role to role, sometimes writing good poetry despite his fears, sometimes writing bad poetry despite his efforts. His mixed imagery of 1: 490–501 demonstrates his attempt to overcome the material reality of landscape even as he appeals to its enlivened core:

> Ye Presences of Nature, in the sky
> Or on the earth! Ye Visions of the hills!
> And Souls of lonely places! can I think
> A vulgar hope was yours when ye employed
> Such ministry, when Ye through many a year
> Haunting me thus among my boyish sports,
> On caves and trees, upon the woods and hills,
> Impressed upon all forms the characters
> Of danger or desire, and thus did make
> *The surface of the universal earth*
> With triumph, and delight, and hope, and fear,
> *Work like the sea*?

The repetition of "thus" suggests a speaker whose control over his verse is shaky, and the simile linking land and sea is forced. It seems to mean that the power of Presences of Nature transforms the static landscape into something as changeable, as "variegated," as the surface of the sea. Do the Presences, then, enliven only the "sky" and the "earth"? If so, why is the sea more atmospherically lively than the earth? And why the emphasis on surfaces? As he works through Book 1, the speaker's confusion is further conveyed through what emerges as a fear of poetry. His attraction to roles and the accompanying inability to choose any one role transmutes into an anxiety over "lengthen[ing] out,/ With fond and feeble tongue, a tedious tale" (1: 646–7). His closing determination to settle on a "theme/ Single and of determined bounds" rather than "work/ Of ampler or more varied argument,/ Where I might be discomfited and lost" (1: 668–9, 670–72) elevates the speaker's story in poetic significance, but it also indicates his anxiety that of all the roles he might seek, that of Poet is most elusive.

Throughout Book 1, the speaker uses the mechanics of poetry to begin to assert his identity as Poet, while equally displaying his anxiety that he might be overcome by those mechanics. By Book 7, the speaker has developed a strategy to deal with his weaknesses: he foregrounds conflict in order to control it. In Book 7, the speaker concentrates on the theater, juxtaposing its artifice to the authenticity of Nature. Underlying his self-conscious use of this comparison, however, is a sense of the drama that adheres to a Poet so concerned to promote the natural. The speaker highlights the artifice of the Book almost immediately, proclaiming "I sang/ Aloud, in Dithyrambic fervour, deep/ But short-lived uproar, like a torrent ..." (7: 4–6). This is the Poet on stage, whose poetry is defined by its structure, rhythmic and imagistic. As the Book continues, the speaker continually resorts to theatrical and spectacular diction with multiple references to "scenes," "the Prompte[r]," "a raree-show," "files of ballads," "the Spectacles/ Within doors," "half-rural Sadler's Wells," the fabric of "theatres," "Hall or Court, Conventicle, or Shop,/ ... public Room or private, Park or Street ...," "public Shows/ The capital City teems with" (7: 108, 190, 245–6, 289, 374, 569–70, 444–5). Just as frequently, the speaker counters this with a naturalizing impulse that smooths artifice into a kind of drama of the real: he "pitche[s his] vagrant tent," "streets with clouds and sky above," "some sequestered nook/ Still as a sheltered place when the winds blow loud," "the Spirit of Nature was upon me here" (7: 60, 160, 186–7). The speaker uses diction to convey his disgust at the city's excesses, even as diction shows how flimsy his control is over his imagery: "Shall I give way,/ *Copying* the *impression* of a *memory*" – the layers of artifice lead directly to "the work of Fancy" (7: 145–6, 148, emphasis added). This is especially evident in lines 244–80, the description of "the Spectacles/ Within doors": the speaker revels in the artifice he describes, "every tree/ Through all the landscape, tuft, stone, scratch minute,/ And every Cottage, lurking in the rocks,/ All that the Traveller sees. ..." The wealth of detail is such that the reader, and the speaker too it seems, forgets the artificiality of what is being described. So that when the speaker moves on to speculate on the stories of those he sees around him, he revels as well in picturing himself as a story-teller, acting vicariously the dramas he sees around him.

This is exacerbated in the highly literary, self-consciously poetic juxtaposing of fairs as we move from Book 7 to 8. The city's dissipation and the country's pure enjoyments stand as a distinctly poetic *device* by which the speaker can make his point about corruption versus wholesomeness. In this Book the speaker sets about making the familiar mysterious, and the mysterious familiar: his poetry works to insist on the inherent interest of the rural after having let himself run away with the fascinations of the city. Hence the fair that opens the Book emerges from "the depth of air/ Ascending" and shepherds and dogs are "girt round with mists" (8: 2–3, 96). Book 8 gives the speaker a chance to romanticize his rural past, to encode his youthful experiences with meaning and drama and mystery, and to assert his ability to translate his past into a meaningful present. In order to do this, the speaker must poeticize the country and nature, and hence his pictures of the rural are more about "unlaborious pleasure" than harsh realities. The speaker's emphasis in Book 7 on the theatrical has trained him to look at that around him, to derive meaning from appearance, and his frequent use of the verb "beheld" underscores his impulse to look. As he looks at his subject, we look at him, and his reliance on poetry to grant meaning to what he sees is matched by the repetition of verbs of observation: "beheld," "mine eyes have glanced," "his Form hath flashed upon me," "I descried," "before mine eyes," and again "beheld" (8: 391, 400, 404, 406, 411, 429). Piling up these verbs in one verse-paragraph, the speaker betrays his limitations: what he sees is what we get.

Wordsworth's manipulations of diction and imagery turn, in Books 9 and 12, directly to the act of writing itself.[67] In Book 9, the speaker's extended metaphor of the river points to the self-conscious artifice of a Poet aware of the need for forceful writing in a poem such as *The Prelude*; his exploration of his poetic development as a "genius" continually returns to his expressive skill, his ability to write poetically, and his consciousness that his self-presentation as divided and conflicted relies on an accumulation of metaphor and imagery. But as with the books discussed above, the speaker again is undercut when Wordsworth (impatient with poetic preciousness?) traps him in a genre dichotomy that encodes its own fictitiousness. Book 9 turns repeatedly to a romance narrative in competition with the "novel."[68] The story of Vaudracour and Julia is shaded by a quest-romance featuring the speaker, whose description of French soldiers and his own involvement with them relies absolutely on a romantic vision of purity.[69] War is, here, a romantic occupation, and the speaker simultaneously a troubadour and a hero. Even the "hunger-bitten Girl" (9: 512) is subsumed to the "tragic Tale" of Vaudracour and Julia. This exemplary romance, however, which the speaker sees as representative of the tragedies brought by war and mistakenly calls a "plain history" (9: 643), is so genre-bound and tied up in the romance of his own excitement at consorting with soldiers that it becomes, in the end, less revealing than the speaker's unthinking repetition: "novel imaginations" (l. 30), "novelties in speech" (l. 82), "novelty and change" (l. 333), "a novel scene" (l. 466). In Book 9, the speaker's failure to grasp the nature of the genre he writes in, and his blind reliance on a word so at odds with his desire to write romance, points to Wordsworth's unveiling of the speaker's subjective excesses.

The Prelude's focus on writing culminates in Book 12. Nearly every verse-paragraph contains either an image of reading or writing or the word "compose"/"composition"; indeed, the fourth uses "composition" twice and "read" once in 21 lines. As the speaker pursues the idea of his own regeneration in Nature and his maturation as a Poet, the Book embeds writing in its very fabric, composing the speaker along with his poetry. The speaker's rote modesty ("I, the meanest of this Band," l. 306) leads directly into an image of Nature as a blank page on which to write:

> ... a Traveller ...
> Upon the Plain of Sarum was I raised;
> There on the pastoral Downs without a track
> To guide me, or along the bare white roads
> Lengthening in solitude their dreary line
> ....
> ... before me on the downy Plain
> Lines, circles, mounts, a mystery of shapes
> ...
> With intricate profusion figuring o'er
> The untilled ground... (9: 313–17, 339–40, 342–3)

The bare, white, trackless plain becomes covered with lines, circles, and other shapes; the image is a highly poetic way of describing the writing process followed by reading what has just been written. And it is a testament to the speaker's self-obsession that he fails to recognize what he has composed. Instead, he falls into "an antiquarian's dream" (l. 348), rehearsing a vision of Druids before dismissing his opportunity with an indifferent "This for the past" (l. 354). O'Neill remarks that in *The Prelude*, "the way the self is constituted finds a mirror in the poem's process of imaginative self-constitution" (p. 53), and suggests that the poem is self-conscious; that is, conscious of itself *as* a poem. That so much of the poem is devoted to images of artifice and writing intimates that the self Wordsworth constitutes is only a *version* of himself as Poet, and a compromised one at that. The speaker whose main concern is the development of his poetic genius both attracts and embarrasses Wordsworth: *The Prelude* ultimately cannot decide whether to support or critique a self so devoted to self. Using poetry in the way that Smith uses history, Wordsworth writes his indecision into his poem, creating a monologue that undercuts the integrity, the subjective and creative wholeness, of the Self-as-Poet.

What is a Poet?

Brooke Hopkins has said that the opening lines of *The Prelude* offer "a perfect version of Keats's 'egotistical sublime', except that ... the passage tends to expose rather than indulge in it" (p. 297). This is a key distinction. Keats, a perceptive reader of poetry, recognizes that Wordsworth is doing something out of the ordinary in his poetry of the Self, but perhaps because the Poet-figure that Wordsworth creates is so coherent; or perhaps because, even by 1818, Keats as a reader has an expectation of what constitutes the "wordsworthian"; whatever the reason, the plausibility of the self-obsessed Poet overtakes the hints at his constructedness. Smith, too, is a victim of her own success; the personalities of the *Sonnets* became subsumed into the one figure most visible to her readers: Smith herself. The performative technique that each poet develops relies on an active readership, rather than a passive one: a readership that reads to learn through analysis and thought.[70] As Slinn puts it:

> Poetry ... depends upon a form of double utterance, by both poet and reader ... [And] if it is to function as critique by foregrounding its verbal activity, it requires a reader actively to realize that, not just by registering its eloquence or illocutionary effect, but by (re)enacting its full discursive process – the whole complex of the poetic act. This [is a] readerly act ... of analysis and understanding as well as enunciation ... [and] requires close analysis of formalist as well as thematic features.... (p. 71)

Reading Smith's and Wordsworth's "autobiographical" poetry closely loosens the tie between author and speaker until the autobiographical becomes the feint on which the poet can base her or his dramatized monologue. And having untied the biographical knot so that it becomes a useful poetic tool, both poets can explore the possibilities poetry offers for a knowing exploration of performed selfhoods.

Smith and Wordsworth use poetry to establish the subjective nature of the speaking "I" because both recognize that poetry only pretends to be natural; both, in other words, comprehend the inherent insincerity of sincere writing, the basic artifice of the authentic. Exploiting the artificial nature of poetry, they respond as well as contribute to the late-eighteenth-century desire for public displays of subjectivity. Smith takes the sonnet forward from the pathos introduced by Gray, for instance, and Wordsworth tells tales in *Lyrical Ballads*; a model for Mary Robinson's more overt style in her 1800 *Lyrical Tales*. Their shorter poems, then, act as rehearsals for, as previews to the more complex interweaving of subjectivities they later pursue. "Beachy Head" and *The Prelude* will refine the dramatized monologue, developing a more nuanced interplay between artifice and subjectivity. There is less critique in these later poems. Smith moves from undermining the passive sufferer of the *Sonnets* to a consideration of voice and tone which leads directly to a display of versions of creative ego. By distinguishing between approaches in "Beachy Head," she dramatizes the voice of the Poet as an amalgam; the poem works best when poetry and history combine fluently. Wordsworth, too, shifts stances: the dis-ease of the curious *Lyrical Ballads* speaker is transformed, in *The Prelude*, into anxiety, communicated at the level of composition. The Poet, that is, becomes dimly aware of his problematic subjectivity and writes accordingly.

Self-exposure, in the Romantic dramatized monologue, is not about exposing the self through autobiography (Forbes' "uniquely authentic self-expression," p. 10), nor does it provide "an example in living, an engagement of the whole being of the poet – his imagination, but also his conscience and his intellect – in the whole of his experience" (Perkins, p. 111). Smith and Wordsworth are both more complex than this. Striving for authenticity, or using poetry to develop a philosophy of life – these, they show, are the concerns of self-conscious, self-identified "Poets," whose egos provide the most fertile ground for growing poetry, whose spontaneous overflows are caught and preserved but not cultivated. Instead, Smith and Wordsworth are engaged in exploring the ramifications of self-exposure; they use poetry exactly because its form allows for experimentation. As they innovate at the level of structure, they demonstrate the vital link between formal concerns and the creation of the voice of the poet. Theirs are experiments with selfhood as well as with structure. To call the subjectivities on view in their dramaticized monologues mere examples of the egotistical sublime, then, is to misread one of the most vital elements of Smith's and Wordsworth's Romanticism: their understanding that poetry, written well, performs Selfhood rather than reflecting Self.

In using poetry to create and model the Romantic poet, furthermore, Smith and Wordsworth show how deeply they understand the malleable nature of this figure. The spectacle of the poet, someone who speaks through the act of writing, whose audience reads in a visual act that is presented as auditory, grows out of a display-oriented society, but Smith and Wordsworth do more than merely react to this trend. They recognize that in order to compose poetry they must also compose the Poet, and they assemble their raw materials from what is to hand: imaginative reconstructions of autobiography, generic convention, the utility of voice, their own skill at constructing and deconstructing poetic form. The very nature of autobiography comes into question, as does the viability of a successful poetic sincerity. Both Smith and Wordsworth seem to understand that committing an identity to print immediately compromises its authenticity, and so instead of making futile attempts to write actuality, they shape an "I" whose "I-ness" they repeatedly destabilize. This is not to deny that for both poets, the personal could be poetic, or to suggest that basing poetry on or writing out of experience did not interest them. But their investment of autobiography with the ideology of performance, and their manipulations of the speaking "I," indicate that both poets enlivened poetry not just with images drawn from life, or from an irrepressible egotism, but also with a strong understanding that, in an age of poetry, the most complex model was that of the Poet.

5
1807: The Art of Poetry on a New Plan

As Chapter 1 argued, Smith and Wordsworth established the Romantic fascination with experimentation by engaging creatively with the physical properties of poetry. Smith's initial, tentative novelties of the late 1780s, and her more assured and thoroughgoing innovations as *Elegiac Sonnets* progressed and enlarged, found their counterpart in Wordsworth's contributions to *Lyrical Ballads*. Both poets created poetic hybrids of resonant, sounding poetry. For both, this activity facilitated an understanding of poetry as fluid, flexible, and changeable. Their willingness to work with their material demonstrates that both poets participated in the period's general interest in understanding causes, effects, and principles, and in so doing bedded in experimentation as a value of Romanticism. Their interest in the possibilities of hybridization is one response to what Sophie Thomas has called "a new disciplinary and classificatory impulse," something she associates in particular with the establishment of museums and public shows that characterize the period.[1] In 1807, both poets published (Smith posthumously) collections of poetry that offered a follow-up to their 1790s poetics: in *Beachy Head: with Other Poems* and *Poems, in Two Volumes*, Smith and Wordsworth moved from hybridity to taxonomy, their books exploring the interrelations between the making of poetry, the naming of poetry, the science of poetry, and the impact of poetry.[2] In this chapter I will explore their presentations of their collections *as* collections: to borrow Stuart Curran's phrase, as "multum in parvo," distilled worlds of imaginative engagement with the process of book-building.[3] Their 1807 work exemplifies the Romantic desire to see into the life of things, and in so doing to understand both the parts and the whole of that life. By combining science and poetry in their collections, both poets make manifest the necessary correlative of Romantic experimentation: Romantic classification, and the ways in which understanding the world proceeds from, and is mirrored by, understanding the self.

It could be argued that what Smith and Wordsworth do in 1807 is mere ekphrasis, descriptive poetry about things, whether works of art or of nature. This may be one reason why, when Wordsworth's poems of 1807 are discussed, scholars tend to focus on the clearly signposted significance of the "Sonnets Dedicated to Liberty," and to a lesser extent on selected "Miscellaneous Sonnets." Similarly, Smith's "Beachy Head" attracts the most attention of all the poems in her volume; as the title poem, and first in the line-up, it is clearly the cornerstone. And, of course, elsewhere in this study I have myself pulled selected poems from both collections to make specific arguments. However, this chapter will consider the volumes as collected wholes, examining them as sums of parts, specifically put together by poets who, whether at the end of a career (and life) or still settling in, were deeply invested in poetry as a system of thinking and imagining. In 1807, what comes to the fore is how this system is energized or activated through the mechanics of the collection. This is why even the lesser-studied poems in the volumes, the poems about places, plants, flowers, birds, and other animals that make up major portions of text, are only ekphrastic superficially. Description is always in the service of the identification of something else, something other to the "thing" at hand. Even as the scientist relies on a system of taxonomy to understand larger issues of the physical world, so too Smith and Wordsworth place their poeticizing of things as means to ends, rather than the ends themselves. If hybridity created a mode for the self-reflexive lyrical ballad, as I showed in Chapter 1, then taxonomy allows for the building of categories from which the poets seek to project their understanding of the world, both inner and outer. The volumes of 1807 have an illustrative and a pedagogic function, but the pedagogy goes beyond merely teaching readers about botany or the concept of liberty. Instead, the volumes display the steps and stages utilized by the poets to *delve into*, *uncover*, and *excavate*; they exemplify the art of making poetry *through* sciences of differing models. For both, the interaction between *ars* and *scientia* underscores the position of their volumes as "works," whether finished, in progress, or somehow both.

In 1807 Smith and Wordsworth crystallize the period's growing interest in and explorations of poetic categorizing. This is different to the attention paid to genre in the earlier decades; then, versatility was on display as poets to greater or lesser extents showed off their skills as sonneteers, odists, balladeers, and so on. Smith's and Wordsworth's own *fin-de-siècle* innovations exemplified and set the trend for complicating and recombining such accepted, and acceptable, forms. Their next step was not to monumentalize their experiments, but rather to reconceive the practice of typing poetry. By 1807, they have made a science of poetry, partly through a poetry of science (poetry wherein knowledge systems and formal taxonomies are emphasized) and partly through a poetics of systems. *Ars*, the Latin for art or skill, also denotes the work of art itself, both the finished product and the process by which the product was finished. It carries whispers of profession (what we do), theory (how we think about what we do), manner of acting (how we do it), cunning (what we think about as we do it), and artifice (what we have made if we think too much).[4] *Scientia*, the Latin for knowledge and understanding, is the endgame: the thorough practice and application of art and skill results in expertise. Modern society has created a schism between ars/art (making) and scientia/science (understanding), but this is not a separation Smith and Wordsworth would acknowledge; rather, the two are coterminous, in that in undertaking the one, the poet achieves the other. Moreover, the reader gains from them a fuller, more whole sense of the world as rendered by the poet. Both Smith and Wordsworth described their volumes specifically as collections, envisioned as made more perfect by being taken as such. Smith by 1805 saw her "local poem" "Beachy Head" as "a member of the collection of all I have written [for the volume] ... it is my ambition ... to make the whole as perfect as it will admit of."[5] Wordsworth in turn described the contents of his *Poems* as "collectively mak[ing] a Poem ... collectively ... fix[ing] the attention upon a subject eminently poetical..."[6] For both, the collective force arose from the interactions of the parts, themselves carefully grouped under categorized headings, as in Wordsworth's *Poems*, or individually concerned with categorizing, as in Smith's *Beachy Head*. The volumes allow the achievement of understanding via the categorizing art that sustains each collection.

Taxonomy is key to the poets' use of category. Dahlia Porter has recently described taxonomy as "the drive to distinguish, separate, and compartmentalize," in the context of what she calls "scientific analogy and literary taxonomy" in the work of Erasmus Darwin. For Porter, "analogy provides the connections missing in dictionary-like taxonomic systems," even as "taxonomy stems the tide of unbounded analogy."[7] Darwin's strict reliance on Linnaean systems requires the leavening of analogy. Smith and Wordsworth, however, use taxonomic distinctions in their volumes as both art and knowledge: for them, categories create overarching thematics rather than imposing rigid borders. Making use of their understanding of the creative enlivening of the hybrid, they in effect re-sequence taxonomy so that it enacts the collection's congregative drive, creating the whole from the parts instead of privileging the parts over the whole. Both poets rest their taxonomies on the cushion of the miscellaneous, Smith with the general heading "Miscellaneous Poems" that opens her collection, Wordsworth with his embedded "Miscellaneous Sonnets" and the general sense of miscellany that pervades the text. The mixed and various, many-sided nature of the miscellany would seem to work against the distinguishing that is integral to the taxonomic, but the poets' vital spark is to make the miscellaneous itself into a taxonomic category. Hence, what had been rigidly normatizing becomes, to use Wordsworth's term, "poetic, and essentially poetic, and why? because it is creative" (Letter to Lady Beaumont, p. 101).

Wordsworth's "creative" is itself a category that carries tones of an imaginative drive, a living force that marries well with his 1807 emphasis on the natural and the organic, and that echoes Smith's thematics of botanical science within *Beachy Head: with Other Poems*. 1807 proves a moment when both poets take from their 1790s poetics (experimental hybridity, states of compromised subjectivity, and explorations of worldly pain and suffering) a comprehensive systematizing of experience, their own and those they assume and assign. The idea of a "system" has been discussed in connection to Wordsworth's poetry ever since the reviews of the *Poems, in Two Volumes*; as Curran notes, "readers immediately discerned a 'system' underlying the volumes. Most of them did not like it ..." ("Multum," p. 234). Most frequently, by contrast, *Beachy Head: with Other Poems* has been discussed (on the few occasions it has been discussed as a whole) as self-evidently lacking a system: *Beachy Head* is "not completed according to the original design," "Flora" and "Studies by the Sea" are transplants from *Conversations Introducing Poetry* but considered by "friends" to be "misplaced in that work" (*Poetry*, p. 153). "Miscellaneous" comes to be seen as "haphazard," accidental, unplanned. However, even as Wordsworth took great care over the placement and order of his poems, sending directions to his printer as to type size, layout, and other formatting details, so too Smith's letters show her to be as concerned with *Beachy Head: with Other Poems* as she had been with any of her earlier volumes, despite her increasing poor health. In other words, the systematic categorizing and ordering of these two collections demonstrates, once again, and in Smith's case for the last time, the poets' establishing participation in what has lately been described as a distinctly Romantic *genre*, rather than a simple organizational principle.[8] With *Beachy Head: with Other Poems* and *Poems, in*

Two Volumes, Smith and Wordsworth explore "system" as a poetics of taxonomy, revealing it as a particular pursuit of Romantic poetry as laid out and graphed in their collections. If, as a variety of scholars have shown, "system" is endemic to the period, then Smith and Wordsworth show it to be integral to a made Romanticism, one that is built even as it grows. These two poets have explored it from the start, but it becomes explicit in 1807.

According to critics, "system" can be read as a process, as an ordering device, and, most intriguingly, as a genre that functions, within the novel, to assume blame for the wrong turnings taken by a culture first energized, and then enervated, by revolution. It is both scientific and sociological: it can regiment and it can free up space for re-framing, renaming. Many theories of systems use the term to connote some form of order(ing) against an external force: hence, in family systems theory, for instance (amended accordingly), "a person [poem] is not a freestanding, constant entity but achieves her or his nature of the moment through interaction ... a family [poetic] system consists of a set of people [poems] and their relationships with one another ... the dynamics among the people [poems] in the system ... [are] not necessarily stable."[9] Similarly, complexity theory, slightly rephrased, holds "that all systems [of poetry] function in an operative field surrounded by two or more types of chaos [readers]; the slightest change of just the wrong/right sort can throw an entire system [of poetry] into disorder."[10] Facetious though it might be, by importing poetry to these admittedly general descriptions one notes two issues key to Smith's and Wordsworth's volumes: the poems work most effectively when taken in the stated order and as a whole, and that effectiveness is subject to the disordering actions of readers who refuse to do that. Wordsworth, I would argue, has the disobedient reader in mind when he reflects to Lady Beaumont on the power of his poems when taken as a group, and their apparent triviality if taken out of context. Smith, too, understands the power of readers to decide her fate based on their comprehension of her poetry. It is the system they employ to render their collections as collectives that can counter such discomposing forces. Put very simply, they order, categorize, notate, and preface their poems so that they *become* systems.

According to Barbara Maria Stafford, what she calls the "systematizing Romantics" created poetry of interlinking sensations that, when read, could both "capture experience in discrete units and as a dream of engulfing immersion."[11] She emphasizes the "creative role" enabled by "the process of perception," a creativity that, as Smith's and Wordsworth's volumes encourage readers to see, comes most wholly when the poetry itself is whole (Wordsworth's creativity that is itself poetic) (Stafford, pp. 321, 320). Siskin follows a different line of argument, but also sees that the reader is taught to read creatively through reading a kind of writing that is itself categorized as literary: another way of describing the pedagogic function of Literature/poetry.[12] And again, this learning comes from, arises from the move toward what Siskin comes to call System: System and Writing being mutually dependent. For Stafford and Siskin, *ars* and *scientia* give rise to a "comparatist generation" for whom "the study of life and the study of the earth were integral to the study of mind and its evolution"; "the work that writing performed was to constitute new classifications systems that could provide *discipline* in ... its distinctly modern sense: control for the sake of growth" (Stafford, p. 335; Siskin, p. 20). For Siskin, writing in a specifically Romantic way creates the category of Literature and types of writing within Literature; it creates differing classes of writers; it emphasizes the centrality not just of experimentation but of identifying, naming, and grouping. It is a movement and a maneuver, and when Smith and Wordsworth publish their volumes in 1807 they not only demonstrate Siskin's argument, they also manifest its poetics. Their volumes participate in the building of writing by instituting poetic disciplining as well as economies of knowledge, which can then be disseminated to readers. Siskin discusses anthologies in *The Work of Writing*, but he does not explore the collection, the "standalone volum[e] of poetry" that he calls "the generic marker of High Romanticism" (p. 12). And yet the collection, as written by Smith and Wordsworth, provides a concerted example of the Romantic "system" of writing.

Stafford and Siskin unpick the complexities of typologies, but the burgeoning field of Romantic Science offers another example of how categories and taxonomies underpin the period. Smith's *Beachy Head: with Other Poems* is itself an example of scientific writing expressed poetically, and, as I will discuss below, this functions as one aspect of its taxonomic imperative. Wordsworth, too, explores a variety of sciences in *Poems, in Two Volumes*, albeit with less rigor than Smith (although his methods, as outlined below, are carefully, artfully scientific). As Noel Jackson summarizes, science functions in the period as an aesthetic quality as well as a category of poetry; Jackson's book is itself a kind of miscellany, a compendium of fascinating insights into how Romantic poetry speaks a specific type of sense perception.[13] Jackson's sense-based "soft" science is balanced by Alan Richardson's "hard" science of the mind; his study of "neural Romanticism" sees the language of organic connection as creating a single interconnected organism. This may be pictured by the brain's systemic connection via the nervous system to the body (meaning that the body functions as a kind of collection), figured by contemporary scientists like Franz Joseph Gall and Johann Gottfried von Herder through nature imagery (the brain as a fruit or flower atop the spine).[14] Richardson "places Wordsworth, at least for a few crucial years, in the midst of one of the most daring intellectual ventures of his era – the reinvention, among naturalistic, physiological, and ecological lines, of the study of human nature" (p. 67); he refers to Wordsworth's "tendency to see the world in terms of 'separate blockish units' (analogous to basic categories)" and explores the poet's controversial statement that "the best part of language" is derived from immersion in rustic life (pp. 205, n. 80; n. 82). Richardson's work shows how deeply the Romantic period was inflected by concerns with *scientific* categorizing, typing, and taxonomizing; Jackson's conveys how an aesthetics of science colored Romantic-period writing. Both demonstrate the tendency of the period to merge and mutually complement art with science, and both find this working, in particular, in Wordsworth (neither mentions Smith at all, despite her clear affinities with their arguments). *Poems, in Two Volumes* do not feature, however, in their discussions, although individual poems from the collection do, an oversight that suggests the subtlety of Wordsworth's 1807 practice.[15] Smith's poems of natural history, and Wordsworth's histories of natural poetry, perhaps fall outside the remit of Romantic Science in part because the field arises from a category differentiated from typical understandings of Romantic poetry's nature-based musings as precisely *unscientific*.

Romantic Science, however, serves to remind us that the period is deeply invested in finding and experimenting with new ways to understand life and being. Smith and Wordsworth use their collections to participate in this culture; moreover, they establish the poetic collection as an exemplar of the art of scientific method.[16] Their taxonomies and their affinities with science are, in fact, a *system* much like the prose genre Siskin has identified. For Siskin, System inhabits the novel almost surreptitiously (it "[takes] cover within other genres"), and once there it "assume[s] causal roles ... rewritten into something that could be blamed" ("Novels and Systems," n.p.).[17] Siskin's theory posits that systems are endemic to the period, and that moreover they coalesce into System and pervade fiction to the point of becoming not only a genre, but (to put words onto Siskin's pages) perhaps even a main character *type*, the villain (and in that way an avatar of taxonomy): "we have The System to blame" ("Novels and Systems," p. 216). The "placement [of systems] within other genres produces effects that become characteristic

Romantic features," such as the "authoritative" I-speaker ("Year," p. 13). Siskin describes the marriage of System and prose as unstable – the one is only "imperfectly" embedded in the other (p. 24) – and quotes Wordsworth's Appendix to the Preface of 1800 (1802):

> a sentiment which ought to be the pervading spirit of a system, detached parts of which have been imperfectly explained in the Preface – [is] namely, that in proportion as ideas and feelings are valuable, whether the composition be in prose or in verse, they require and exact one and the same language. ("Year," p. 24)

Drawing attention to Wordsworth's use of "ought," Siskin proposes that Wordsworth's sentiment both underlies "the ongoing centrality ... of system" and establishes the discomfort of its embedding ("Year," p. 24). Hence, like a piece of grit that stubbornly refuses to pearlesce, System wars with its host.

Siskin's fascinating thesis makes it plain that when Smith and Wordsworth engage with systems/System in their collections, they are participating in one of the period's main modes, whether it is expressed through science or genre. But Siskin's emphasis on prose begs the question: what happens if the host genre is poetry? Smith and Wordsworth make "system" integral to their collections; *collection* becomes a specific system mode. For them, "system" is something to use rather than something to blame. The information system that Siskin attaches to the novel underpins their collections, but constructively. It allows Smith and Wordsworth to build their collections and to cohere the parts, and to impart the process of cohesion. This is not merely a Johnsonian "'reduc[tion]' of 'many things' into a 'regular' and 'uni[ted]' 'combination' and 'order,'" which Siskin opposes both to the "essay" and to the Romantic period's particular take on System ("Novels and Systems," p. 204). Smith and Wordsworth do not reduce and distill; rather, they grow their collections as reflections of their "own mind[s]" and of the natural world, and its possible forms of knowledge, all of which contribute to their "moods." Collecting their poetry together, then, for both poets, means that categories, taxonomies, and contents are not mechanical means of division but necessary elements of the projects, evidence of the skill that goes into the art (*ars*), and underpinning and activating the expert understanding that is the result (*scientia*).

Like "system," collecting and collections have come under increased scholarly scrutiny recently. The practice is usually discussed in terms of science: museums or closets, filled with things, specimens, "disparate items [that] were of interest either because they were rare, or because they were typical."[18] Collecting itself, as an activity, was spurred by "the urge to master ... that fuels the collector's desire."[19] The resulting compendiums or miscellanies themselves gave rise to the urge to classify, if only to make sense of the collection: "taxonomy as a way to map variety," variety itself the outcome of "Romanticism's preoccupation with representation and representability – with the problem of relating parts to wholes or even finding wholes for those parts."[20] Judith Pascoe's work most cogently sums up what she calls the "entanglement of literary and collecting aesthetics" (p. 22). Concentrating mainly on collectible *things*, Pascoe notes the enduring association of Romantic poetics deriving from, for example, readings of Wordsworth "as enacting an escapist aesthetics, one that permits the poet to retreat from obdurate physical reality," and that this might reasonably be opposed to "the activity of collecting" (p. 4). Indeed, Pascoe cites Wordsworth himself as evincing a "specific distaste for the collecting impulse" (p. 4).[21] But she also notes, in a departure from the prevailing notion of the collector as desiring mastery over a subject, that Romantic collecting could be "driven also by Wordsworthian modes of longing ... which suffuse romantic poetry more generally" (p. 4). Thus, the Romantic collector became a kind of poet – and in a culture increasingly interested in collecting things, the Romantic poet who chose to publish a collection in essence transformed the poems themselves into collectible items: species of things, albeit intangible ones.[22] Simultaneously, their "thingness" worked to ally the principles of collecting with the literary collection.

The period's interest in gathering objects that gave rise to enthusiastic collecting of specimens is closer to the system of literary collecting, then, than the utter difference in type of things collected might otherwise allow. The one is concrete, measurable, and tactile, the other existing at a remove from tangibility; and yet the collection, as assembled by Smith and Wordsworth, exactly fulfills the needs of its adopted system. Rather than objects, Smith and Wordsworth assemble a collection of ideas, following a mode of "system" that requires the specificity of an ordered contents. As I have noted, few scholars have treated *Poems, in Two Volumes* as a whole; only Curran has given extended attention to the volumes as specifically collected. And no readers have approached *Beachy Head: with Other Poems* in its entirety; even Dahlia Porter, who has pertinently called the collection "a true miscellany," concentrates on the poem "Beachy Head" rather than the collection as a whole.[23] In part this is because it can be quite a challenge to cover sufficiently an entire collection of poetry and maintain coherence and, perhaps, the reader's attention. In addition, for each poet their work of 1807 contains gem-like examples of the best they were capable of, attracting scholarly attention (with the scholar in the position of the antiquary or specialist whose interest in a cabinet of curiosities focuses on one or two pieces of especial interest). However, as Neil Fraistat has established, it is through a comprehensive approach that the structure of a collection gradually reveals itself: the pattern is inherent in the order of the poems. Fraistat has argued that, in the Romantic period particularly, there is a plethora of collections self-consciously styled as such, and that the period is distinctively concerned with coherence and structure within pieces of sustained writing. As he notes, "thoughtful poets developed structural symmetries and synchronic connections in their books by spreading thematically related pieces throughout ... [P]oems condition each other's meaning so that no resolution in the book is left unquestioned."[24] Interestingly, Fraistat locates these thoughtful poets mainly in what has been called the "second-generation" Romantics – Shelley and Keats (along with the later Wordsworth) – and he emphasizes what he calls "open-ended, organic structures" which mandate the questioning of resolutions (p. 44). This is "the most distinctively high Romantic use of the volume" (p. 44). Writing in 1985, Fraistat draws his conclusions before Smith becomes visible on the critical stage, but nonetheless his argument is suggestive in its concentration on the "high Romantic" and the later years; in other words, the most purely, self-consciously literary collections published after 1807. Indeed, Wordsworth's *Poems* of 1815 claim more space than *Poems, in Two Volumes*. But Fraistat's observations and understanding of the impact and the function of the collection point out the centrality of 1807 and Smith's and Wordsworth's joint, if independent, construction of what becomes representatively Romantic.

Smith and Wordsworth exploit and perfect a format that, as Barbara Benedict has shown conclusively, is by the Romantic period a well-established genre: the "literary anthology." Benedict, however, defines the anthology or miscellany as containing work by many hands, a collection of disparate pieces; she focuses on the development of the anthology into an artefact that "reprint[ed] material in different settings and according to different principles ... Texts bec[ame] dehistoricized, depoliticized, and hence 'timeless,' immortal, or, in other words, eternally contemporary."[25] Benedict notes that by the middle of the eighteenth century, "collections [that is, anthologies] designed by powerful critics and booksellers ... centralize literary values and rank authors." Robert Dodsley's *Collection of Poems* (1748–58), for instance, "define[s] contemporary taste," setting itself as the "touchstone of literary taste" (pp. 33, 157, 159). Benedict does not consider the collection assembled and composed by the single poet, in part because her study deals only briefly with the late eighteenth century. Her discussion, however, adds to the equation the cultural association of the miscellany or anthology as setting and arbitrating literary taste, and by extension literary value. If this is one effect of a certain kind of collection, then Smith and Wordsworth can be seen to be drawing on the cultural authority of the miscellany, itself devoted to timeless classics of literature, to underpin and characterize their own collections (and their mutual use of the word "miscellaneous" comes to mind). By implicitly drawing on the social pre-eminence of the style or type of volume popularized by Dodsley and his forerunner Dryden, Smith and Wordsworth with their volumes of 1807 intervene in the establishment of literary taste and position themselves as its arbiters. And by simultaneously drawing on the figure of the collector – whose mission is to find and display exemplars and rarities – they effectively merge these literary and thing-based activities. They make, and do, a system that draws on but crucially and transformatively enhances existing modes. In other words, they reclassify the anthology as the personal and reflective collection, while maintaining the cultural authority (and capital) that Benedict shows it had accrued by the period. And in so doing, they bring to the surface the internal organizing principles that Fraistat demonstrates are integral to the collection.

The collector of things quite often is also a hoarder, allowing only the most limited access to his or her array of special items. Smith and Wordsworth, however, assemble their collections of poems specifically for dissemination. Smith's certainty that it is by the value of her poetry that she will be remembered, and her expressed wish to "make the whole [of *Beachy Head: with Other Poems*] as perfect as it will admit of" (*Letters*, pp. 705–706), are matched by Wordsworth's conviction that the collective value of his *Poems, in Two Volumes* will only emerge when readers "fix the attention" on them (*Letters*, p. 100). The world as disciplined by the poets in their volumes is broken down so that it may be reconstituted and thereby understood. It is not just that "the poems cohere as an extended self-portrait of the poet" (Fraistat, p. 33), although that may function as a means; instead, the portraits of self, plants, animals, places, and states of being "turn from a meaning that is putatively literal by making its figurality manifest" (Kelley, p. 234). *Things* become *ideas*, and ideas coalesce around different forms that in the end cohere: taxonomies leading to the creation of species. The doubling of Romantic taxonomy and Romantic poetics, according to Kelley, allowed interaction between these parts and wholes, and by extension between the self and the world (p. 249). Thus, when Smith and Wordsworth create collections reliant on taxonomies, no matter the difference in labels or tags, they render the collection seamless, and also perfect its readiness to be read.[26] Taxonomized poetry assists readers in making sense of the system the volumes themselves embody; the making and the doing (which then becomes the reading) of poetry literalizes *ars* and *scientia* on the page and recreates its mechanics in the experience of the reader.

Poems on Flowers

Smith's well-established interest in botanical poetry has led to "Beachy Head," and to a (surprisingly) lesser extent "Flora," receiving the most attention when critics examine *Beachy Head: with Other Poems*.[27] "Beachy Head" itself, of course, is about much more; as a number of scholars have suggested, myself included, in many ways it acts as a collection or compendium of Smith's poetic career to date, containing overt and more subtle references to her dominant poetics of sorrow and loss as well as echoes and indirect quotations from her earlier poetry.[28] In this way it emblematizes the structure and function of the entire collection, inferring the several layers in which the parts, combined, create the most coherent whole.[29] This has been noted, as well, in *Poems, in Two Volumes*, where in each section the parts cohere to form the whole. The *group* is what matters: "each group in *Poems, in Two Volumes* must create its own context or fall into miscellany" (this is what Stuart Curran calls their "composite unity," p. 238).[30] Having noted this, it is interesting that both Smith and Wordsworth scatter flower poems throughout their collections. Wordsworth, as he does with his other particularized poems, crosses and recrosses his own borders: his flower poems occupy space in the opening section, in "Moods of my Own Mind," in "Blind Highland Boy," and in the "Miscellaneous Sonnets." Smith's "Flora," "The Horologe of the Fields," and "A Walk in the Shrubbery" create and immediately transcend boundaries, with the complexity of "Flora" creating a kind of aide -mémoire for the other two poems.

'Flora" may be seen to contain the field of Linnaean botany, "us[ing] poetic figures derived from botanical names" (Kelley, "Romantic Exemplarity," p. 224), and, as Kelley argues, this "has everything to do with contemporary debates about botanical taxonomy and nomenclature" (p. 238).[31] More than this, though, "Flora" figures the poeticizing of taxonomy itself. Its figurative personification recalls Darwin, but where Darwin provocatively humanized his plants, and in so doing made it tantalizingly easy to forget their botanical nature, Smith in "Flora" absolutely mandates a creative, poetic state of mind before the poem itself can even be contemplated; before the flower can be seen, the poet and the reader must enter the botanical realm. It is Fancy's "magic pencil" that can "teach [the poet] to describe/ The enchanting goddess of the flowery tribe," which then allows the poet to "teach" the reader about a kind of poetic escapism via a note quoting Cowper: "The spleen is seldom felt where Flora reigns" (p. 189, ll. 9, 13–14). Once "the vision comes," the poet immerses herself in a world devoted to the careful categorization of types and species (p. 190, l. 21). The poem is a detailed and intricate revelation of a botanical world wherein not only Flora and her flowery attendants gain prominence, but also the insects and other plant life on which flowers depend. The poem creates and then supports an approach to knowledge that is derived from taxonomy, which itself arises from exactly the visionary nature of the activity. Something has happened within the poetry: via Fancy and her "magic pencil," a collection of personified creatures can flourish. "Flora" devises "an antepast of Paradise" that, the poem suggests, is possible even outside of "the poet's dream" (p. 196, l. 228; p. 195, l. 202). Smith uses an image that is similar to Wordsworth's in "Tintern Abbey," where the memories of a happy past in Nature can provide sustenance for the imagination weighted down by life's travails. The poem closes with an appeal that illustrates how poetic magic can function off the page:

> O! fairest of the fabled forms! that stream
> Dress'd by wild Fancy, thro' the poet's dream,
> Still may thy attributes of leaves and flowers,
> Thy garden's rich, and shrub-o'ershadow'd bowers,
> And yellow meads, with Spring's first honours bright,
> The child's gay heart, and frolic step invite;
> And, while the careless wanderer explores,
> The umbrageous forest, or the rugged shores,
> Climbs the green down, or roams the broom-clad waste,
> May Truth, and Nature, form his future taste!
> ....
> But most for those, by Sorrow's hands oppress'd,
> May thy beds blossom, and thy wilds be dress'd,
> And where by Fortune and the world forgot,
> The mourner droops in some sequester'd spot,
> ...
> Yet the dear image seeks not to forget,
> But woos his grief, and cherishes regret;

Loving, with fond and lingering pain, to mourn
O'er joys and hopes that never will return; –
Thou, visionary power! Mayst bid him view
Forms not less lovely, and as transient too;
And while they soothe the wearied pilgrim's eyes,
Afford an antepast of Paradise.
(pp. 195–6, ll. 201–10, 215–18, 221–8)

This turn is not unproblematic, especially given the poem's emphasis on vision and magic. An "antepast to Paradise" might function like fairy food: insubstantial and malnourishing. And the link to Paradise embeds as well the loss and despair associated with an Eden always already lost. But the poem's ending suggests, nonetheless, that the "poet's dream" need not be confined to the privileged few, that any "careless wanderer" may experience the leap from an appreciation and love for the "things" of Nature to the ideas resident within them: that is, the creative construct of flowers. This allows for the ardently desired transformation of pain to pleasure.[32] The poem makes the change: even as the Poet enters this world of dream only to find it taxonomically anchored in the world of Nature, the reader follows.

Taken in isolation, "Flora" offers an entrance to a classically enhanced botanical world, but as part of a collection, it begs to be seen in relation to its counterparts. "The Horologe of the Fields" and "A Walk in the Shrubbery" both explicitly connect the passage of human-time to the correct understanding of flower-time. They individually explore specific named floral species while also cementing the connection, in the three flower poems, between the instability of past and present and the precision of the botanical. "Horologe" contrasts "a magnificent French timepiece" with a variety of flowers whose petals open and close at specific times each day. The artificial splendor of the French clock successfully disguises the "hours mispent, and murder'd time" (l. 8); it tells not time, but occasion ("moments wing'd with new delights," l. 4). The auditor of the poem, "Emily," is encouraged to see that, although deprived of such "works of art," she benefits from Nature, but only if she uses an "observant eye" (ll. 10, 14). Then, "unveil'd," will appear "faithful monitors, who tell/ How pass the hours and the seasons by" (ll. 14, 15–16). The poem ranges through terrestrial and oceanic flowers, stopping to reveal how each performs its botanical duty and in that way substantiates its very existence. The poem renders a complicated figuring that assigns each example both a personified and a taxonomic identity: so flowers "rest lovely heads," their "faces unveil," "lift soft eyes," and so on, while also obeying their botanical imperatives as observed by the variety of experts Smith cites in her notes (ll. 24, 42, 56). The result is the naturalizing of time itself, which is neither artificially masked as with the French clock, nor irrecoverable as in "Flora." Instead, close attention to flower-time, repetitive and trustworthy, means that the observer is provided with a constancy not possible in human-time. As each flower opens and closes at its allotted period, again and again, it offers "sweet remembrancers" that overcome Time's "ceaseless pace": "Yet lose we not the fleeting hours,/ Who still their fairy footsteps trace,/ As light they dance among the flowers" (ll. 67, 69, 70–72). "Horologe" offers a contrasting view to "Flora," which could only see the past *as* past, and Flora's role as provider of moments of retreat through memory.[33] Perhaps because "Flora" exists only within the poet's visionary dream, it cannot bring the poet any continuing pleasure: it is always lost in the past. "Horologe," though, privileges a constant present achieved by a Nature not concerned with human-time at all, and in ignoring time's "winged moments," it overcomes them.

It is "A Walk in the Shrubbery" that reveals this attempt to substitute flower-time for human-time as fundamentally flawed: the two are simply incompatible. Again opening by contrasting two states, here the florist's cultivated bulb with the botanist's wild specimens, the poem enables an understanding of the qualities of the Rock Rose by comparing and contrasting it with the functions and appearances of "fruit buds," laburnum, and lilac, each of which is both distinctly itself and of a piece with some aspect of the others. The Rock Rose, "whose flowers expand, and fall off twice in twenty-four hours," is then itself linked to "the poet's favourite Rose," which holds its bloom and its beauty "beyond a second day ... still lingering in decay" (ll. 49, 50, 52). And then the poem moves abruptly back to human-time, and fulfills the problematics of "Flora." This poem's speaker is neither the poet of "Flora" nor the solace-giver of "Horologe": here Smith constructs a "moralizing Botanist" who strains the botanical metaphor to reflect on friendships that have "flourished for an hour at noon,/ But leave no trace when overblown" *and* to grieve over being "replaced by a Succession" of ever-competing blooms (ll. 12, 59–60, 68). The Rock Rose provides the diversion of "Flora" and the solace of "Horologe," but its transformation into poetic device at the end of "Walk" leaves it hanging between categories, a conflicted taxonomy. The care with which flowers have been poeticized until the last four stanzas of "Walk" only becomes apparent when the three poems are read as a collection, and thus permitted to infuse each other. The poems take the reader from the visionary magic of personified flowers straight through to the disenchantment of human relationships. With "Walk" in place, the solace of "Horologe" becomes only temporary. Like a triptych, each poem contains its own subject and then opens up to reveal the bigger picture, which is that the comfortable stability and reliability of the floral realm will never overcome the thoughtless indifference of the human.

Wordsworth's flower poems arrange themselves into a small country bouquet. There are three in the opening section ("To the Daisy," "To the Small Celandine," "To the same Flower"), three in "Moods of my Own Mind" ("The small Celandine," "[I wandered lonely]," "[Who fancied what a pretty sight]"), and two in "The Blind Highland Boy" ("To the Daisy," "To the same Flower").[34] Curran notes Wordsworth's "systematic insistence" on "unadorned simplicity" (p. 236), and in many ways these flower poems draw our attention to their simplicity: they are small, inconspicuous, and unadorned with Smith-style science. Instead, they ask to be noticed precisely because of their ubiquity. The Lakes are scattered with celandines, daisies, snowdrops, and daffodils, but in the poems we are invited to see just *this* one: what David Ginsberg calls "envisioning it beyond the mundane" as opposed to "displaying an object as we normally see it."[35] This, following Aristotle, he names *epideixis*, and he argues that this is a guiding principle of *Poems, in Two Volumes*, where the reader is asked to look, and then look again, at a previously indistinguishable something until "the bystander is transformed into a beholder" (p. 117) and until the unnoticed is noticeable and worth noticing. For most readers, the flower poem that attracts notice is "[I wandered lonely]," often called simply "Daffodils" in a redaction that focuses on the flowers but not on the point of the poem as one of a cross-category group. Indeed, the poem is usually divorced even from its partner, "[Who fancied]," which directly follows it and shares the same meter, stanza form, and rhyme scheme. Both poems assign to a group of flowers (daffodils and snowdrops) a particular function: to solace and remind human beings of "where life is wise and innocent." "[I wandered]," like "Flora," gives flowers a specific mnemonic identity, although Wordsworth's brevity and simplicity of expression are in strong contrast to Smith's classical formulations. "[Who fancied]," like "Horologe," presents flowers as maintaining a constancy and purity lost to the human world. This is emphasized when the speaker's speculations over who might have "set" (rather than "planted") the snowdrops in their place around a rock (a child, a maid, a matron, an old man) are answered by the "Flora"-like "whisper'd" information that "It is the

Spirit of Paradise/ That prompts such work, a Spirit strong" (ll. 5, 13, 15–16).[36] The poem, and "[I wandered]," do not lack figuring devices (the snowdrops are set like a "Coronet" on the "Head" of a "little Rock"; the daffodils, famously, dance and laugh), but they contain none of the botanical science of Smith's flower poems; instead, they rely on a taxonomy of appearance and affect: small, dancing, laughing, innocent.

Wordsworth's three daisy poems pull together the first section of *Poems, in Two Volumes* and the last: "To the Daisy" opens the entire collection and its counterparts anchor the mid-section of "The Blind Highland Boy." The poems share meter and stanza form, and are linked by Wordsworth's note to the second two: "The two following Poems were overflowings of the mind in composing the one which stands first in the first Volume" (*P2V*, p. 238). Wordsworth chose to separate and distinguish them, while simultaneously conjoining them; he reminds his readers in Volume 2 of the poem that opens the collection, pulling together not only the poems but the volumes as well. And each poem offers a linked but subtly developing take on the purpose of the daisy itself. In "To the Daisy," the flower serves to keep the poet stable and earth bound; it represents the mood of his maturity:

> In youth from rock to rock I went
> From hill to hill, in discontent
> Of pleasure high and turbulent,
>   Most pleas'd when most uneasy;
> But now my own delights I make,
> My thirst at every rill can slake,
> And gladly Nature's love partake
>   Of thee, sweet Daisy! (ll. 1–8)

'Flora" again comes to mind as the poet charts an emotional movement from "wooing" grief and "cherishing" regret to delighting in Nature. Where this is the endpoint in "Flora," however, Wordsworth begins his poem with this development, and credits the daisy with enlivening his imagination: "A hundred times .../ .../ Have I derived from thy sweet power/ Some apprehension;/ Some steady love; some brief delight;/ Some memory that had taken flight;/ Some chime of fancy wrong or right;/ Or stray invention" (ll. 41, 43–8). This makes sense in an inaugural poem, but Wordsworth continues the theme when he returns to the daisy in Volume 2: "Oft do I sit by thee at ease,/ And weave a web of similies,/ Loose *types* of *Things* through all degrees,/ *Thoughts* of thy raising" (ll. 9–12, emphasis added). The daisy takes on exactly the taxonomic power of *Poems, in Two Volumes* as a whole, and in so doing it not only creates poetry but fulfills the promise that in putting together a collection of poems, Wordsworth will effect the transformation of "Things" to ideas (or, as he expresses it, "thoughts"). It is no surprise, then, that "To the same Flower" (or "To the Daisy 3") sees the elevation of the daisy from sparker of poetry to a kind of proselytizer for the power of collected thoughts:

> Thou wander'st the wide world about,
> Uncheck'd by pride or scrupulous doubt,
> With friends to greet thee, or without,
> Yet pleased and willing;
> Meek, yielding to the occasion's call,
> And all things suffering from all,
> Thy function apostolical,
> In peace fulfilling. (ll. 17–24)

Not even "Flora" so thoroughly personifies a flower; and this transformation only makes sense if the poem is read after the other two. Comforter/inspiration, co-poet, signifier of Poet: the daisy acquires a new taxonomy as a result of completing its function within the poet's floral catalogue.

The three poems to the celandine are as interesting for what they don't do. The first two, in the opening section to *Poems, in Two Volumes*, carry out a daisy-like evaluation of the flower as representative both of itself and of its own poetic value. The poems thus enlarge on the idea offered by "To the Daisy" and confirmed by "[I wandered]" and "[Who fancied]"; they take their place in the taxonomy. Wordsworth provides a hasty contextual catalogue at the start of "To the Small Celandine" that, as above, gestures toward but at the same time dispenses with the precise botanical taxonomies with which Smith is concerned.[37] For Wordsworth, the flower is there to confirm the poetry: the speaker implicitly contrasts his ability to notice the flower, which allies him with the "thrifty Cottager," to the inattention of the "Poets, vain men in their mood!" who "never heed them" (ll. 37, 33, 35). Having come to love the celandine, the speaker reconstitutes them from "careless Prodigals" to "Prophet[s] of delight and mirth," and celebrates his own "hymns in praise of what I love!" (ll. 30, 57, 64). But there is a problem. Whether it is the poetry escaping the speaker's control, or the fact that the celandine is itself too changeable to be seen properly *even* by the speaker, this flower does not stay put within its category. The daisy poems offer a firm narrative trajectory that collects them together, despite the pages in between. The celandine, on the other hand, is in its first poem a "kindly, unassuming Spirit!" (l. 42), only to become in its second (which immediately follows) "arch and wily" (l. 31). And the speaker of the first poem, perhaps identifying too closely with his discovery ("There's a flower that shall be mine/ .../ I'm as great as [great astronomers]/ Since the day I found thee out," ll. 7, 13–14), is himself a slippery being:

> Prophet of delight and mirth,
> Scorn'd and slighted upon earth!
> Herald of a mighty band,
> Of a joyous train ensuing,
> Singing at my heart's command,
> In the lanes my thoughts pursuing,
> I will sing, as doth behove,
> Hymns in praise of what I love! (ll. 57–64)

Does the speaker categorize the celandine, or himself? Who, exactly, is the prophet, the herald; who sings at whose command? The poem superficially celebrates the humble celandine, which accepts its own slights and is content with the "good enough." But the second poem increases the level of anxiety expressed by the speaker that no one notices the celandine, even as he reads a "book/ Only read perhaps by me," so that the conclusion that "Praise it is enough for me,/ If there be but three or four/ Who will love my little Flower" rings hollow (ll. 27–8, 46–8). This tone contrasts strongly with the triumphalism of the first poem, and it suggests that all is not as it should be in the world of the celandine, a suspicion confirmed in "The Small Celandine." This poem is found in "Moods of my Own Mind," and it redounds to suggest that the first two poems are also, in some way, mood poems. "The Small Celandine" takes a completely different form to the first two, but it has in common a tone of anxiety and ambivalence. Where the first two construct a personal relationship between the speaker and the flower, albeit a troubled one, this third poem presents the celandine as an abjected Thing stripped of its ability to "close self-shelter" itself from "hailstones" and "blasts" (ll. 8, 5, 6). The speaker creates an object lesson from the sight:

> To be a Prodigal's Favorite – then, worse truth,
> A Miser's Pensioner – behold our lot!

> O Man! that from thy fair and shining youth
> Age might but take the things Youth needed not! (ll. 21–4)

But he precedes this thought wrested from the Thing of the flower with a vengeful and splenetic satisfaction in the celandine's changed condition: "I smiled that it was grey" (l. 20).

The three celandine poems lack the clarity of the other flower conjunctions, and yet they operate as a group nonetheless. What they offer, however, is a more Smith-like movement from avoidance and denial to anger, drawn from the celandine's typing as itself changeable, unknowable, and, ultimately, dying. Curran notes that the "development of the two volumes is ... a continual readjustment of perspective between the simple and complex, the quotidian and cosmic" (p. 236). When examining the flower poems as collections within the collection, it becomes clear that poems about flowers are not about genus or species, although they are about a taxonomy. The flowers offer an instance of the poetic mind in its various guises; they are part of Nature when they are things, and part of the poet when they are ideas. The science that Wordsworth relies on in the flower poems is not botany, but, like Smith, Wordsworth moves from a static taxonomy to a fluid poeticizing that springs from his presentation of certain parts of nature. For both, the collection creates the poems, rather than the other way round.

Poems on Birds and Beasts

Reading Romantic natural history through Adorno and against Hegel, Theresa Kelley proposes that "the array of species and that ongoing instability that they brought to the classification of natural history may offer to Romanticism [a] kind of freedom," a freedom to weave "local particulars" into "grand historical narratives."[38] In writing of birds and beasts, Smith and Wordsworth invoke systemic categorizing that works both within and across poetic borders: the local, the individual poem, combines with its likenesses until something new emerges, a collectible that "emphasizes the mental impulse of patterning itself" (Curran, p. 250). In terms of sheer numbers, Wordsworth's collection has the clear advantage: his seven poems on birds and eight on beasts (if the category is enlarged to include insects and worms) outweigh Smith's three on birds and single poem on a beast (if the figure of friendship as love without wings admits of such a description). However, Smith's poems provide a guiding trope for both collections: two of her bird poems are explicitly based on fables, with their attendant morals, and this structure informs Wordsworth's as well. Fascinatingly, in writing of birds and beasts the two poets devise a remarkably similar mode of interpretation, that these representations of living creatures enact, not so much the figuring of the poet, but the figuration of a poetics derived from human, or humanized, relationships.

Wordsworth's poems at first glance image their birds and beasts in fairly standard ways: thus, birds represent the freedom to fly away from and transcend earthly cares, dogs fulfill their destiny as emblems of fidelity, butterflies are allied to transience and the swift passage of time. In their separate categories, the birds and beasts are perhaps the main cause of Francis Jeffrey's dismissal of their "low, silly and uninteresting subjects."[39] However, this strict taxonomy gives way to a more nuanced combination of the "local" into the "grand." Almost every poem refers in some way to a brother, a sister, a lover, or some form of interaction between things or ideas. The word "brother" appears in "The Redbreast and the Butterfly," "To a Sky-Lark," "The Green Linnet," and "Tribute to the Memory of the Same Dog." "Sister" or "Emmeline" is focal in "The Sparrow's Nest" and both poems named "To a Butterfly." A child ("Laura") features in "The Kitten and the Falling Leaves" and a lover ("Lucy") in "[Among all lovely things]."[40] Relationships, whether conflicted or supportive, are important in "The Redbreast and the Butterfly," "[O Nightingale]," "[Yes! full surely]," "Fidelity," "Incident, characteristic of a favourite dog," and "Tribute." Only "To the Cuckoo" stands outside this pattern, although the poem's thrust, a comparison between present and past with the cuckoo as the linking constant, creates its own form of relationship. "To the Cuckoo" acts as the exception that proves the rule: its reference to the bird as "an invisible Thing" and the bird's ability to transform "the earth we pace" into "an unsubstantial, faery place" seems to dissolve the poem from within (ll. 29, 31). It is balanced by "Yes! full surely," another cuckoo poem which reflects with some panic on "voices of two different Natures" (l. 16): that of the cuckoo and its echo, the one emerging from Nature, the other from a debased human nature, a contrast spun into a moral exhorting readers to "listen, ponder, hold [the echoes from beyond the grave] dear;/ For of God, of God they are!" (ll. 23–4).

Wordsworth's animal poems create an emergent pattern of a chain of being that is self-generated by the experience of reading the poems, an example of the process described by Curran as "the reader [being] drawn by identification to discern the complex of patterning and to become mentally renewed in the process of a further self-projection and return" (p. 250); that is, reading poems that make up the idea of selfhood from the things of nature, and then reading one's own self into that. The last poem in the sequence is "Yes! full surely," with its dualistic refrain, but the penultimate bird and beast poem, "Tribute," encapsulates the point of its type:

> For love, that comes to all; the holy sense,
> Best gift of God, in thee was most intense;
> A chain of heart, a feeling of the mind,
> A tender sympathy, which did thee bid
> Not only to us Men, but to thy Kind:
> Yea, for thy Fellow-brutes in thee we saw
> The soul of Love, Love's intellectual law ... (ll. 29–35)

The poems create a cross-species sympathy ("for thy Fellow-brutes") that asserts an "intellectual law": love is not a mere feeling but the indicator of life itself. This kind of argument is not suited to flower poems; it requires, simply put, a nervous *system*, the route by which physical being performs thought (Wordsworth gives this power, in some form or another, to all his birds and beasts). Scattering his birds and beasts throughout *Poems, in Two Volumes* (they feature in the opening section, "Poems Composed During a Tour," "Moods of My Own Mind," and "The Blind Highland Boy"), Wordsworth uses them to form a chain of feeling and "chain of heart" that links all in the family of nature.

Smith does something similar with her bird poems, two of which she sublinks as "Fables." I have argued elsewhere that in her fables (which also include "The dictatorial owl" and "The jay in masquerade" from *The Natural History of Birds*, 1807), Smith follows her sources La Fontaine, Pilpay, and Aesop and uses animals to dramatize human foibles.[41] However, her fables are more than simply translations, which would have been the easy route given her facility with French and her ill health at the end of her life. Instead, she calls attention to the fables as history, providing a lengthy note on La Fontaine and including references to Pilpay and Aesop in the titles. She then rewrites her sources, fleshing out the stories, adding motivation and psychological depth, transforming her fabulous beasts into humans in beasts' clothing. For her, as for Wordsworth, birds are not separate and distinct creatures from humans, but rather a variation on the type: her taxonomy uses the literary category of the fable to figure the metaphorical function of her animals. Thus "The truant dove" acts out the base behavior of the straying husband, who then redeems himself by humbly returning home (but not before the poem has some revenge, subjecting him to loss of influence, attacks by a hawk and a cat, and a wing broken by a sportsman's bullet). Wordsworth's "chain of heart" seems in operation in "The truant dove," since despite their abandonment his wife and children take him back and, "by the best physician, Love,/ His wounds were heal'd" (p. 183, ll. 248–9). Both this fable and its match, "The lark's nest," direct their morals squarely at "the *bipeds without plumes*": "So love your wife, and know when you are well" ("Dove," p. 183, l. 262), and the lengthier

> For very true it is, that none,
> Whatever be his station,
> Lord of a province, tenant of a mead,
> Whether he fill a cottage, or a throne,
> Or guard a flock, or guide a nation,
> Is very likely to succeed,
> Who manages affairs by deputation. (p. 187, ll. 144–50)

The Fables thus offer one subset in the category of bird and beast poems, creating a chain of being through figuration and allowing for a kind of decisiveness to emerge regarding the similarities between birds and beasts, or, rather, one particular type of beast. Smith does not shy away, in these two poems, from specifying a category of men whose selfishness and shortsightedness render them, essentially, bird-brains, but her method is not to bestialize men by presenting them as animals; rather, she humanizes the bird so that she may derive from this literal figuration the idea of types and the relationships between such types.

This becomes clearer in Smith's "The Swallow," which, like many of Wordsworth's bird poems, operates on one level to associate the bird with its attendant season:

> The welcome guest of settled Spring,
> The Swallow too is come at last;
> Just at sunset, when thrushes sing,
> I saw her dash with rapid wing,
> And hail'd her as she pass'd. (ll. 6–10)

And, as in "The Redbreast and the Butterfly," "To the Cuckoo," and "Yes! full surely," on this level the bird functions as an emblem, an idea by which the speaker can muse on Nature's mysterious and instinctive knowledges. The starting point, as throughout *Beachy Head: with Other Poems*, is scientific: the poem explores a number of competing explanations for the swallow's migratory nature and its disappearance during the winter months. In this way the poem is about taxonomy: the speaker attempts to understand the bird and its habits by contemplating its possible different categories of existence. The poem sets up a system of interpretation, bringing in through "fable" an "Indian Sage" who by legend could "translate the wild bird's song" (ll. 16, 20). "Fable" connects the poem by association, if not by pure function, to the preceding bird poems, and a note reminds the reader that "there are two or three fables that relate the knowledge acquired by some Indian recluse, of the language of birds" (*Poetry*, p. 187). The speaker, by invoking precedent, also assumes this translational power, and the rest of the poem lays out the speaker's repeated theories about "what our *vain systems* only guess,/ [To] know from what wide wilderness/ You came across the sea" (ll. 23–5, emphasis added). The speaker soon co-opts the bird's narrative potential: "I wish ... I might learn from thee" transmutes into a series of hypotheticals (l. 21, 22). Is the bird from Africa, or Asia? Does it "ply ... [its] pinions strong" "the vast and pathless ocean o'er," or does it "hide, tho' none know when or how,/ In the cliff's excavated brow" (ll. 43, 42, 48–9)? How does it know when to return, or when to awake? Each stanza poses a question, and, depending on the answers, each stanza has the potential to reconstruct the swallow into a different type of bird: migrant or hibernating? Responsive to stimuli or to instinct? From the opening lines, which merely welcome a confirmation of spring's arrival, the poem proceeds through fable and story-telling to arrive not at an answer, but rather (and rather oddly, given the scientific underpinning of the volume) at the conclusion that

> Alas! how little can be known,
> Her sacred veil where Nature draws;
> Let baffled Science humbly own,
> Her mysteries understood alone,
> By *Him* who gives her laws. (ll. 66–70)

In other words, the poem's speculation not only cannot be answered, but, it transpires, should not be answered. The bird is by design mysterious; its laws are untranslatable. The only way, it seems, that we can "know" the bird's nature is by recombining it into human form. It is, therefore, fabulous: an unknowable idea, if an observable thing. As Kelley has suggested, at a certain level the drive to classify and order within Romantic culture begins to undo itself: "particulars and abstractions need each other and they need to be intrinsically in contest"

("Romantic Histories," p. 312). Smith's "The Swallow" shows that it is only through fable that birds may be brought into the realm of human understanding. Thus the poem both inhabits its taxonomy (bird poem, fable poem) and comments on its futility.

All this leads the reader to Smith's single "beast" poem, if such it may be called. In "On the Aphorism, *'L'Amitié est l'Amour sans ailes,'*" Smith creates another *"biped without plumes,"* although this one is not the errant human male:

> Friendship, as some sage poet sings,
> Is chastened Love, depriv'd of wings,
> Without all wish or power to wander;
> Less volatile, but not less tender:
> Yet says the proverb – 'Sly and slow
> Love creeps, even where he cannot go;'
> To clip his pinions then is vain,
> His old propensities remain;
> And she, who years beyond fifteen,
> Has counted twenty, may have seen
> How rarely unplum'd Love will stay;
> He flies not – but he coolly walks away. (ll. 1–12)

As in "Walk," the poem arrives at the conclusion that despite all efforts to categorize, understand, and order, the idea can and will contrive to escape one's understanding. Friendship refuses its category and reverts to Love; Love refuses its identity and abandons its object. The truant dove learns his lesson and returns to his patient wife, but Love itself is the most fabulous of the beasts Smith poeticizes. Reading the four poems as a group allows for the thread of fable and the fabric of disillusion to produce the opposite of Wordsworth's chain of the heart: Smith's poems typify instead a chain of heartlessness, all the stronger for being complete.

Miscellanies

Wordsworth classifies his poetry openly and deliberately; Smith uses classification as a guiding principle for her poems. Smith makes an overt and tropic use of varying forms of science; Wordsworth establishes himself (or a written version) as a guiding model. In thus taxonomizing their poems they hand at least some of the responsibility of making sense of their systems to the readers, who are encouraged to follow the tags and labels provided and in so doing take on the role of the collector themselves. *Poems, in Two Volumes* and *Beachy Head: with Other Poems* use naming, placing, categorizing, and making actively, drawing in the reader curious to understand the clue to the miscellany. I have dwelt on flowers, birds, and beasts, but both collections are also concerned with presenting types of people, exemplary figures, and states of being. In the case of Wordsworth, these aspects have perhaps garnered the most sustained attention (beggars, gypsies, Alice Fell, resolution, independence, and intimated immortality), although "Beachy Head," as the most studied poem in Smith's volume, contains thoroughly realized examples of each (and this may well be the reason it has attracted the most attention). Such types tend, as well, to correlate to many readers' ideas of what constitutes serious poetry, meaningful poetry. As my discussion has shown, however, once their collective nature is recognized and factored into the analysis, the "low and silly" poems reveal their significance.

Smith and Wordsworth follow a system wherein parts and wholes work together. Their notes, for instance, are spoken in a different tone to the poetry (and, as I argued in Chapter 4, Smith's notes to "Beachy Head" can even be spoken by a different figuration), but they are nonetheless integral to it; the explanations and information they offer function not unlike a miniature *catalogue raisonné*. In "Flora," for instance, Smith anchors the scientific fancies of the poem with references to a more knowable world: supplying common names of plants alongside the Linnaean classification makes sense of her figures. Thus "Scutellaria guards the martial brows" is notated "Scutellaria galericulata. – small skull cap" (*Poetry*, p. 191). The notes might take the reader even further into the science: "Rich was the purple vest Floscella wore,/ Spun of the tufts the Tradescantia bore" is glossed

> Tradescantia virginica.—The silk-like tuft within this plant appears to the eye composed of very fine filaments; but on examining one of these small silky threads through a microscope, it looks like a string of Amethysts. (*Poetry*, pp. 191–2)

"Purple vest" is justified by the scientific method described in the note. Smith is equally careful to distinguish between her poetry and her science even as she links them; the note immediately preceding refers to Smith's *poetic* method: "The Dragon-fly, or as it is called in the southern countries [i.e., counties], the Horse-stinger, though it preys only on other insects. Several sorts of these are seen about water; but its introduction here is a poetical license, as it does not feed on, or injure flowers" (*Poetry*, p. 191). "Flora," like most of the poems in *Beachy Head: with Other Poems*, is copiously notated; the notes offer the reader the fuller knowledge they need to comprehend the poetry. In the case of the fables, they alert the reader to the need to read them as a typed group: headed "Notes to the Fables," the extensive comments refer to both "Dove" and "Lark" simultaneously. Their accompanying "Additional Notes to the Fables" enlarge on "the varieties of pigeons here named" and, as the notes to "Flora" do, illustrate the science that enlivens the poetic figures (*Poetry*, pp. 177–8). Even the notes, then, preserve the collective tone. And when Smith goes on to observe that these "varieties are produced by art from the common pigeon ... [Pigeon] Fanciers are to Ornithologists, what Flower Fanciers are to Botanists" (*Poetry*, p. 178), she gestures back to the botanical science attached to "Beachy Head," and forward to "Flora" and, in particular, "Walk," where the initial note states that a "Florist ... has very different pursuits and purposes from a Botanist" (*Poetry*, p. 205).

Wordsworth appends notes to *Poems, in Two Volumes* as well, but these are seldom discussed. They can be hard to distinguish: for example, the Cornell edition of *Poems, in Two Volumes* combines Wordsworth's notes with his later notes to the *Poems* of 1815, his musings to Isabella Fenwick, and textual notes by the editor.[42] I commented above (in a note) on the striking resemblance of Wordsworth's self-defense against charges of plagiarism to Smith's; Wordsworth's notes also share with Smith's a concern with accuracy and contextual information that explain and annotate the poetry. Although his notes are much less extensive than Smith's (perhaps because his titular classifying is so much more), they perform the same function, and in many cases in the same way. Where Smith uses a note to explain scientific provenance or protocol, Wordsworth, especially in the notes to Volume One, uses his to enlarge on his sources and inspirations: "a Cumberland tradition," "[t]he story of this Poem is from the German of Frederica Brun," "See Carver's Description of his Situation upon one of the Lakes in America" (Darbishire, pp. 164, 165). He is precise, like Smith, as to his facts: "From a passage in Skelton, which I cannot here insert, not having the Book at hand" (p. 166).[43] The fuller notes to Volume Two also include some limited natural and local history, as well as a very long note to "Song, at the Feast of Brougham Castle" that calls to mind Smith's masterly note in "Beachy Head" discussed in Chapter 4. This note, which carries over six pages, quotes from and paraphrases a number of historical sources ("Thus far is chiefly *collected* from Nicholson and Burn," p. 340, emphasis added) and bolsters this with "my own knowledge" and "a word upon the subject of those numerous and noble feudal Edifices, spoken of in the Poem" (p. 340). His notes, like Smith's, form their own collection-within-a-collection; Wordsworth, like Smith, clearly considered them necessary to the full and nuanced understanding of the poems. Both poets supplement the systems underpinning their poetry with notated nods to the known and knowable world, demonstrating the process by which knowledge becomes art.

Jared Curtis has remarked that in *Poems, in Two Volumes* Wordsworth "tried, with varying degrees of success, to aid the reader's response to his poems" through the guidance implicit in the patterns and shapes of the sections (Introduction, *P2V*, p. 38). Smith, too, sought an "original design" for *Beachy Head: with Other Poems* that would arise from the nature of poetic interplay. The collections were to speak as and for the poets and speak to the readers, establishing the classical relevance of a poetry that would not lose its voice, that would "tell [their] name[s] to distant ages," as Smith phrases it in "To my Lyre." To "tell" means not only to relate, narrate, or inform; it also means to count or reckon, to place in order, to account for and esteem: to count for something. If one's name is told then one is placed within a group: in the case of Smith (and Wordsworth), one becomes part of a taxonomy of poets. Categories, once set, speak to each other across their borders; enlarged and enhanced, the miscellany is reconstituted as its own *raison d'être*.

Many critics have remarked on Wordsworth's categorizing and systematizing within *Poems, in Two Volumes*, from Francis Jeffrey onward; similarly, as discussed above, critics have described "Beachy Head," on its own, as a kind of container or compendium of Smith's poetics. As I have suggested in this chapter, however, this is not merely superficial, an arranging device. It is, rather, inherent to the collections themselves. Through the poetry they write and the arrangements they control (even if, in Smith's case, death wrested this control from her), Smith and Wordsworth transform mere ordering into an enactment of artistic, poetic taxonomizing. Smith, using botany and other sciences, does this in what we might call a disciplined way; Wordsworth, using deceptively slight headings and topics, creates a domestic science that utilizes enthusiasm in place of a purer method. Their system transforms the inert collection of things into an enlivened collection of ideas, reframing what might have been merely a portrait of the writing self into a blueprint by which the reading self can be reconstructed. What they do is integral to the period, integral to a self-made Romanticism. But it is most thoroughly explored by Smith and Wordsworth, who from the start have displayed an experimental imperative that culminates in 1807, when the hybridizing of the 1790s creates the conditions necessary for the full examination of categories, newly improved.

Within this imperative, *scientia* merges with *ars*, and making with doing. Whether it is the poetry of science or the science of poetry, Wordsworth and Smith use the collection to explore what it means to write sequenced poetry, poetry that pushes past its own compositional borders, that proceeds in conversation with its fellows. From the experience of seeing what hybridities make possible, Smith and Wordsworth in the first years of the nineteenth century move, not just onward, but *inward*: they write poetry that, once in place within the collection, gains multiple identifications. Of course, within any collection certain poems will claim a reader's attention, and it is not always possible to read a collection in full, every time. *Poems, in Two Volumes*, it must be said, is lengthy; it relies on spaces between its subsets as textual rest areas. And it relies on readers content to "turn over leaves," as Wordsworth himself is recorded as doing with Smith's *Sonnets*, as they examine the contents. Both collections, however, treat the parts of a whole as exactly that: not as individual, discrete, disconnected, and random selections, susceptible to dismemberment. After all, few readers take the chapters of novels out of order or piecemeal. The narratives constructed within *Beachy Head: with Other Poems* and *Poems, in Two Volumes* mark the point where disciplinarity calls attention to itself, announces its status as science, and becomes subsumed within art. Siskin notes that the developing energies of disciplinarity in the later Romantic period coalesce around the goal of "naturaliz[ing] *truth* ... even as they regrouped those forms according to different modes of accessing that truth: the strategic commingling of description and data in the social sciences, the hermeneutic interplay of the creative and the critical in the humanities, and the hypothesizing of what is not yet known in the natural sciences" (*Work of Writing*, p. 19). I would suggest that each of the disciplines he describes is present in these two collections, that each brings its own disciplinary requirements, and that each is embedded in the other: taxonomies in the service of crossing their own boundaries.

Conclusion

Paul Hamilton, in unpacking the layers of "Wordsworth and Romanticism," observes that "William Wordsworth's centrality to any review of English Romantic period writing continues fundamentally undisturbed."[1] His essay astutely distinguishes between the Wordsworthian, in its Victorian and later, critical guises, and Wordsworth, while the poet and poetics he describes align very closely with those central to this book's argument. Yet throughout his essay his points of reference, whether contemporary or posthumous, English or European, are male (with the sole exception of Anna Seward, who merits a brief mention for her dislike of Wordsworth's thematics in *Poems, in Two Volumes*). This suggests that the Romanticism Hamilton deals with is still the Romanticism of convention, defined by a limited canon of poets, with Wordsworth still the "most memorable" (p. 227). Indeed, within *The Cambridge Companion to Wordsworth*, and Wordsworth scholarship in general, the comparative approach (unless it is with Coleridge) remains confined mainly to footnotes and indices. In this *Companion*, for instance, Smith is indexed because Wordsworth read her *Elegiac Sonnets*, and because her second novel *Ethelinde* (1790) is subtitled *The Recluse of the Lake*, the lake in question being Grasmere.[2] It has been the aim of my book, however, exactly to disturb, fundamentally, Wordsworth's uncontested centrality to Romanticism, and instead to create a twinning that situates Smith and her contemporary poet as co-writers of a Romanticism responsive to poetic form, cultural and social history, developments in literary convention, and the querying of convention itself. More can be said, and should be said, about, for instance, the poets' championing of childhood, their constructions of themselves as parents, their understanding of the public nature of writing, their ambivalent personal politics and their engagements with and retrenchments from the radical tenets of Revolution, their visits to France, their shared sense of social responsibility: the list is long. That is not to say that their contemporaries did not also work within such parameters and ask similar questions. What is strikingly apparent, however, is that no other pairing, whether proximate or virtual, shared so many ideas and thematics, so consistently, during a period of such concentrated and fruitful co-writing.

After 1806, the year of Smith's death, Wordsworth's poetry and his articulations of his poetics shift ground. This has been ascribed to the response his *Poems, in Two Volumes* met with: the accusations of childish simplicity, for instance, and the unseemly concentration on self as Man of Nature. Over the next few years, Wordsworth concentrated his efforts on the ambitious philosophical poem *The Excursion*, the very poem that divided his Victorian readers into the "Wordsworthians" and the true readers, if one follows Matthew Arnold. When he publishes what has been called his first "collection" in 1815, but what, in light of Chapter 5 above, should more properly be called his first "collected poems," he has developed a new tone, especially in relation to his readers. Whereas his earlier addresses relied on readers astute enough to follow a marked path without the presence of a guide (something akin to a walker following a blazed trail: the way is plain for those with eyes to see it, but the walker's choice, even to go wrong, is tacitly assumed), his "Preface" and "Essay, Supplementary to the Preface" for the *Poems* of 1815 take a much firmer line. Readers are now most thoroughly guided, and those who won't follow are pretty much dispensed with; Wordsworth runs through a version of literary history so that he may point out the divergences between true and popular poetry. Many poets have been popular; only a few have been true. From here, Wordsworth classes his readers as distinctly, and as finally, as he now classes his poems. And whereas in *Poems, in Two Volumes* innovation arose from the interplay of classes and disciplines, and the fluidity with which poems spoke across nominal divisions, the *Poems* of 1815 follow a rigid classification that Wordsworth justifies and rationalizes in his "Preface," which itself, in laying out the orders of poetry, returns to the kind of standardizing found in Newbery, Blair, and others. Wordsworth reinscribes exactly the kind of authoritative classifying his *Lyrical Ballads* queried.

This is not to make the familiar argument about decline, or to elevate the Arnoldian great period of approximately 10 or 15 years over the last 35 of Wordsworth's poetic career. It is, however, to suggest another influence on his creative development than the reactions of the critics he lambasts in the first paragraph of his 1815 "Preface," subsequently dropped.[3] Smith's death deprives Wordsworth of his creative co-writer, and by 1815 he has chosen to be the director of his readers' taste, actively managing their responses rather than hopeful of bringing them to full critical development. His Imagination/Fancy distinction and his return to fixed poetic forms function as a recantation of the experimentation that fed his poetry up until 1807. It is a different Wordsworth who writes after 1807, and it is the loss of Smith as much as the hostility of the critics that provokes this change. It would, of course, be useful if somewhere in his letters or his sister's records of the period there was explicit mention of grieving ("Beloved William is turning over the leaves of Mrs. Smith's sonnets once again. How much he misses her!"). But the older Wordsworth is chary of admitting any form of influence or creative debt, other than to Milton, and while Carlyle might well exaggerate, it is telling that as he recounts his meeting with Wordsworth in 1835, he notes to several correspondents that Wordsworth appeared to need to be poetically pre-eminent: "it seems also rather to grieve him that you have any admiration for anybody (but him)."[4] It is equally telling, then, that it is in this same period that Wordsworth publicly acknowledges his interest in Smith, by then well on her way to insignificant "poetess" status, in his note to "Stanzas Suggested in a Steamboat off Saint Bees' Head, on the Coast of Cumberland" (1833) and in his advice to Dyce in 1830 that she be included in his *Specimens of British Poetesses* (the irony of the anthology's title is evident). As remarked in the Introduction, Wordsworth links his poem with Smith's "Saint Monica": "The form of stanza in this Poem, and something in the style of versification, are *adopted* from the 'St. Monica', a poem of much beauty upon a monastic subject, by Charlotte Smith: a lady to whom English verse is under greater obligations than are likely to be either acknowledged or remembered" (emphasis added). Wordsworth's use of "adopted" conveys a greater sense of "obligation," as well as of attachment, than the more expected "adapted" would. He has not only referred to, made creative use of, the poem; he declares its kinship with his own. Both acknowledgment and remembrance are effected through this choice of word.[5]

"Saint Monica" itself acts to establish a kind of kinship. St. Monica's feast day is 4 May, Smith's own birthday, and she is the patron saint of women in difficult or abusive marriages. The poem is one of decay and loss; its Abbey, a "dismantled scite," is an emblem for its own historiography. As the poem rehearses past activities associated with the Abbey, it also situates the place as a marker of change: from its original foundation and its intercessionary mission, through the destruction of the Reformation, to its current state as ruin and site both of local superstition and local rumination by "a pensive stranger" who marks "the silent, slow, but ever active power/ Of Vegetative Life, that o'er Decay/ Weaves her green mantle, when returning May/ Dresses the ruins of Saint Monica" (ll. 75, 87–90). The poem ends by allowing Nature the longevity and even permanence denied the works of human hands:

> Oh Nature! ever lovely, ever new,
> He whom his earliest vows has paid to you
> Still finds, that life has something to bestow;
> And while to dark Forgetfulness they go,
> Man, and the works of man; immortal Youth,
> Unfading Beauty, and eternal Truth,
> Your heaven-indited volume will display,
> While Art's elaborate monuments decay,
> Even as these shatter'd aisles, deserted Monica! (ll. 94–102)

Smith obfuscates the poetic truisms of "immortal Youth,/ Unfading Beauty, and eternal Truth" by consigning all, despite their adjectives of permanence, to "dark Forgetfulness," and she complicates the signifiers of literature ("art") and Nature by giving to Nature a "volume" and to art merely a "monument." For all that Saint Monica has stood for in the past, it is now subsiding to Nature, which alone maintains its significance. Throughout the *Beachy Head* volume, nature is preferred to (human) culture, but in "Saint Monica" Nature provides the *only* solace; even poetry, being monumental and subject to decay, is insufficient. Wordsworth's incorporation of "Saint Monica" to the margins of his "St. Bees' Head" thus undergirds his reflections on the rising of new forms of human thought and endeavor ("the new-born College of St. Bees," l. 153) with the inevitability of their own subsiding. At the same time, it over-writes Smith's conviction of such an inevitable end with a kind of benedictory hopefulness:

> Alas! the Genius of our age, from Schools
> Less humble, draws her lessons, aims, and rules.
> To Prowess guided by her insight keen
> Matter and Spirit are as one Machine;
> Boastful Idolatress of formal skill
> She in her own would merge the eternal will:
> Better, if Reason's triumphs match with these,
> Her flight before the bold credulities
> That furthered the first teaching of St. Bees. (ll. 154–63)

The two stances are not easy to reconcile, yet still they co-exist within "St. Bees' Head" and read backward to "Saint Monica."

It has been the aim of this book to establish that the Smith/ Wordsworth interchange is central to the poetry of each and to the establishment of one of the most familiar and studied forms of Romanticism. The "Wordsworthian" may have changed its aspect over the years, but it has always been used as shorthand for what readers find within Wordsworth's poetry, for something specific to his work that has altered conceptions of British poetics even for those for whom Wordsworth is tangential. The library shelves sagging under the weight of articles and monographs with "Wordsworth" and "Romanticism" in the title demonstrate, as well, the close coupling that has become a critical norm. And yet, as so much of what Wordsworth wrote developed from his readings of Smith, should we be more forthright about turning to the Smithian instead? If the relationship was one of simple influence, then probably so. Certainly, the more than quarter century that separates "Saint Monica," and Smith's death, from "St Bees' Head" attests to her enduring currency for Wordsworth. But it is not simply about influence, and emphatically not about a greater talent finding in a lesser one the seeds for his artistic development. From 1784 until 1807, British poetry blossomed through the joint practice of its two most substantial artists, a mutual rejuvenatory poetics that wrote into existence what we now call Romanticism.

Notes

Introduction

1. 'Wordsworth's Poetry to 1798," in *The Cambridge Companion to Wordsworth*, ed. Stephen Gill (Cambridge: Cambridge University Press, 2003): 22–37, p. 22. Wu also observes that the boy Wordsworth was offered Cowper's *The Task* and Burns' *Poems*, and tinges of both these other early sources resonate within his poetry.
2. See *Journals of Dorothy Wordsworth*, ed. Mary Moorman (Oxford: Oxford University Press, 1971), p. 164, entry for 24 December 1802.
3. By "not-seeing" I mean the poem's conceit that the speaker "sees" Williams, which contributes to its theatrical tone. This is furthered by the possibility that the first lines – "She wept. – Life's purple tide began to flow/In languid streams through every thrilling vein; /Dim were my swimming eyes ..." – dramatize a shift from third to first person, so that the "she" is also the "I" whose eyes swim with tears.
4. 'Dear delicious pain," say Carol Landon and Jared Curtis, is drawn from William Hayley's *Triumph of Temper* (1781) (*EPF*, p. 396). Wu, however, notes that Wordsworth probably did not read Hayley until 1786, after he would have read the similar phrase in Smith's *Elegiac Sonnets* of 1784 (*Wordsworth's Reading 1770–1799* [Cambridge: Cambridge University Press, 1993], pp. 72, 127).
5. See "Wordsworth and Charlotte Smith," *The Wordsworth Circle* 1 (1970): 85–103, reprinted in *The Wordsworth Circle* 35.2 (2004): 80–91. This very important article treats Smith's influence on the young Wordsworth seriously, and is essential reading. However, it does not take further its insights, and (perhaps inevitably) concludes by re-establishing the poetic hierarchy of major (Wordsworth) and minor (Smith).
6. *The Poems of Charlotte Smith* (Oxford: Oxford University Press, 1993), p. xix.
7. See *Charlotte Smith: Romanticism, Poetry and the Culture of Gender* (Manchester: Manchester University Press, 2003), pp. 166–7.
8. *The Collected Letters of Charlotte Smith*, ed. Judith Stanton (Bloomington: Indiana University Press, 2003), p. 38, entry for [27 November 1791].
9. See Christopher C. Nagle, *Sexuality and the Culture of Sensibility in the British Romantic Era* (Basingstoke: Palgrave Macmillan, 2007), p. 176, n. 26. Nagle provides one of the very few serious treatments of Wordsworth's sonnet on Williams' tears (pp. 62–7).
10. In 1830, Wordsworth "advised Alexander Dyce to include her in his *Specimens of British Poetesses*" (Wu, "Wordsworth's Poetry," p. 127).
11. A close comparison of the two poems shows how closely Wordsworth follows "Saint Monica": Wordsworth also incorporates many of Smith's images as well as her stanza form and "style of versification." There are teasing hints in "Saint Monica" that, even as her poem still resonated for Wordsworth so long after its publication, Smith had a similar receptiveness

to Wordsworth's *An Evening Walk*. Wordsworth provides a note to his use of "gill" in l. 72: "Gill is also, I believe, a term confined to this country [eg. the Lakes]" (*EW*, p. 36). In "Saint Monica," Smith uses the word "gill" in l. 38 and notates it thus: "Gill is a word understood in many parts of England, and more particularly in the North ..." (*Poetry*, p. 203). See below for a fuller discussion of Smith's possible uses of *An Evening Walk*. See the Conclusion for a fuller discussion of "Saint Monica" and "St. Bees' Head."

12. There has been the occasional notation of Wordsworth's debt to Smith, the fullest being Hunt's 1970 survey of stylistic and other similarities noted above. It is remarkable how little impact this article has made. At the time, of course, Wordsworth as the major writer and Smith as a minor poetess could exist only within a single paradigm of greater and lesser. Subsequent notices, by Curran as cited, myself, and other critics noted throughout this book, have usually done little more than assert affinity. It is the task of this book to demonstrate the affinities and justify the assertion, as well as acknowledge the debt owed to the scholarly community.
13. The single most important source for understanding how Wordsworth came to be seen, understood, and constructed in the nineteenth century is Stephen Gill, *Wordsworth and the Victorians* (Oxford: Oxford University Press, 1998).
14. See "The Romantic Emergence: Multiplication of Alternatives and the Problem of Systematic Entrapment," *Modern Language Quarterly* 39 (1978): 264–83, p. 267.
15. Anne D. Wallace discusses the stereotype of the isolated genius in "Home at Grasmere Again: Revising the Family in Dove Cottage," *Literary Couplings: Writing Couples, Collaborators, and the Construction of Authorship*, eds. Marjorie Stone and Judith Thompson (Madison: University of Wisconsin Press, 2006): 100–23, p. 100. The Barrett quotation is from Gill, *Wordsworth and the Victorians*, p. 10. See also Carl Woodring, "Wordsworth and the Victorians," *The Age of William Wordsworth: Critical Essays on the Romantic Tradition*, eds. Kenneth R. Johnston and Gene W. Ruoff (New Brunswick: Rutgers University Press, 1987), 261–75. The very title of this collection emphasizes the critical trend to read Romanticism through Wordsworth.
16. See Charles Richard Sanders, "Carlyle and Wordsworth," *Browning Institute Studies* 9 (1981): 115–22, pp. 116–17. The emphases are Carlyle's.
17. See *Revision and Romantic Authorship* (Oxford: Oxford University Press, 2002), 19–77.
18. In *Wordsworth's Bardic Vocation, 1787–1842*, Richard Gravil summarizes fifty years of critical reconstructions of Wordsworth:

> The construction of an Idealist Wordsworth, Cartesian/Kantian/Hegelian in his thinking, concerned more with imagination than with nature or history, was as David Bromwich has suggested, largely a work of the sixties and seventies. The further and even more fictive construction, upon that doubtful base, of something called a 'Romantic Ideology', in which the Romantic Poet is *in flight from* the ruins of history, occupied much of the eighties [punctuation the text's].

The Romantic Poet presumably being Wordsworth still, Gravil's description participates in the critical shorthand under discussion.

19. I am grateful to my anonymous reader for helping me to see this more clearly.
20. Stephen Gill, "Wordsworth's Poems: The Question of Text," *Romantic Revisions*, eds. Robert Brinkley and Keith Hanley (Cambridge: Cambridge University Press, 1992): 43–63, p. 43.
21. See "British Romanticism as a Cognitive Category," *Romanticism on the Net* 8 (1997), http://www.erudit.org/revue/ron/1997/v/n8/005767ar.html. Accessed 5 July 2010.
22. For a thorough discussion of the workings of gender within Smith's poetry, which also gives an overview of discussions that focus on the poetry as expressions of femininity, see my *Charlotte Smith: Romanticism, Poetry, and the Culture of Gender*. The first ten to fifteen years of scholarship on Smith emphasized her position as a woman writer, but as the study of writing by women matures, scholars are beginning to explore the very nature of the label "women's writing." For a volume of essays devoted to the question, see *The History of British Women's Writing, 1750–1830*, ed. Jacqueline Labbe, vol. 5 of *The History of British Women's Writing*, gen. eds. Jennie Batchelor and Cora Kaplan (Basingstoke: Palgrave Macmillan, 2010).
23. See "'Tell My Name to Distant Ages': The Literary Fate of Charlotte Smith," *Charlotte Smith in British Romanticism*, ed. Jacqueline Labbe (London: Pickering and Chatto, 2008): 203–17, p. 204.
24. See "The Sorrows of Mrs. Charlotte Smith," *Cornhill Magazine* 15 (1903): 683–96, p. 691.
25. The quote is from Stuart Curran (cited in n. 5), whose work galvanized Smith studies. Curran also led the scholarly project to republish of all of Smith's poetry and prose in *The Works of Charlotte Smith*, 14 vols. (London: Pickering and Chatto, 2005–8). Several of Smith's novels are also now available in convenient paperback, mainly from Broadview Press.
26. Theresa Kelley, in noting Bishop Hunt's article, observes that "Hunt argues in his ... essay that Wordsworth is far the better poet than Smith. I might agree, yet I would also turn the point differently. As Hunt amply demonstrates, Smith's poetry offered Wordsworth motifs, phrases, and even some metrical choices that we now identify as 'Wordsworthian.' If one's scholarly concern is to recognize what poetic habits are typically Romantic or Wordsworthian and so on, who generated those habits is a question that merits consideration." See "Romantic Histories: Charlotte Smith and 'Beachy Head,'" *Nineteenth-Century Literature* 59.3 (2004): 281–314, p. 286, n. 15.
27. September: Sonnets I and VII; October: Sonnet V; December: Sonnets II and XI. See *Poetry*, pp. 218–19, for details.
28. See "Wordsworth's *Lyrical Ballads* in Their Time," *From Sensibility to Romanticism: Essays Presented to Frederick A. Pottle* (London: Oxford University Press, 1965): 357–72, p. 357. Ryskamp, seeking to define the lyrical ballad, links the ballad with the song and cites Donne's *Songs and Sonets* as likely to be known to Wordsworth and his educated readers. Although Ryskamp notes that a "sonet" is merely "a song or short poem" (p. 358), given the presence of a "Song" in Smith's *Elegiac Sonnets* and the clear line that can be drawn from her song to Wordsworth's, the Donne title is suggestive (although for different reasons than those interesting Ryskamp). See Chapter 1, pp. 15–17, 32–3, for a discussion of the two poets' use of the song.

29. See *The Invention of Evening: Perception and Time in Romantic Poetry* (Cambridge: Cambridge University Press, 2006). Besides Wordsworth, Miller's book focuses on Coleridge, Shelley, and Keats, and later writers like Tennyson, Eliot, and Stevens. As welcome as its discussion of the undervalued *Evening Walk* is, the book remains in thrall to conventional Romanticism.
30. See *William Wordsworth: The Poems, Volume One*, ed. John O. Haydon (Harmondsworth: Penguin, 1977), p. 926.
31. See *Wordsworth's Reading 1770–1799* (Cambridge: Cambridge University Press, 1993), p. 128. In *Early Poems and Fragments, 1785–1797*, Carol Landon and Jared Curtis also note Wordsworth's copying of these "two further sonnets by Charlotte Smith, ones that were first published in her novel *Celestina* in 1791 and reproduced in the *European Magazine* in July of that year" (Ithaca: Cornell University Press, 1997) p. 677.
32. Neither Stuart Curran's 1993 edition of Smith's poems, nor my own from 2007, note the Beattie allusion in Sonnet LIX.
33. "Infant Zephyr" is also found in "The Cave of Poverty, a Poem Written in Imitation of Shakespeare," by Mr. [Lewis] Theobald (London, 1715); "low muttering" – without the dash – is found in Thomson's "Summer," from *The Seasons* (l. 853), and again in Beattie's *Judgement of Paris* (1765).
34. *Gentleman's Magazine* (March 1794): pp. 554–5, quoted in Thomas Pfau, *Wordsworth's Profession: Form, Class, and the Logic of Early Romantic Cultural Production* (Stanford: Stanford University Press, 1997), p. 99.
35. See Chapter 2, pp. 67–74, for a full discussion of the poets' use of figures.
36. See Jan Plug, "Romanticism and the Invention of Literature," *Idealism without Absolutes: Philosophy and Romantic Culture*, eds. Tilottama Rajan and Arkady Plotnisky (Albany: State University of New York Press, 2004): 15–38, p. 23.
37. As this Introduction has predicated, and for the purposes of clarity and brevity, unless otherwise indicated "Romanticism" stands for the version critics rely on when they place Wordsworth at its heart.
38. See *The Crisis of Literature in the 1790s: Print Culture and the Public Sphere* (Cambridge: Cambridge University Press, 1999), p. 241.
39. General Introduction, *The Works of Charlotte Smith*, 14 vols. (London: Pickering and Chatto, 2005–7), vol. I, p. xxv.

Chapter 1

1. *Disowned by Memory: Wordsworth's Poetry of the 1790s* (Chicago: University of Chicago Press, 1998), pp. ix–x.
2. The quotation is from Melissa Bailes, "The Evolution of the Plagiarist: Natural History in Anna Seward's Order of Poetics," *Eighteenth-Century Life* 33.3 (2009): 105–26, p. 109.
3. See Anna Seward, *Letters of Anna Seward: Written Between the Years 1784 and 1807. In Six Volumes.* (Edinburgh: Constable and Co., 1811), 2: 287; review of *Lyrical Ballads* by Robert Southey, *Critical Review*, 2nd series, XXIV (October 1798): 197–204, in *Lyrical Ballads*, eds. R.L. Brett and A.R Jones (London: Routledge, 1991), p. 322.
4. As U. C. Knoepflmacher observes, "new forms of belief – and new literary forms – can be hewn out of contraries." Knoepflmacher's special issue

of *Studies in English Literature* assigns to the Victorian period the kind of productive, experimental hybridity that this chapter finds in Smith and Wordsworth. See "Editor's Preface: Hybrid Forms and Cultural Anxiety," *SEL* 48.4 (2008): 745–54, p. 746.

5. Smith, "Preface to the First and Second Editions" (*Poetry*, p. 10).
6. See Robinson, "*Elegiac Sonnets*: Charlotte Smith's Formal Paradoxy," *Papers on Language and Literature* 39.2 (2003): 185–220.
7. See, for instance, John E. Jordan, *Why the* Lyrical Ballads*?* (Berkeley: University of California Press, 1976), p. 99 *passim*; Mary Jacobus, *Tradition and Experiment in Wordsworth's* Lyrical Ballads *(1798)* (Oxford: Clarendon Press, 1976), pp. 188–91.
8. Key texts on *Lyrical Ballads* and *Elegiac Sonnets* may be found in the Bibliography.
9. For an astute and thorough investigation of the print culture of the period, see William St. Clair, *The Reading Nation in the Romantic Period* (Cambridge: Cambridge University Press, 2004).
10. Both write for money: Smith's financial need is well known and thoroughly documented in her letters and paratexts. In 1799 Wordsworth notes that "I published those poems for money and money alone" (*The Letters of William and Dorothy Wordsworth*, ed. Ernest de Selincourt, 5 vols. (Oxford: Clarendon Press, 1967): I, p. 267.
11. In other words, the "elder writers" provide the jumping-off point.
12. For ease of reference, throughout this chapter I refer to *The Art of Poetry* as Newbery's. However, its authorship is unclear; it is first published as *The Art of Poetry Made Easy ... Being the Seventh Volume of the Circle of the Sciences* (London: for J. Newbery, 1746), and then republished as *The Art of Poetry on a New Plan* (London: for J. Newbery, 1762). This is the version discussed in this chapter. See also Hugh Blair, *Lectures on Rhetoric and Belles Lettres*, 3 vols. (Dublin: Whitestone et al., 1783). I am grateful to Bill Overton for the bibliographic clarification on Newbery.
13. As Stuart Curran shows, Smith heavily populated her poems with many of these figures through allusion and quotation. See "Intertextualities," in *Charlotte Smith in British Romanticism*, ed. Jacqueline Labbe (London: Pickering and Chatto, 2008), pp. 175–88.
14. See Warton, *The History of English Poetry, from the Close of the Eleventh to the Commencement of the Eighteenth Century* (London: J. Dodsley; J. Walter; T. Becket; J. Robson; G. Robinson, and J. Bew; and Messrs. Fletcher, at Oxford, 1774–81), 4 vols., vol. I, pp. v, ii, iii.
15. Wordsworth's famous description of poetry as "the spontaneous overflow of powerful feeling, recollected in tranquillity" owes much to Blair's historicizing.
16. Here I refer to her self-portraits as mother, bereaved wife, etc., that I explored in greater length in *Charlotte Smith: Romanticism, Poetry and the Culture of Gender*. I am of course aware of, and have indeed made, the counter-argument that in displaying her "personal" griefs so openly, Smith is anything but feminine. However, given Newbery's association of the elegy with a feminized stance, it may be that even Smith's public mourning takes on a more feminine cast than hitherto realized.
17. See *Charlotte Smith*, pp. 64–90, for a full description of Smith's linguistic feint.

18. As I make clear in *Charlotte Smith*, this "person" is a textual creature, embodied by Smith's efforts to personalize her, but nonetheless separate. This artifice will be explored in greater length in Chapter 4.
19. "At last I knew/ Porphyria worshipped me; surprise/ Made my heart swell, and still it grew/ While I debated what to do./ .../ [I] strangled her" (Robert Browning, "Porphyria's Lover" [1836], ll. 32–5, 41).
20. Even the combination of literature and science undertaken by Erasmus Darwin separates the two disciplines on the page: poetry and notes coexist but do not mingle. For an important new reading of Darwin's method that proposes an alternative view, see Dahlia Porter, "Scientific Analogy and Literary Taxonomy in Darwin's *Loves of the Plants*," *ERR* 18.2 (2007): pp. 213–21.
21. This functions even at the level of allusion, since in broad outline the poem resembles "The Despairing Damsel" by "Mr. Gay" (John?), which Newbery identifies as a song (II: 48).
22. In *The Historicity of Romantic Discourse* (New York: Oxford UP, 1988), Clifford Siskin notes that during the Romantic period, "the self was *made* to feel by being re-made into an active agent – one whose primary activity is feeling and whose cultural status is as high as that feeling is deep. A significant depth signals a consumer of literature (and vice versa); a self even more profound, of course, can produce it" (p. 67). A poem like "Elegy," which uncovers and justifies feeling buttressed by form, seems to exemplify his point.
23. The avalanche is foreshadowed in line 1: "Where cliffs arise by winter crown'd," but this only becomes apparent after the fact; another instance of self-reflexivity, here concentrated on a knowing use of poetic device.
24. In an essential article, Robert Mayo shows the female exiles, vagrants, and abandoned lovers and mothers were a common subject in the 1790s. See "The Contemporaneity of the *Lyrical Ballads*," *PMLA* 69 (1954): 486–522. See also Chapter 2 for a differently focused reading of this poem.
25. The name "Phoebe" resonates on a variety of literary and natural levels that we can be reasonably sure Smith would be aware of. Her status as a pastoral character is captured by Shakespeare in *As You Like It*, while she also features in the first Endymion poem in English, Drayton's *Endimion and Phoebe* (1595). The name is given to Leda's and Leucippius' daughters; she is also associated with the moon in Greek myth, and also with Artemis. "Phoebe" is also a genus of the laurel family. Smith's character, then, is herself a kind of hybrid.
26. See Chapter 2 for a full discussion of how the "real" can intrude on the world of the poetic.
27. Although, as Nicholas Roe observes, "*Lyrical Ballads* may be thought of as bringing together contrary movements of the age so that tradition *or* experiment ... may not be a choice we are obliged to make," for most critics this is exactly the point of departure and of conclusion. See "Renewing *Lyrical Ballads*," in *1800: The New Lyrical Ballads*," eds. Nicola Trott and Seamus Perry (Basingstoke: Palgrave, 2001): 224–38, p. 235.
28. It is possible that Newbery would class the ballad as a kind of song, in which case Wordsworth creates a tautology.
29. Barbara Hardy says that the lyric "isolates feeling in small compass and so renders it at its most intense," which points to its generic resemblance to the sonnet. See *The Advantage of Lyric* (London: Athlone Press, 1977), p. 1.

30. Jacobus, in discussing Blair, notes that the "renewal of the pastoral eclogue informs Wordsworth's developing concept of narrative," and refers to *The Ruined Cottage* and "The Brothers" (p. 168).
31. I refer, of course, to "Michael," "The Last of the Flock," "We are Seven," and "Anecdote for Fathers."
32. This functions at a material level, among others; the poem is the fifth in the volume, after three by Coleridge and "Lines left upon a Seat in a Yew-tree."
33. In this way, Smith herself is both an "elder writer" and a Master.
34. Kenneth Johnston sees these distinctions between the two volumes: "in 1798 the great danger was mental breakdown, caused by apparent rejection from English society itself," whereas in 1800 the concentration is on "a suddenly perceived loss of love, in a relationship, a family, or a community." See "Wordsworth's Self-Creation and the 1800 *Lyrical Ballads*," in *1800: The New Lyrical Ballads*: 95–122, p. 98.
35. She maintains a separation between "author" and speaker in her own poem by including an "I" in the note who is patently not the speaker of the poem.
36. I would not want to suggest that Coleridge, for instance, or Southey, or Robinson is not also writing new-style poetry. But Coleridge and Southey do not invent new forms, and Robinson's *Lyrical Tales* clearly derive from her reading of the *Lyrical Ballads*. Only Smith and Wordsworth seem to recognize actively the power of combining forms to produce something else altogether.

Chapter 2

1. I am grateful to the anonymous reader of this chapter, whose full and generous comments helped immeasurably as I formulated the concepts of the real and the transcendent.
2. See, for instance, John Barrell, *Imagining the King's Death: Figurative Treason, Fantasies of Regicide 1793–1796* (Oxford: Oxford University Press, 2000) and *The Spirit of Despotism: Invasions of Privacy in the 1790s* (Oxford: Oxford University Press, 2006); Harriet Guest, *Small Change: Women, Learning, Patriotism, 1750–1810* (Chicago: University of Chicago Press, 2000); Saree Makdisi, *Romantic Imperialism: Universal Empire and the Culture of Modernity* (Cambridge: Cambridge University Press, 1998) and *William Blake and the Impossible History of the 1790s* (Chicago: University of Chicago Press, 2003); Jon Mee, *Dangerous Enthusiasm: William Blake and the Culture of Radicalism in the 1790s* (Oxford: Oxford University Press, 1992) and *Romanticism, Enthusiasm and Regulation: Poetics and the Policing of Culture in the Romantic Period* (Oxford: Oxford University Press, 2003); and the other sources cited in this chapter.
3. M. O. Grenby even sees Smith as an anti-Jacobin writer on the basis of *The Banished Man*; see *The Anti-Jacobin Novel: British Conservatism and the French Revolution* (Cambridge: Cambridge University Press, 2001).
4. "Local Transcendence: Cultural Criticism, Postmodernism, and the Romanticism of Detail," *Representations* 32 (1990): 75–113, p. 76, emphasis added.

5. Susan Wolfson, "The Language of Interpretation in Romantic Poetry: 'A Strong Working of the Mind,'" in *Romanticism and Language*, ed. Arden Reed (London: Methuen, 1984): 22–49, pp. 22, 23.
6. Bromwich, *Disowned by Memory: Wordsworth's Poetry of the 1790s* (Chicago: University of Chicago Press, 1998). David Simpson's work is also important to this chapter: as he notes in *Wordsworth's Historical Imagination: The Poetry of Displacement*, Wordsworth's speakers in the earlier poetry are alienated subjects, and the poetry is "a writing that continually falls short of what it aspires to be, but reveals in that falling short its greatest intelligence and its most coherent messages" (p. 2). In contrast, I argue that the poetry *wants* to achieve such heights, but that the very tools by which it makes the attempt, highly poetic gestures toward art and artifice, in the end dismantle the structure for both poets.

   In the interests of readability, for the remainder of the chapter I will dispense with the quotation marks around "real." I emphasize, however, that within my argument the concept is as much a device as it is a worldly state of being.
7. *The Artifice of Reality: Poetic Style in Wordsworth, Foscolo, Keats, and Leopardi* (Madison and Milwaukee: The University of Wisconsin Press, 1964), p. 128.
8. See Gerald R. Bruns, "Wordsworth at the Limits of Romantic Hermeneutics," *The Centennial Review* special issue: *Wordsworth and the Modern World*, ed. A. C. Goodson, 33.4 (1989), 393–418, p. 403.
9. This chapter differentiates between transcendence as social and political praxis and the version that becomes so strongly associated with the later Wordsworth: a rising above corporeal and worldly concerns, a search for imaginative unity and coherence. However, seeds of this later turn are scattered throughout the work under discussion here, in particular as found in *The Ruined Cottage*, and especially as found in critical analyses of the poem. It may be significant that neither Simpson nor Bromwich spends a great deal of time on this poem.
10. Bromwich and Simpson find in the Wordsworth of the 1790s a capacity for irony that allows him to shift the burden of interpretation onto the reader – who then, according to his or her own capacity for irony, gets or misses the point. While not wishing to reject this reading, for my purposes it lends Wordsworth a certainty about his poetic practice that, as I argued in the previous chapter, I would not locate to the 1790s. The experimental Wordsworth may well be working his way toward certainty and irony, but the poems under discussion in this chapter share with Smith's a persistent return to a starting point of attempted engagement with pain, suffering, and deprivation, only to find, in the act of poeticizing, an equally persistent refusal by such raw states to be aestheticized, regularized, or normalized.
11. To overwrite, as on p. 53 above, is to substitute one reading for another; to underwrite would be to fail to achieve a full and convincing picture of the subject. To unwrite is a more conscious act, and has to do with praxis: the poems' continual turn to the mode of transcendence, followed by the collapse into event – into description.
12. The question of who speaks the poems continues to be pertinent. Like Simpson and Bromwich, I read Wordsworth's speakers as not-Wordsworth; unlike Bromwich, I interpret the poems as less about moral states than about

the ramifications of telling event through story. Most critics of Smith read her 1790s output as personal to her voice, which I contest in this chapter. For instance, most recently Harriet Guest reads *The Emigrants* as "assert[ing] the *poet's* sympathy for the emigrants" while "the complex verse-paragraphs ... enable the *poet* to articulate a difficult poetics which must constantly shift its ground, and repeatedly qualify its position." See "Charlotte Smith, Mary Robinson and the First Year of the War with France," in *The History of British Women's Writing, 1750–1830,* ed. Jacqueline Labbe, vol. 5 of *The History of British Women's Writing,* gen. eds. Jennie Batchelor and Cora Kaplan (Basingstoke: Palgrave, 2010): 207–30, pp. 214, 215 (emphasis added).

Both poets, I think, would take issue with some of the claims for sincerity and authenticity that have been made for them; see Chapter 4 for a discussion of their manipulations of sincerity. Within this chapter, the 1790s poems might be said to set up an early disenchanting of the sincerity topos.

13. For instance, l. 20: "Death vindicates the insulted rights of Man."
14. See Alan Liu, *Wordsworth: The Sense of History* (Stanford: Stanford University Press, 1989), p. 388.
15. For this reason the novel of sensibility declines swiftly in the 1790s, so that by 1801 Maria Edgeworth can use sensibility as shorthand for an extreme naïveté, bordering on insanity, in the character of Virginia in her novel *Belinda*.
16. See Antje Blank, "Things as They Were: The Gothic of Real Life in Charlotte Smith's *The Emigrants* and *The Banished Man*," *Women's Writing* 16.1 (2009): 78–93, p. 84.
17. As I discuss below, she is both a figure and a Figure, functioning to draw the reader into a picture of war-enabled violence; see p. 70.
18. "Local Transcendence," pp. 96, 97. It should be noted that Liu writes as much against this formulation as for it.
19. See "'The Mild Dominion of the Moon': Charlotte Smith and the Politics of Transcendence," in *Rebellious Hearts: British Women Writers and the French Revolution*, eds. Adriana Craciun and Kari Lokke (Albany: State University of New York Press, 2001): 85–108, p. 86.
20. Even the settings on what could be a disinterested eminence are compromised when Smith turns her, and our, attention to "the buildings, new and trim/ With windows circling towards the restless Sea,/ Which ranged in rows, now terminate my walk" (p. 127, I: 87–9).
21. This, of course, characterizes only a few of the sonnets, most of which play in a variety of ways with the identity/ies of their speaker; see my *Charlotte Smith: Romanticism, Poetry and the Culture of Gender.*
22. See, for instance, J. Robert Barth, "Wordsworth and Hopkins: In Pursuit of Transcendence," *Renascence: Essays on Values in Literature,* 48.3 (1996): 174–89.
23. See "Wordsworth and the Ideology of Romanticism," in *New Historical Literary Study: Essays on Reproducing Texts, Representing History*, eds. Jeffrey Cox and Larry J. Reynolds (Princeton: Princeton University Press, 1993), 178–98; p. 189.
24. See *Wordsworth's Poetry: 1787–1814* (Cambridge: Harvard University Press, rep. 1987), pp. 125, 122.
25. *European Magazine* 24 (1793): 41–5, p. 42 (unsigned review).

26. See Chapter 4 for a full discussion of this idea.
27. See "By Way of Introduction: Voice, Text, Mediality: Romantic Self-Positioning," in *Romantic Voices, Romantic Poetics*, eds. Christoph Bode and Katharina Rennhak (Trier: Wissenschaftlicher Verlag Trier, 2005): 7–20, pp. 9, 12–13.
28. For convenience I am identifying the speaker as female – although this in itself reifies the poet/speaker link, and should be taken under advisement.
29. The speaker notes that such figures "too oft defor[m]" the landscape (p. 141, II: 204).
30. This speaker, of course, is not yet aware of war, other than of the fighting on the Continent; in November 1792 war had not yet been declared. But the poet who publishes the poem in 1797 is. It is worth noting that this volume also included, under the title "Fragment, descriptive of the Miseries of War," the vignettes of the terrorized mother (stopping before her death) and her husband, the "wild raving Maniac." Unsurprisingly, Smith shows more insight than the speaker of "The Female Exile."
31. *Wordsworth*, p. 187. Bromwich calls *Salisbury Plain* "the poem that captures Wordsworth's state of mind in 1793" (p. 11), which seems to underestimate the distancing effect not only of years, but also of the poem's revisions and its competing points of view.
32. My argument, below, is in sympathy with Simpson's, who notes "the possible tensions between the personae of narrator and poet, whereby the 'happiness' of the one is not clearly endorsed by the other." He sees "the phenomenon of displacement" as "a feature of subjectivity itself." See *Wordsworth's Historical Imagination*, p. 14. My discussion centers on the 1799 version of the poem, MS.D in *RC*.
33. See Jerome McGann, "Romantic Responses to the Death of Beauty," in *Repossessing the Romantic Past*, eds. Heather Glen and Paul Hamilton (Cambridge: Cambridge University Press, 2006): 226–43, p. 230.
34. See Duncan Wu, "Wordsworth's Poetry to 1798," in *The Cambridge Companion to Wordsworth*, 22–37, p. 33. Wu also calls *Salisbury Plain* "essentially an anti-war poem" (p. 33).
35. See Peter Thorslev, "German Romantic Idealism," in *The Cambridge Companion to British Romanticism*, ed. Stuart Curran (Cambridge: Cambridge University Press, 1993): 74–94, p. 94.
36. A similar real-world response is Simpson's: "the portrayal of Margaret's husband ... is marked by a complex awareness of the terrible effect of unemployment on the moral and domestic life ... [and] the psychological stresses resulting from prolonged unemployment ..." (pp. 192, 193). It is significant that Simpson focuses on Margaret's *husband* as a representation of real-life emotional brutalization, although in so doing he overlooks Margaret's own descent into "psychological stress."

    Another way to approach the poem's uneasy shifts of tone is to read its subject through Wordsworth's own desire to find an expression for his moral psychology (Bromwich's term) that does not capitulate to the market – that preserves itself from commercial attractiveness. In this reading, the poet Wordsworth wants to set an example for a kind of intervention that operates outside commercial imperatives. This is akin but adjacent to my argument, since I maintain that although the poem ultimately fails to voice its lesson articulately, the failure is not the poet's, but rather the poem's. My argument seeks to detach Wordsworth's "moral psychology" from the artifice relied on by the Pedlar and his companion. I am grateful to my anonymous reader for suggesting this train of thought.

37. The "gaunt wolves" who "in armies howl" may also owe something to the "gaunt monsters of the howling waste" who stalk *The Emigrants* (p. 142, II: 238).
38. In *Wordsworth and the Figurings of the Real* (Basingstoke: Macmillan, 1982), Simpson explains that the "Romantic writers ... worked within the orbit of a crisis in which the figured and the real were coming to be more closely identified. What is regarded as the real has already been figured or processed by the mind." Further, "it is the mind that sees, not the eye. The mind ... selects and composes such sense data as it receives into particular codes of significance, elements of meaning" (pp. xix, ix). Simpson's references to an epistemology that conflates a perceived object with the meaning generated by perceiving it situates his use of "figuring" as a philosophical mode of comprehension. In my reading, Smith and Wordsworth work within but also against a system that reconciles too easily the thing with the meaning assigned to it. In these poems, the two confront this system of seamless signification by writing moments of crisis, where the figured and the real merge on the page.
39. Theresa Kelley has noticed how Smith "invokes the language of taxonomy to prompt readers' sympathy for 'affliction's countless tribes,'" focusing on the contemporary use of "tribe" "to refer to classes of plants and animals as well as human groups." See "Romantic Exemplarity: Botany and 'Material' Culture," in *Romantic Science: The Literary Forms of Natural History*, ed. Noah Heringman (Albany: State University of New York Press, 2003): 223–54, pp. 235–6. Kelley's argument illustrates a complementary variety of emblematizing in the poem, although she shows it to work to a more viable extent.
40. Liu's figuring of Wordsworth draws more, perhaps, on his later poetry, but the experimental Wordsworth of the 1790s also shows an interest in the transcending effects of the "historical imagination," to borrow Bromwich's term.
41. This scene bears direct resemblance to Smith's half-sighed-for "lone Cottage, deep embower'd/ In the green woods" (p. 126, I: 41–3).
42. L. 61. Although the poem places the line in quotation marks, as if it is directly drawn from Gray, Smith's note provides the actual wording. It seems that this actor has not learned his lines thoroughly.
43. See Kevis Goodman, *Georgic Modernity and British Romanticism: Poetry and the Mediation of History* (Cambridge: Cambridge: Cambridge University Press, 2004), p. 123.
44. As Gill phrases it, "the sufferings of Margaret and the Pedlar's instruction in how to read them" (*William Wordsworth*, p. 686, n. 31).
45. Within the arguments put forward by Bromwich and Simpson, Margaret stands as a test and the Pedlar as testmaster. By presenting the Pedlar as, in the end, not worthy of trust (an understanding achieved through appreciating Wordsworth's ironic presentation of the Pedlar as unreliable), the poem justifies its reduction of Margaret. The reader is invited to measure up the inadequacies of the figures within the poem. I would suggest that this does not *in itself* require the abjection of Margaret – it only requires the Pedlar

to read her actions as abjected. However, the poem gives authority to the Pedlar's representation of Margaret's artistic value, of her actual degeneration. In other words, it overdoes it.

46. As Bromwich says, "the poignant confession of intimacy has been converted into a picturesque opportunity" (p. 151): a photo op.
47. Smith avoids this dilemma exactly by writing her monstrous mother in *The Emigrants* as a stock character – her rote nature does not allow her to carry the weight assigned to Margaret, despite the latter's departures from maternal perfection.
48. As Simpson says, "as soon as representation ... becomes selective, then the assumption of a commonly available world is threatened" (p. xii).
49. See "Politics, History and Wordsworth's Poems," in *The Cambridge Companion to Wordsworth*, 196–212, p. 198.
50. See "Literature and Politics," in *The Cambridge Companion to English Literature, 1740–1830*, eds. Thomas Keymer and Jon Mee (Cambridge: Cambridge University Press, 2004): 43–60, p. 44.

Chapter 3

1. For instance, the website for Bignor Park, the erstwhile Turner family estate, now features information on Smith, supplied by myself, along with Sonnet XXII: "Written at Bignor Park in Sussex, in August 1799" (see http:// Wordsworthw.bignorpark.co.uk/index2.php, accessed 9 June 2010).
2. 'Wordsworth, Inscriptions and Romantic Nature Poetry," ed. Geoffrey Hartman, *Beyond Formalism: Literary Essays 1958–1970* (New Haven: Yale University Press, 1970), p. 222.
3. See, for instance, Judith Pascoe, *Romantic Theatricality: Gender, Poetry and Spectatorship* (Ithaca: Cornell University Press, 1997); Celeste Langan, *Romantic Vagrancy: Wordsworth and the Simulation of Freedom* (Cambridge: Cambridge University Press, 1995); Anne Wallace, *Walking, Literature and English Culture: the Origins and Uses of Peripatetic in the Nineteenth Century* (Oxford: Clarendon Press, 1993); and Robin Jarvis, *Romantic Writing and Pedestrian Travel* (Basingstoke: Macmillan, 1997).
4. See "Wordsworth and the Naming of Places," *Essays in Criticism* 39 (1983): pp. 196–216, p. 198.
5. See "Place Deixis and the Schematics of Imagined Space: Milton to Keats," *Poetics Today* 26 (2005): 386–432, p. 389.
6. See also Christoph Bode, "By Way of Introduction: Voice, Text, Mediality – Romantic Self-Positioning," in *Romantic Voices, Romantic Poetics: Selected Papers from the Regensburg Conference of the German Society for English Romanticism* (Trier: Wissenschaftlicher Verlag Trier, 2005), pp. 7–20.
7. See *Romantic Geography: Wordsworth and Anglo-European Spaces* (Basingstoke: Macmillian, 1998), p. 3.
8. See *Atlas of the European Novel, 1800–1900* (London: Verso, 1998), p. 3.
9. See *Wordsworth Writing* (Cambridge: Cambridge University Press, 2007), p. 80.
10. Bennett opens his chapter on inscription poems by observing that they "are notable not only for the way they record or comment on their materiality ... but also for the way that they assert a certain act and a certain temporality, that of

writing itself" (pp. 79–80). Where he sees this as "impos[ing] a fundamental and fundamentally significant or meaningful distance between the poem and the title by which it is named and defined *as* an act of writing" (p. 80), I read it as signaling a fundamental aspect of the poem's geography, and therefore integral to its locale.

11. There is a further distinction made by Smith, in that some of her poems are "supposed to have been written," which opens an additional space to explore; see below, p. 84.
12. 'I will build a fane/ In some untrodden region of my mind,/ .../ And in the midst of this wide quietness/ A rosy sanctuary will I dress/ With the wreath'd trellis of a working brain" ("Ode to Psyche," ll. 50–51, 58–60). While neither "written" nor "composed," Keats' poem nonetheless captures the moment where insubstantial thought becomes substantiated object.
13. Timothy Clark makes a similar point when he writes a "text projects or performs its own act of utterance ... speaking from out of a non-existent place." See *The Theory of Inspiration: Composition as a Crisis of Subjectivity in Romantic and Post-Romantic Writing* (Manchester: Manchester University Press, 1997), p. 23.
14. Although in service of a different point, Hartmann also links Wordsworth's and Smith's written lines when he notes that "lengthiness of title as well as the emerging significance of place and date might also have been influenced by the journalistic broadside ballad which tended toward concrete and elaborate titles"; he cites this Smith sonnet as a counterbalance to Wordsworth's "Yew Tree." See "Wordsworth, Inscriptions, and Romantic Nature Poetry," p. 209, n. 5.
15. It is a critical commonplace that the Spenserian sonnet is the most difficult to write effectively, because it limits the available rhyme so severely and requires an unusual level of elegant interweaving.
16. Sonnet LXII is also a "written" poem, one of a group that is multiply inscribed: the transplanted novel poems. Written by Smith the novelist in the guise of a novel's character, they are then relocated to the *Elegiac Sonnets* where their writer is simultaneously Smith-novelist, Smith-poet, novel-character, and poem-speaker.
17. The autumn poems are mixed. XII features a Petrarchan/Shakespearian rhyme scheme, *abba cddc effe gg*, arranged as two quatrains and a sestet. XXXII is Smith's only purely Petrarchan sonnet, *abba abba cdecde*, laid out without division into stanzas. XLVI and LXXXVII are both irregular, *abab acac cdcd ee* and *abab cddc effe gg* (or *ff* through near-rhyme) respectively, and both are unbroken into stanzas. As a group, they present the potential for change, but not the full-blown version: winter growth?
18. Discussed also in Chapter 2, p. 33.
19. It is interesting to note that Smith, too, develops in this way; most of her "written" poems are found in Volume II of *Elegiac Sonnets*.
20. "The Critique of Romantic Solipsism in Tennyson's 'The Palace of Art,'" *The Review of English Studies* 57 (2006): 707–20, p. 707.
21. Christopher Rovee, "Solitude and Sociability: *Wordsworth on Helvellyn*," *Literature Compass* 1 (2004); Beth Lau, "Placing Jane Austen in the Romantic Period: Self and Solitude in the Works of Austen and the Male Romantic Poets," *ERR* 15 (2004): 255–67, p. 255.

22. Clara Tuite and Gillian Russell, eds., *Romantic Sociability* (Cambridge: Cambridge University Press, 2002), p. 4.
23. "Communal Romanticism," *ERR* 15 (2004): 329–34, pp. 329–30. Cox presents this formulation as that current when he "was taught Romanticism" (p. 329).
24. *Revision and Romantic Authorship* (Oxford: Oxford University Press, 1996), pp. 2–3.
25. *Godwin's Political Justice* (London: Duckworth, 1986), p. 164.
26. This idea is explored in more detail in Chapter 4, below.
27. This point is brilliantly argued by Simon Parkes. See "Home from the Wars: The Revenant Soldier in the Romantic Period," unpub. PhD thesis, University of Warwick, 2009.
28. It is interesting to note the verbal echo of *The Emigrants*: "while yet/ England had charms for me" (p. 128, ll. 156–7).
29. But see Chapter 4 for a contrasting reading of this poem.
30. Moreover, he, like certain other of Wordsworth's solitaries (for instance in "The Discharged Soldier"), wanders at night along public ways, and excites the attention of dogs. He seems transplanted from *Lyrical Ballads* to "Beachy Head."
31. Significantly for my argument, in 1815 Wordsworth changed "written" to "composed."
32. See *Wordsworth's Great Period Poems: Four Essays* (Cambridge: Cambridge University Press, 1986), Chapter 1: "Insight and oversight: reading 'Tintern Abbey,'" pp. 14–57.
33. This echo has also been noted Bishop C. Hunt in "Wordsworth and Charlotte Smith," *The Wordsworth Circle* 1 (1970): 85–103; and Kari Lokke in "Charlotte Smith and Literary History: 'Dark Forgetfulness' and the 'Intercession of St. Monica,'" *Women's Studies* 27.3 (1998): 259–80. However, neither has noted the significance of the time span.

Chapter 4

1. See *Romantic Theatricality: Gender, Poetry and Spectatorship* (Ithaca: Cornell University Press, 1997).
2. In *Wordsworth in his Major Lyrics: The Art and Psychology of Self-Representation* (Columbia: University of Missouri Press, 2001), Leon Waldoff follows a similar line of thought to great effect, tracing in what he calls the major lyrics "a speaker [who] presents a self-dramatizing performance and attempts, through the dramatics of his utterance, to transform the sense of individual self represented in a moment of lyrical expression" (p. 8). Whereas I, in this chapter, label Wordsworth's and Smith's relevant poems "dramatized monologues," Waldoff calls the poems he discusses "dramatic lyrics." Our approach differs, however, in that Waldoff is interested in teasing out motives using a psychoanalytic methodology: "the persistent concern [the speaker] shows with self-transformation and self-realization require a way of defining and conceptualizing his subjectivity that will give greater recognition to the psychological dimension of his experience" (p. 10). In my reading, it is not about what the *speaker shows*, rather it is what the *poem reveals* about the speaker that is the issue.

3. Letter to Richard Woodhouse (27 October 1818), in *Selected Poems and Letters by John Keats*, ed. Douglas Bush (Boston: Houghton Mifflin, 1959), p. 279.
4. For a detailed discussion of Smith's strategies in her Prefaces, see my *Charlotte Smith: Romanticism, Poetry and the Culture of Gender*, Chapter 1. Judith Pascoe also notes that Smith "narrow[s] the distance between author and narrator of her poems" in the increasing detail of the Prefaces (p. 17).
5. Parrish included this essay in Chapter 3 of *The Art of the Lyrical Ballads* (Cambridge: Harvard University Press, 1973). Parrish sees Smith's "Apostrophe to an Old Tree" as the inspiration for "The Thorn," p. 106.
6. The ethics of portraying others have been finely nuanced by Simpson and Bromwich, whose ideas about the ironic function of double-voicing inform this chapter. However, for my purposes "irony," with its knowing detachment, is too limiting a mode; instead, this chapter explores what might be called a more *studious*, hypothetizing engagement. For Smith and Wordsworth, although equally ill at ease with the period's fascination with celebrity and cult-making, nonetheless also subject their personae to the conditions of the market as they tease out the parameters of the Poet.
7. See *Poetry*, explanatory notes, for details.
8. Wordsworth, of course, also made use of the *European Magazine* in March 1787 to house his first published effort, the sonnet on H. M. Williams, which he signed "Axiologus" ("a Greek compound for 'Words-Worth'" says John O. Hayden in *William Wordsworth: The Poems Volume One* [1982; London: Penguin, 1977], p. 923).
9. Wordsworth's many periodical poems in the 1790s were a virtual secret until well into the twentieth century. See, for instance, N. B. Bauer, "Wordsworth's Poems in Contemporary Periodicals," *Victorian Periodicals Review* 11 (1978): 61–76.
10. Robert Langbaum, *The Poetry of Experience: The Dramatic Monologue in Modern Literary Experience* (London: Chatto and Windus, 1957), pp. 25, 33.
11. David Perkins, *Wordsworth and the Poetry of Sincerity* (Cambridge: Belknap Press of Harvard University Press, 1964), pp. 2, 210, 84.
12. Lionel Trilling, *Sincerity and Authenticity* (London: Oxford University Press, 1972), p. 2.
13. William Galperin, *Revision and Authority in Wordsworth: The Interpretation of a Career* (Philadelphia: University of Pennsylvania Press, 1989), p. 66.
14. Leon Guilhamet, *The Sincere Ideal: Studies on Sincerity in Eighteenth Century English Literature* (Montreal: McGill-Queen's University Press, 1974), p. 276.
15. "Beachy Head," p. 164, l. 346.
16. Frances Ferguson, *Wordsworth: Language as Counter-Spirit* (New Haven: Yale University Press, 1977), p. xiv.
17. Sheila Kearns, *Coleridge, Wordsworth, and Romantic Autobiography: Reading Strategies of Self-Representation* (Madison: Fairleigh Dickinson University Press, 1995), p. 25; Elizabeth Fay, *Becoming Wordsworthian: A Performative Aesthetics* (Amherst: University of Massachusetts Press, 1995), pp. 2, 16.
18. Deborah Forbes, *Sincerity's Shadow: Self-Consciousness in British Romantic and Mid-Twentieth-Century American Poetry* (Cambridge: Harvard University Press, 2004), p. 34.
19. Fay's excellent book is second only to Pascoe's in opening new ways to read Wordsworth. Where our arguments differ is in her emphasis on Dorothy as

an equal partner in the creation of "Wordsworth"; for her, "Wordsworth" hides a double, William/Dorothy identity. By contrast, I see a multiple Wordsworth/"Wordsworth"/ Wordsworth-as-"Wordworth" aesthetic informing his meta-autobiography.

20. Alan Sinfield, *The Dramatic Monolgue* (London: Methuen, 1977), pp. x, 45. Sinfield refers to the "simple sincerity of the Romantic poetic 'I'" (p. 60).
21. See Pascoe, who views the peripatetic Wordsworth as spectacle, and links his impromptu rural performances with those of strolling players and minstrels (p. 196 *passim*). See also *Romanticism and Celebrity Culture, 1750–1850*, ed. Tom Mole (Cambridge: Cambridge University Press, 2009).
22. In a related remark, E. R. Harty states that "even in those cases where the poet *intends* to speak in his own voice, to express his own thoughts and feelings, by employing a poetic genre he automatically abdicates his right to be so construed." Harty's view, that poetry as a genre is inherently artificial, is one that I am sympathetic to, although I think that both Smith and Wordsworth exploit the dramatic potential of poetry rather than are subject to it. See "Voice and Enunciation in the Dramatic Monologue and the Lyric," *Unisa English Studies* 28 (1990), 14–21, p14.
23. I would not want to argue that *all* of the two poets' autobiographical work is dramatized; for Wordsworth, especially, there is a clearly documented investment in the personal nature of his writing. But to explore the ways in which their poetry undercuts even as it creates the highly personalized Romantic Poet takes further the critical understanding of the interplay between the "real" and the imagined that is explored in Chapter 2.

    There are ways in which my argument bears resemblance to those made by Bialostosky, Simpson, and Bromwich, who read Wordsworth's presentation of suspect speakers in many of his poems as evidence of his self-consciously "inscrutable acts of impersonation" (with thanks to my anonymous reader for this elegant phrase). My discussion perhaps places more emphasis on how Wordsworth mines the meta-autobiographical for material – on the artistic license he allowed himself over his use of Self. In light of this, it is pertinent to note that neither Bromwich nor Simpson discusses *The Prelude*.
24. See *The Collected Letters of Charlotte Smith*, ed. Judith Stanton (Bloomington: Indiana University Press, 2003). Smith was a copious letter-writer, as were many accomplished women of her time, and great caches of her letters have survived, with new ones continuing to turn up since the publication of Stanton's magisterial edition. See, for instance, my "Gentility in Distress: A New Letter by Charlotte Smith," *The Wordsworth Circle* XXXV (2004), 91–3. In addition, a new group of 93 letters to Smith's publisher Cadell was unearthed in the East Sussex Public Record Office in 2006 and is now being thoroughly studied. See also Harriet Guest and Judith Stanton, "'A smart strike on the nerves': Two letters from Charlotte Smith to Thomas Cadell, With a Title Page," *Women's Writing* 16.1 (2009), 6–19.
25. I discussed some of these personae in *Charlotte Smith*, which is mainly concerned with the gendering of the Selves Smith concocts. See also Jacqueline Labbe, "The Seductions of Form in the Poetry of Ann Batten Cristall and Charlotte Smith," *Romantic Form*, ed. Alan Rawes (Basingstoke: Palgrave Macmillan, 2007), 154–70.

26. A clear novelistic analogue to this speaker is Orlando Somerive in *The Old Manor House*, who spends most of the novel being buffeted by the winds of what he regards as fate, but which the text's narrator presents as arising from his own limitations. See my edition of the novel (Peterborough, ON: Broadview Press, 2001) for a discussion of Orlando as passive hero.
27. Pascoe also makes this point: Smith "narrows the distance between author and narrator of her poems" through her paratexts (p. 17).
28. As I argue in *Charlotte Smith*, the pains Smith takes in her paratexts to situate herself as aged and scarred by her troubles disallows any easy identification of herself and the attractive ingénues portrayed in the plates. See pp. 1–22 for further discussion.
29. In this way my discussion picks up from that in Chapter 3: with Smith's poems, the addition of another factor – here, the plate, and an examination of the rhyme scheme – reveals additional layers of meaning, each awaiting a different lens.
30. "*Elegiac Sonnets*: Charlotte Smith's Formal Paradoxy," pp. 200, 185.
31. Smith uses the term in the Preface to the First Edition of the *Sonnets*, and Robinson notes that "in the eighteenth century, the kind of sonnet that Smith writes – three quatrains and a couplet, like Shakespeare's – was a bastardized form" (p. 186, n. 1). As I note in Chapter 3, Sonnet XII features a mixed Shakespearian/Petrarchan structure; its "irregularity" is in fact highly regulated.
32. Most critics discuss this poem in terms of its suggestive content as developed by a woman writer. Its actual generic continuity is less remarked. See, for instance, Stella Brooks, "The Sonnets of Charlotte Smith," *Critical Survey* 4.1 (1992): 9–21; Deborah Kennedy, "Thorns and Roses: the Sonnets of Charlotte Smith," *Women's Writing* 2.1 (1995): 43–53; Adela Pinch, *Strange Fits of Passion: Epistemologies of Emotion, Hume to Austen* (Stanford: Stanford University Press, 1996); Esther Schor, *Bearing the Dead: The British Culture of Mourning from the Enlightenment to Victoria* (Princeton: Princeton University Press, 1994).
33. In this context it is interesting that one of Smith's contemporary readers, John Thelwall, singled out Sonnet XLIV for its generic completeness: "Perhaps it is not saying too much to declare, that in the narrow compass of these fourteen lines, are included all the requisites of good poetry: vivid painting, numerous harmony, sublimity of thought and expression, and pathos of sentiment" (quoted in Robinson p. 193, n. 11).
34. "Poetry and Culture: Performativity and Critique," *New Literary History* 30 (1999), 57–74; p. 66. While Slinn, Pascoe, and Fay all talk about "performativity," Pascoe and Fay emphasize performativity *in* poetry where Slinn theorizes about the performativity *of* poetry. My argument effectively synthesizes these two positions: Smith, in writing dramatized monologues, shows the performance of the persona to be performance, but she also demonstrates the essential suitability of poetry to the creation of performance.
35. As Chapter 3 discusses, "written" has a particular valency, suggesting both the physical act of writing and the artefact it produces. "Supposed to have been written" occupies an indeterminate space between the concrete and the abstract.
36. From the first to the eighth edition, the sonnet, and the four following, are entitled "From the novel of Celestina" and "From the same." From the

ninth edition on, Smith switches to the titles noted in my discussion of the poems.

37. As I discuss in *Charlotte Smith*, most of Smith's Augusta sonnets have a romantic, rather than a maternal tone. See pp. 75–81.
38. Sonnet LXII also originates in a novel, *The Old Manor House*, published two years after *Celestina*.
39. Although not included among the Werther sonnets, Sonnet LXX revisits the "story of the Lunatic" Smith references in Sonnet XXI: "Supposed to be written by Werter." This connection has not, as far as I am aware, been made yet, and it opens up intriguing possibilities concerning the date of composition for Sonnet LXX as well as her understanding of the five-act nature of the Werther sonnets. See *Poetry*, p. 230, n. 50.
40. Since *Celestina* was published in 1791, this date seems almost pointedly to emphasize the continuity between Sonnets LIII and LIV.
41. See, for instance, Leon Guilhamet as quoted on p. 110 as he elaborates, for Wordsworth, poetry connects readers to "truth": the "real language of men" equates with the "real feelings of men" and "poetry, as communicator of feeling, is the humanizing quality in truth" (pp. 271–2, 274).
42. In 1798, the anonymous single author stands in, of course, for the partnered Wordsworth and Coleridge. In 1800, the newly "out" W. Wordsworth silently encompasses the now-marginalized Coleridge. 1800, in this way, marks the first time the autobiographical Wordsworth can be read as such by his readers.
43. I use "Song" as exemplary of the short sequence of "Strange fits of passion," "Song," and "A slumber did my spirit seal," but the argument could be applied to any of these poems. As Chapter 1 shows, "Song" is particularly open to being re-viewed.
44. Following Chapter 1, another way to approach this movement – where form effectively undoes content – is to refer to the result achieved by the experiment undertaken in both *Elegiac Sonnets* and *Lyrical Ballads*: self-reflexivity.
45. The change in 1800 to "practice" signals this version's transfer of culpability from the speaker to Edward, reinforced in the revision of line 46 from "Hung down his head, nor made reply" to "He blush'd with shame, nor made reply."
46. Letter to unnamed correspondent, Oct. 17 [?1826]; *Letters of William and Dorothy Wordsworth: the Later Years*, Part 1 (1821–1828) (Oxford: Clarendon Press, 1978), p. 486.
47. *The Prose Works of William Wordsworth*, eds. W. J. B Owen and Jane Worthington Smyser, 3 vols. (Oxford: Clarendon, 1974), II. 125. Quoted in Brooke Hopkins, "Wordsworth's Voices: Ideology and Self-Critique in *The Prelude*," *Studies in Romanticism* 33 (1994), p. 279, n. 2.
48. Jean Deubergue, "Time, Space, and Egotistical Sublime: The *Unity* of 'Tintern Abbey,'" *Bulletin de la Faculté des Lettres de Strasbourg* 47 (1969): 203–16. Although Deubergue's stance may strike readers as outdated, it is worth comparing to Deborah Forbes', quoted above (p. 111).
49. Galperin, pp. 76, 79. See also David Perkins, who views the poem as a self-parody: "One might say that he had composed his verse in distaste of the public and found a further reason for distaste in the reception he encountered" (p. 151). Mary Jacobus also sees the poem as self-projection in *Tradition and Experiment in Wordsworth's* Lyrical Ballads *(1798)*.

50. The resonances with "Nay, we'll go/ Together down, sir" ("My Last Duchess," 53–4) are telling; Browning, at least, seems to have picked up on the poem's inherent drama as well as its darkness.
51. This identification is also, of course, shored up by Smith in "Beachy Head"; see Chapter 3. See also Hunt.
52. It is also worth noting the echo of the repetitions "fair and more fair" and "think, and think, and think again."
53. See *The Character of the Poet: Wordsworth in* The Prelude (Princeton: Princeton University Press, 1971), p. 29.
54. In *William Wordsworth, A Life* (2001; Oxford: Oxford University Press, 1989), Gill situates the poem as one of "Wordsworth's greatest autobiographical poems" which "seizes imperiously on the 'facts', to forge a poetic fiction with which to convey essential truth" (p. 152).
55. Forbes argues, following Galperin, that doubt is the element that threatens to disable the poem, but that Wordsworth abandons this, thus showing the sincerity of doubt. However, by composing a dramatized monologue, Wordsworth avoids the awkwardness of introducing, only to abandon, a key trope; instead, the uncertainty regarding doubt functions as another way in which his obsessed speaker exposes his own limitations.
56. See "*Beachy Head*: The Romantic Fragment Poem as Mosaic," in *Forging Connections: Women's Poetry from the Renaissance to Romanticism*, eds. Anne K. Mellor, Felicity Nussbaum, and Jonathan Post, *Huntington Library Quarterly* 7 (2002), 119–46.
57. For a discussion of these identities that emphasizes Smith's gender play, see Chapter 5 of *Charlotte Smith*, "Locating the Poet in 'Beachy Head'" (142–64).
58. The next chapter will treat at length the collection *Beachy Head, with Other Poems*; as noted on p. 157 below, "Beachy Head" functions as a microcosm for the collection as a whole, and one of its main exhibits is precisely its collection of voices.
59. See "The Case of William Wordsworth: Romantic Invention versus Romantic Genius," *Rhetorical Traditions and British Romantic Literature*, eds. Don Bialostosky and Lawrence Needham (Bloomington: Indiana University Press, 1995): 122–38, p. 130.
60. A close analogue to this technique can be found, of course, in Coleridge's later version of "The Rime of the Ancient Mariner," where the marginal glosses are presented as composed by a later reader of the poem itself.
61. Throughout this section I read the notes' placement as chosen or approved by Smith. It must at least be acknowledged, however, that they could be purely down to the typesetter. By summer 1806 Smith notes in a letter to William Davies that all but "the close of the local poem ... the notes & two short poems, [and] a long preface" have been sent to the printer, which suggests that she is taking her usual care over the volume's progress through the publication process (letter to William Davies, 11 July 1806, in Stanton, *Collected Letters*, p. 740).
62. In the next note, smugglers are "a hardy and athletic race of men"; later, the authority represented by books on the subjects of natural history, botany, and poetry are called into question (pp. 160, 165, 166, 170, for example). The Poet, meanwhile, carries on exploring the possibilities of imagery: the smuggler follows a "clandestine traffic .../ The crook abandoning"; fossilized

seashells "with the pale calcareous soil/ Mingl[e], and see[m] of resembling substance"; "flies ... lightly sport/ In the green shade" (ll. 182–3, 374–5, 446–7).

63. Again, Kelley describes Wordsworth in Book 5 of *The Prelude*.
64. Michael O'Neill, *Romanticism and the Self-Conscious Poem* (Oxford: Clarendon, 1997), p. 60; Theresa M. Kelley, "The Case of William Wordsworth: Romantic Invention versus Romantic Genius"; Brooke Hopkins, "Wordsworth's Voices: Ideology and Self-Critique in *The Prelude*"; Abbie Findlay Potts, *Wordsworth's* Prelude*: A Study of its Literary Form* (Ithaca: Cornell University Press, 1953), p. 362. And yet most critics still want to read the poem as autobiographical. For a reading that highlights the text's competing voices, see Chris Jones and Li-Po Lee, "Wordsworth's Creation of Active Taste," *Romanticism and Victorianism on the Net* 54 (2009), "the narrator demonstrates the processes of imagination but in ways that reveal its artifice." http://www.erudit.org/revue/ravon/2009/v/n54/038764ar.html?lang=en. Accessed 21 June 2010.
65. See *The Oxford Authors: William Wordsworth* (1988; Oxford: Oxford University Press, 1984), p. 727.
66. Jones and Lee also use a Bahktinian approach. For Hopkins, the Victorian dramatic monologue is more concerned with the relationship between the voice of the author and that of the speaker.
67. As he has shown in his shorter poetry, "writing" carries strong resonances; see Chapter 3. See also Andrew Bennett, who observes that for Wordsworth "the act of writing is troubling, difficult, even traumatic; it both produce[s] a poetic self and, at the same time, disturb[s] any possibility of a coherent articulation of such a self" (*Wordsworth Writing*, p.12).
68. As with the other Books, it is deeply indebted to genre-derived diction: theatre, chivalry, heroic. This turn also takes further the 1790s trope of realism discussed in Chapter 2, but to different effect: the speaker's need to romanticize is highlighted.
69. It is not just the meek Officer who "through events/ Of that great change wandered in perfect faith,/ As through a Book, and old Romance or Tale/ Of Fairy" (9: 305–8).
70. As noted in Chapters 1 and 5, both poets predicate much of their more novel conceptualizations on a readership willing and able to read deeply and think about what they have read, in tandem with the poet.

Chapter 5

1. "'Things on Holiday': Collections, Museums, and the Poetics of Unruliness," *ERR* 20.2 (2009): 167–75, p. 167.
2. It is interesting to note that, also in 1807, the *Edinburgh Review* concluded that Kasper Friedrich Wolff's theory that biological forms were not, after all, "inherent and immutable" was "the only true theory of generation" (quoted in U. C. Knoepflmacher, "Editor's Preface: Hybrid Forms and Cultural Anxiety," *SEL* 48.4 (2008): 745–54, p. 745). By 1807 there was consensus about the viability of hybridity, in the *Edinburgh* at least. It was time for the next step.

3. "Multum in parvo": much in little. See Curran, "Multum in Parvo: Wordsworth's *Poems, In Two Volumes* of 1807," in *Poems in Their Place: The Intertextuality and Order of Poetic Collections*, ed. Neil Fraistat (Chapel Hill: University of North Carolina Press, 1986), 234–53.
4. The Greek equivalent, *techne*, connotes as well the knowledge of how to do things; hence its modern derivation, technique. David P. Haney has argued that for both Wordsworth and Coleridge, technique took the status of mere workmanship: "Wordsworth exalts the ethical force of poetry even as he denigrates the poet's work as mechanical techne." My point is partly that, in 1807, the "poet's work" is precisely where Wordsworth finds the "force of poetry," especially if "ethical" is taken to mean the integrity or wholeness of the project. See "Aesthetics and Ethics in Gadamer, Levinas, and Romanticism: Problems of Phronesis and Techne," *PMLA* 114.1 (1999): 32–45, p. 33.
5. Letter to Thomas Cadell, Jr. and William Davies, August 18, 1805. See *The Collected Letters of Charlotte Smith*, ed. Stanton, p. 705.
6. Letter to Lady Beaumont, May 21, 1807. See *The Letters of William Wordsworth: A New Selection*, ed. Alan G. Hill (Oxford: Oxford University Press, 1984; repr. 1990), p. 100.
7. Porter, "Scientific Analogy and Literary Taxonomy in Darwin's *Loves of the Plants*," *European Romantic Review* 18.2 (2007): 213–21, pp. 214, 219.
8. I refer to Cliff Siskin's work, especially "The Year of the System," in *1798: The Year of the* Lyrical Ballads, ed. Richard Cronin (Basingstoke: Macmillan, 1998), 9–31; and "Novels and Systems," *Novel* 34.2 (2001), pp. 202–16.
9. See Paul C. Rosenblatt, *Metaphors of Family Systems Theory: Toward New Constructions* (New York and London: Guilford Press, 1994), pp. 59, 51. See also Ingrid Broszeit-Rieger, "Family Systems Theory and 'The Man of Fifty Years' in Goethe's *Wilhelm Meister's Journeyman Years*," *Romanticism and Parenting: Image, Instruction and Ideology*, ed. Carolyn A. Weber (Newcastle: Cambridge Scholars Publishing, 2007), 74–86, p. 76.
10. Rodney Farnsworth, *Mediating Order and Chaos: The Water-Cycle in the Complex Adaptive Systems of Romantic Culture* (Amsterdam: Rodopi, 2001), p. 11.
11. "Romantic Systematics and the Genealogy of Thought: The Formal Roots of a Cognitive History of Images," *Configurations* 12 (2004): 315–48, pp. 318, 341. Stafford links "sensation" with "an evaluative response," writing that sensation "allows us to establish relations with other selves, things, surroundings" (p. 318). The sensations engendered by the reading process, especially a systemic one, thus capture the interactive mode of collected poetry, always at risk of dissolving into disconnected chaos. "Engulfing immersion," for my purposes, suggests plunging oneself into the collection's wholeness.
12. *The Work of Writing: Literature and Social Change in Britain, 1700–1830* (Baltimore: Johns Hopkins University Press, 1998), p. 6 *passim*. Siskin's work on the classifications of disciplines in the period, and his follow-up work on System, has proved invaluable for this chapter.
13. See *Science and Sensation in Romantic Poetry* (Cambridge: Cambridge University Press, 2008). See also *Romantic Science: The Literary Forms of Natural History*, ed. Noah Heringman (Albany: State University of New York Press, 2003).
14. See *British Romanticism and the Science of the Mind* (Cambridge: Cambridge University Press, 2001), p. 13 *passim*. Gall images the brain as a fruit, Herder as a flower (p. 35).

15. Jackson notes that, by 1815, Wordsworth's *Poems* "aim ... to describe and to produce in the reader an experience of consentaneous response that will serve as the basis for poetic healing" (p. 156). Wordsworth makes it explicit in 1815 that his readers should experience specific reactions to his work; in this way, it might be said, *scientia* overtakes *ars*; the creative reader has become a cowed one. The poet, too, has become enthralled by his own taxonomies, whereas in 1807 he could still present them without fanfare.
16. Tangential to this, but still apt, is the growing concern that writing itself be disseminated rigorously and with all necessary acknowledgments. As Tilar Mazzeo intimates in *Plagiarism and Literary Property in the Romantic Period* (Philadelphia: University of Pennsylvania Press, 2007), theories of what constituted plagiarism in the period function as another form of categorizing; she focuses on key terms like "novelty" and "indebtedness." Both, I would suggest, can be seen as taxonomies.

    To this end it is curious that both Smith and Wordsworth point out, in 1807, coincidental literary overlaps with another poet in their notes. For Wordsworth, the danger surrounds his poems "To the Daisy," of which he notes

    > This poem, and two others to the same Flower, which the Reader will find in the second volume, were written in the year 1802; which is mentioned, because in some of the ideas, though not in the manner in which these ideas are connected, and likewise even in some of the expressions, they bear a striking resemblance to a Poem (lately published) of Mr. Montgomery, entitled, a Field Flower. This being said, Mr. Montgomery will not think any apology due to him; I cannot however help addressing him in the word of the Father of English Poets.
    >
    > "Though it happe me to rehersin –
    > That ye han in your freshe songis saied,
    > Forberith me, and beth not ill apaied,
    > Sith than ye se I doe it in the honour
    > Of Love, and eke in service of the Flour."

    Smith offers a similar vindication in her extensive "Notes to the Fables":

    > There is nothing I am more desirous of avoiding, even in a trifle like this, than the charge of plagiarism. I must in the present instance defend myself by stating, that so long since as April 1805, Mr. Johnson was in possession of the MS. Copy of this Fable. In July 1806, a friend brought with her from London, a volume called "The Birds of Scotland, with other Poems" [by Mr. Graham], in which I read, what, if my fable [of the Lark] had been first published, I might perhaps have thought very like an imitation.

    Smith quotes from both poems, and goes on to say "[t]he extreme resemblance of these passages may be accounted for, however, by the observation very justly made, that natural objects being equally visible to all, it is very probable that descriptions of such objects will be often alike." She then "remark[s] another coincidence" linking her Lark with Graham's Wren (*Poems*, pp. 177–8, note).

    Both poets remove their poems from others' systems.

17. See http://0-lion.chadwyck.co.uk.pugwash.lib.warwick.ac.uk/searchFulltext.do?id=R01614872&divLevel=0&area=abell&forward=critref_ft, accessed 27 July 2010.
18. Sophie Thomas, "'Things on Holiday': Collections, Museums, and the Poetics of Unruliness," *European Romantic Review* 20.2 (2009): 167–75, p. 169.
19. Andrea Henderson, "Passion and Fashion in Joanna Baillie's 'Introductory Discourse,'" *PMLA* 112.2 (1997): 198–213, p. 202. Judith Pascoe, on the other hand, challenges this association between the urge to collect and the urge to dominate, instead interpreting collecting as an enactment of self-sustaining fantasies. See *The Hummingbird Cabinet: A Rare and Curious History of Romantic Collectors* (Ithaca: Cornell University Press, 2006), p. 173.
20. Theresa M. Kelley, "Romantic Exemplarity: Beauty and 'Material' Culture," *Romantic Science*, ed. Noah Heringman (Albany: State University of New York Press, 2003): 223–54, p. 225.
21. Wordsworth's hesitation seems more directed at the commonly random nature of the thing-based collection, yet even here he can see some value. As *The Prelude* (1805) has it:

    Amid this gaudy congress, framed
    Of things by nature most unneighbourly,
    The head turns round, and cannot right itself;
    And, though an aching and a barren sense
    Of gay confusion still be uppermost,
    With few wise longings and but little love,
    Yet something to the memory sticks at last
    Whence profit may be drawn in times to come. (3: 661–8)

    Wordsworth's odd elocution – using the conjunction "and" (l. 4 above) to lead to a point seemingly at odds with the previous lines – suggests that the useful memorability the passage ends by noting actually arises from the unsettling, dizzying nature of the "gaudy" collection. If so, then this collection of things has more in common with his collection of thoughts in *Poems, in Two Volumes* than at first appears. In addition, the profitable memories arising from the experience bear a close resemblance to those retained as "beauteous forms" with which the weary speaker consoles himself "in lonely rooms" ("Tintern Abbey," ll. 22, 25). It might also be noted that "gaudy," while primarily carrying its meaning of showy or tastelessly luxurious, may also be defined as "immaterial" (OED); in other words, as intangible as the poems in a collection.
22. Pascoe, p. 4 *passim*. Henderson makes a similar point when she notes that "[i]n Baillie's 'Discourse,' passions function as discrete items available for inventory, display, and sale" (p. 199).
23. See "From Nosegay to Specimen Cabinet: Charlotte Smith and the Labour of Collecting," in *Charlotte Smith in British Romanticism*, ed. Jacqueline Labbe (London: Pickering and Chatto, 2008): 29–44, p. 40. Porter goes on to read *Beachy Head* as itself "a meditation on the work of collecting" (p. 44).
24. *The Poem and the Book: Interpreting Collections of Romantic Poetry* (Chapel Hill: University of North Carolina Press, 1985), pp. 37, 44.

25. *Making the Modern Reader: Cultural Mediation in Early Modern Literary Anthologies* (Princeton: Princeton University Press, 1996), pp. 6–7.
26. Heather I. Sullivan describes "the mystical vision of nature held by Novalis: everything in the world is connected in an overall unity and it is our task to seek out and participate in the harmonious patterns of becoming"; in other words, to realize the powerful nature of the collection. "Collecting the Rocks of Time: Goethe, the Romantics and Early Geology," *European Romantic Review* 10.3 (1999): 341–70, p. 350.
27. See, for instance, Kelley, "Romantic Exemplarity"; Kelley, "Romantic Histories: Charlotte Smith and 'Beachy Head,'" *Nineteenth-Century Literature* 59.3 (2004): 281–314; Kelley, "Romantic Interiority and Cultural Objects," *Romanticism and Philosophy in an Historical Age*, ed. Karen Weisman, *Romantic Praxis*: http://www.rc.umd.edu/praxis/index.html; Donelle Ruwe, "Charlotte Smith's Sublime: Feminine Poetics, Botany, and *Beachy Head*," *Prism(s): Essays in Romanticism* 7 (1999): 117–32; Donna Landry, "Green Languages? Women Poets as Naturalists in 1653 and 1807," in *Forging Connections: Women's Poetry from the Renaissance to Romanticism*: 39–61; Judith Pascoe, "Female Botanists and the Poetry of Charlotte Smith," *Re-Visioning Romanticism: British Women Writers, 1776–1837*, eds. Carol Shiner Wilson and Joel Haefner (Philadelphia: University of Pennsylvania Press, 1994): 193–209.
28. I made this argument in *Charlotte Smith*; see especially Chapter 5. It is becoming an accepted reading of the poem, given the number of readers who have noticed her technique: John Anderson calls the poem a "mosaic" in "*Beachy Head*: The Romantic Fragment Poem as Mosaic," in *Forging Connections: Women's Poetry from the Renaissance to Romanticism*, pp. 119–46. Porter says it is a "composite stitched together from pieces of her earlier works" ("From Nosegay to Specimen Cabinet," p. 42). Donelle Ruwe makes a similar point in "Charlotte Smith's Sublime: Feminine Poetics, Botany, and *Beachy Head*."
29. Anne D. Wallace also argues that the poem is invested in categorizing, either positively (through botany), or negatively (through geology). See "Picturesque Fossils, Sublime Geology? The Crisis of Authority in Charlotte Smith's *Beachy Head*," *European Romantic Review* 13 (2002): 77–93, p. 77. In other words, the poem provides the paradigm for the volume as a whole. I will not discuss it directly in this chapter, however, given its prominence in Chapter 4.
30. Curtis, *P2V*, p. 37. He clearly uses "miscellany" pejoratively.
31. Porter also notes that "Flora" "fuses the poet's 'dear delusive art' of weaving 'fantastic garlands' ... with the language and forms of empiricist science" ("Nosegay," p. 38). Both Kelley and Porter concentrate on the poem in isolation from its collection.
32. It should be noted that the poem endorses a Nature-fueled amelioration of woe while at the same time suggesting that a devotion to "fond and lingering pain" can be self-indulgent. "Fond" is a notoriously tricky word, carrying intimations of mild madness as well as of affection. Moreover, "wooing" grief and "cherishing" regret suggest a certain impatience with such solipsistic sorrow. Maxwell Wheeler has argued that Smith's political rhetoric in her novels can be "ambivalent"; the ending to a fervent poem like "Flora" is similarly ambivalent. See "Charlotte Smith's Historical Narratives and the English Subject," *Prism(s): Essays in Romanticism* 10 (2002): 7–18.

33. It could be said that this is the drawback in "Tintern Abbey" as well: even as memories of one's past self compensate for the losses of the present, and provide fodder for others as well when trouble hits, yet they are never more than memories, and the "abundant recompense" the poet asserts is continually troubled by his grammar: "I would believe" rather than "I do believe."
34. Although "To the —" in "Miscellaneous Sonnets" contains references to unspecified flowers, its lack of named detail sets it outside the group.
35. "Wordsworth's *Poems, in Two Volumes* (1807) and the Epideictic Tradition," in *Rhetorical Traditions and British Romantic Literature*, eds. Don H. Bialostosky and Lawrence D. Needham (Bloomington: Indiana University Press, 1995), 108–21, p. 116.
36. So, too, "Flora" ends with its "antepast of Paradise": the floral memories offer a foretaste of Heaven, the snowdrops are "set" by its Spirit.
37. But he also supplies Smith-style botanical identification in his note to the title: "Common Pilewort" (*P2V*, p. 79).
38. See "Romantic Histories: Charlotte Smith and 'Beachy Head,'" *Nineteenth-Century Literature* 59.3 (2004): 281–314, p. 311.
39. Jeffrey's review inspired what Curtis calls "the common charge of triviality" (*P2V*, p. 34). See *Edinburgh Review*, October 1807, in *The Romantics Reviewed: Contemporary Reviews of British Romantic Writers: Part A – The Lake Poets*, ed. Donald Reiman (New York: Garland, 1972), vol. 2: 437–38.
40. Without belaboring the point, it is worth noting that Emmeline is also the name of Smith's protagonist in her first novel (*Emmeline*, 1788), while Laura is a main character in *The Young Philosopher* (1798).
41. For an extended discussion, see my "'The absurdity of animals having the passions and the faculties of man': Charlotte Smith's Fables (1807)," *European Romantic Review* 19 (2008): 157–62.
42. The most accessible version is Helen Darbishire's edition of 1914, which separates Wordsworth's notes from the Editor's and does not attach the Fenwick additions. See *Wordsworth: Poems, in Two Volumes 1807*, ed. Darbishire (1952; Oxford: Clarendon Press, 1914).
43. Smith makes a similar remark in a note in "Beachy Head": "I had often heard of the elephant's bones at Burton, but never saw them; and I have no books to refer to" (*Poetry*, p. 167).

Conclusion

1. "Wordsworth and Romanticism" in *The Cambridge Companion to Wordsworth*, ed. Stephen Gill (Cambridge: Cambridge University Press, 2003): 213–29, p. 214.
2. Kenneth Johnston's description of the novel as "featur[ing] the adventures of a party of stylish London gentry in a fictitious Grasmere Abbey" errs on the side of parody, although it is true that Grasmere Abbey is fictitious. See "Wordsworth and *The Recluse*," *The Cambridge Companion to Wordsworth*: 70–89, p. 75.
3. It is notable that this first paragraph is tonally very similar to Smith's own prefaces excoriating the lawyers and trustees she held responsible for her family's financial travails; the following could easily have come from, for

instance, Smith's own Preface to Volume II of her *Elegiac Sonnets*, suppressed after the first 1797 edition. Compare the following two extracts:

> ... the ignorance of those who have chosen to stand forth as my enemies, as far as I am acquainted with their enmity, has unfortunately been still more gross than their disingenuousness, and their incompetence more flagrant than their malice.

> ... these persons ... have conquered or outlived all sensibility of shame; they are alive neither to honesty, honor, or humanity; and at this moment, far from feeling compunction for the ruin they have occasioned, one shrinks from the very attempt to make such redress as he might give ... while the other uses such professional subterfuges as are the disgrace of his profession ...

Although their targets are different, their language occupies the same lexical terrain (the first extract is from Wordsworth, the second from Smith. See *William Wordsworth: Selected Prose*, ed. Hayden, p. 505; *Poetry*, p. 67).

4. Carlyle makes this observation in his Journal, entry for 17 March 1835, quoted in Charles Richard Sanders, "Carlyle and Wordsworth," p. 116.
5. In the next note to "St Bees' Head," Wordsworth apparently records another obligation, this time through allusion. In speaking of the ratification of religious rites of grieving, the note reads

> No reflecting person, however, can view without sorrow the abuses which rose out of thus formalising sublime instincts, and disinterested movements of passion, and perverting them into means of gratifying the ambition and rapacity of the priesthood. But, while we deplore and are indignant at these abuses, it would be a great mistake if we imputed the origin of the offices to prospective selfishness on the part of the monks and clergy: "they" were at first sincere in their sympathy, and in their degree dupes rather of their own creed, than artful and designing men. Charity is, upon the whole, the safest guide that we can take in judging our fellow-men, whether of past ages or of the present time.

This bears resemblance to a note in *The Emigrants*: "nothing is father from my thoughts, than to reflect invidiously on the Emigrant Clergy, whose steadiness of principle excites veneration, as much as their sufferings compassion. Adversity has now taught them the charity and humility they perhaps wanted, when they made it a part of their faith, that salvation could be obtained in no other religion than their own" (*Poetry*, p. 128).

Bibliography

Anderson, John. "*Beachy Head*: The Romantic Fragment Poem as Mosaic." *Forging Connections: Women's Poetry from the Renaissance to Romanticism*. Eds. Anne K. Mellor, Felicity Nussbaum, and Jonathan Post. *Huntington Library Quarterly* 7 (2002): 119–46.

Backscheider, Paula. *Eighteenth-Century Women Poets and Their Poetry: Inventing Agency, Inventing Genre*. Baltimore: Johns Hopkins University Press, 2005.

Bailes, Melissa. "The Evolution of the Plagiarist: Natural History in Anna Seward's Order of Poetics." *Eighteenth-Century Life* 33.3 (2009): 105–26.

Barrell, John. *Imagining the King's Death: Figurative Treason, Fantasies of Regicide 1793–1796*. Oxford: Oxford University Press, 2000.

Barrell, John. *The Spirit of Despotism: Invasions of Privacy in the 1790s*. Oxford: Oxford University Press, 2006.

Barth, Robert. "Wordsworth and Hopkins: In Pursuit of Transcendence." *Renascence: Essays on Values in Literature,* 48.3 (1996): 174–89.

Barth, Robert. *Romanticism and Transcendence*. Columbia: University of Missouri Press, 2003.

Bate, Jonathan. "Wordsworth and the Naming of Places." *Essays in Criticism* 39 (1983): 196–216.

Bauer, N. B. "Wordsworth's Poems in Contemporary Periodicals." *Victorian Periodicals Review* 11 (1978): 61–76.

Behrendt, Stephen. "Placing the Place in Wordsworth's 1802 Sonnets." *Studies in English Literature* 35.4 (1995): 641–67.

Benedict, Barbara. *Making the Modern Reader: Cultural Mediation in Early Modern Literary Anthologies*. Princeton: Princeton University Press, 1996.

Bennett, Andrew. *Wordsworth Writing*. Cambridge: Cambridge University P, 2007.

Bialostosky, Don. "Genres from Life in Wordsworth's Art: *Lyrical Ballads 1798*." *Romanticism, History, and the Possibilities of Genre: Re-forming Literature 1789–1837*. Eds. Tilottama Rajan and Julia M. Wright. Cambridge: Cambridge University Press, 1998, pp. 109–21.

Blair, Hugh. *Lectures on Rhetoric and Belles Lettres*. 3 vols. Dublin: for Messrs Whitestone, Colles, Burnet, et al., 1783.

Blank, Antje. "Things as They Were: The Gothic of Real Life in Charlotte Smith's *The Emigrants* and *The Banished Man*." *Women's Writing* 16.1 (2009): 78–93.

Bode, Christoph. "By Way of Introduction: Voice, Text, Mediality: Romantic Self-Positioning." *Romantic Voices, Romantic Poetics*. Eds. Christoph Bode and Katharina Rennhak. Trier: Wissenschaftlicher Verlag Trier, 2005, pp. 7–20.

Bromwich, David. *Disowned by Memory: Wordsworth's Poetry of the 1790s*. Chicago: University of Chicago Press, 1998.

Broszeit-Rieger, Ingrid. "Family Systems Theory and 'The Man of Fifty Years' in Goethe's *Wilhelm Meister's Journeyman Years*." *Romanticism and Parenting: Image, Instruction and Ideology*. Ed. Carolyn A. Weber. Newcastle: Cambridge Scholars Publishing, 2007, pp. 74–86.

Bruhn, Mark J. "Place Deixis and the Schematics of Imagined Space: Milton to Keats." *Poetics Today* 26 (2005): 386–432.

Bruns, Gerald R. "Wordsworth at the Limits of Romantic Hermeneutics." *The Centennial Review* 33.4 (1989): 393–418.

Cambridge Companion to Wordsworth, The. Ed. Stephen Gill. Cambridge: Cambridge University Press, 2003.

Clark, Timothy. *The Theory of Inspiration: Composition as a Crisis of Subjectivity in Romantic and Post-Romantic Writing*. Manchester: Manchester University Press, 1997.

Collected Letters of Charlotte Smith, The. Ed. Judith Stanton. Bloomington: Indiana University Press, 2003.

Cooke, Michael G. "The Mode of Argument in Wordsworth's Poetry." *Romantic and Victorian: Studies in Memory of William H. Marshall*. Eds. W. Paul Elledge and Richard L. Hoffman. Rutherford: Fairleigh Dickinson University Press, 1971, pp. 95–109.

Cox, Jeffrey. "Communal Romanticism." *European Romantic Review* 15 (2004): 329–34.

Curran, Stuart. "Multum in Parvo: Wordsworth's *Poems, In Two Volumes* of 1807." *Poems in Their Place: The Intertextuality and Order of Poetic Collections*. Ed. Neil Fraistat. Chapel Hill: University of North Carolina Press, 1986, pp. 234–53.

Curran, Stuart. "Wordsworth and the Forms of Poetry." *The Age of William Wordsworth*. Eds. Kenneth R. Johnston and Gene W. Ruoff. New Brunswick: Rutgers University Press, 1987, pp. 155–32.

Curran, Stuart. "Intertextualities." *Charlotte Smith in British Romanticism*. Ed. Jacqueline Labbe. London: Pickering and Chatto, 2008, pp. 175–88.

Danby, John. *The Simple Wordsworth: Studies in the Poems 1797–1807*. London: Routledge and Kegan Paul, 1960.

Deubergue, Jean. "Time, Space, and Egotistical Sublime: The *Unity* of 'Tintern Abbey.'" *Bulletin de la Faculté des Lettres de Strasbourg* 47 (1969): 203–16.

Duckling, Louise. "'Tell My Name to Distant Ages': The Literary Fate of Charlotte Smith." *Charlotte Smith in British Romanticism*. Ed. Jacqueline Labbe. London: Pickering and Chatto, 2008, pp. 203–17.

Duff, David. "Wordsworth and the Language of Forms." *La questione Romantica: Aesthetics, Philosophy and Politics*. Ed. Annamaria Sportelli. *Rivista interdisciplinare di studi romantici* 10 (2001): 61–71.

Dupré, John. *Humans and Other Animals*. Oxford: Oxford University Press, 2002.

Farnsworth, Rodney. *Mediating Order and Chaos: The Water-Cycle in the Complex Adaptive Systems of Romantic Culture*. Amsterdam: Rodopi, 2001.

Fay, Elizabeth. *Becoming Wordsworthian: A Performative Aesthetics*. Amherst: University of Massachusetts Press, 1995.

Ferguson, Frances. *Wordsworth: Language as Counter-Spirit*. New Haven: Yale University Press, 1977.

Forbes, Deborah. *Sincerity's Shadow: Self-Consciousness in British Romantic and Mid-Twentieth-Century American Poetry*. Cambridge: Harvard University Press, 2004.

Fraistat, Neil. *The Poem and the Book: Interpreting Collections of Romantic Poetry*. Chapel Hill: University of North Carolina Press, 1985.

Galperin, William. "Anti-Romanticism, Victorianism, and the Case of William Wordsworth." *Victorian Poetry* 24:4 (1986): 357–71.

Galperin, William. *Revision and Authority in Wordsworth: The Interpretation of a Career*. Philadelphia: University of Pennsylvania Press, 1989.

Gamer, Michael. "Confounding Present with Past: Romanticism, *Lyrical Ballads*, and Gothic Romance." *Poetica* 39–40 (1993): 111–38.

Gill, Stephen. *Wordsworth's Poetry: 1787–1814*. Cambridge: Harvard University Press, 1987.

Gill, Stephen. "Wordsworth's Poems: The Question of Text." *Romantic Revisions*. Eds. Robert Brinkley and Keith Hanley. Cambridge: Cambridge University Press, 1992: 43–63.

Gill, Stephen. *Wordsworth and the Victorians*. Oxford: Oxford University Press, 1998.

Gilmartin, Kevin. *Writing Against Revolution: Literary Conservatism in Britain, 1790–1832*. Cambridge: Cambridge University Press, 2007.

Ginsberg, David. "Wordsworth's *Poems, in Two Volumes* (1807) and the Epideictic Tradition." *Rhetorical Traditions and British Romantic Literature*. Eds. Don H. Bialostosky and Lawrence D. Needham. Bloomington: Indiana University Press, 1995, pp. 108–121.

Goodman, Kevis. *Georgic Modernity and British Romanticism: Poetry and the Mediation of History*. Cambridge: Cambridge: Cambridge University Press, 2004.

Gravil, Richard. *Wordsworth's Bardic Vocation, 1787–1842*. Basingstoke: Palgrave Macmillan, 2003.

Grenby, M. O. *The Anti-Jacobin Novel: British Conservatism and the French Revolution*. Cambridge: Cambridge University Press, 2001.

Guest, Harriet. *Small Change: Women, Learning, Patriotism, 1750–1810*. Chicago: University of Chicago Press, 2000.

Guest, Harriet. "Charlotte Smith, Mary Robinson and the First Year of the War with France." *The History of British Women's Writing, 1750–1830*. Ed. Jacqueline Labbe. Basingstoke: Palgrave, 2010, pp. 207–30.

Guest, Harriet and Judith Stanton. "'A smart strike on the nerves': Two letters from Charlotte Smith to Thomas Cadell, With a Title Page." *Women's Writing* 16.1 (2009): 6–19.

Guilhamet, Leon. *The Sincere Ideal: Studies on Sincerity in Eighteenth Century English Literature*. Montreal: McGill-Queen's University Press, 1974.

Hamilton, Paul. "Wordsworth and Romanticism." *The Cambridge Companion to Wordsworth*. Ed. Stephen Gill. Cambridge: Cambridge University Press, 2003, pp. 213–29.

Haney, David P. "Aesthetics and Ethics in Gadamer, Levinas, and Romanticism: Problems of Phronesis and Techne." *PMLA* 114.1 (1999): 32–45.

Hardy, Barbara. *The Advantage of Lyric*. London: Athlone Press, 1977.

Harris, Wendell. "Romantic Bard and Victorian Commentators: The Meaning and Significance of Meaning and Significance." *Victorian Poetry* 24:4 (1986): 455–69.

Hartman, Geoffrey. *Beyond Formalism: Literary Essays 1958–1970*. New Haven: Yale University Press, 1970.

Harty, E. R. "Voice and Enunciation in the Dramatic Monologue and the Lyric." *Unisa English Studies* 28 (1990): 14–21.

Henderson, Andrea. "Passion and Fashion in Joanna Baillie's 'Introductory Discourse.'" *PMLA* 112.2 (1997): 198–213.

Hoagwood, Terence Allan. "Fictions and Freedom: Wordsworth and the Ideology of Romanticism." *New Historical Literary Study: Essays on Reproducing Texts,*

Representing History. Eds. Jeffrey Cox and Larry J. Reynolds. Princeton: Princeton University Press, 1993, pp. 178–98.

Hopkins, Brooke. "Wordsworth's Voices: Ideology and Self-Critique in *The Prelude*." *Studies in Romanticism* 33 (1994): 279–99.

Hunt, Jr., Bishop C. "Wordsworth and Charlotte Smith." *The Wordsworth Circle* 1 (1970): 85–103.

Inventing the Individual: Romanticism and the Idea of Individualism. Ed. Larry H. Peer. Provo: Brigham Young University Press, 2002.

Jackson, Noel. *Science and Sensation in Romantic Poetry*. Cambridge: Cambridge University Press, 2008.

Jacobus, Mary. *Tradition and Experiment in Wordsworth's* Lyrical Ballads *(1798)*. Oxford: Clarendon Press, 1976.

Jarvis, Robin. *Romantic Writing and Pedestrian Travel*. Basingstoke: Macmillan, 1997.

Johnston, Kenneth. "Wordsworth's Self-Creation and the 1800 *Lyrical Ballads*." *1800: The New Lyrical Ballads*. Eds. Nicola Trott and Seamus Perry. Basingstoke: Palgrave, 2001, pp. 95–122.

Johnston, Kenneth. "Wordsworth and *The Recluse*." *The Cambridge Companion to Wordsworth*. Ed. Stephen Gill. Cambridge: Cambridge University Press, 2003, pp. 70–89.

Jones, Chris and Li-Po Lee. "Wordsworth's Creation of Active Taste." *Romanticism and Victorianism on the Net* 54 (2009). http://www.erudit.org/revue/ravon/2009/v/n54/038764ar.html?lang=en. Accessed 21 June 2010.

Jordan, John E. *Why the* Lyrical Ballads? Berkeley: University of California Press, 1976.

Journals of Dorothy Wordsworth. Ed. Mary Moorman. Oxford: Oxford University Press, 1971.

Jung, Sandro. "Some Notes on the 'Single Sentiment' and Romanticism of Charlotte Smith." *Connotations* 9.3 (1999/2000): 269–84.

Kearns, Sheila. *Coleridge, Wordsworth, and Romantic Autobiography: Reading Strategies of Self-Representation*. Madison: Fairleigh Dickinson University Press, 1995.

Kelley, Theresa. "The Case of William Wordsworth: Romantic Invention versus Romantic Genius." *Rhetorical Traditions and British Romantic Literature*. Eds. Don Bialostosky and Lawrence Needham. Bloomington: Indiana University Press, 1995, pp. 122–38.

Kelley, Theresa. "Romantic Exemplarity: Botany and 'Material' Culture." *Romantic Science: The Literary Forms of Natural History*. Ed. Noah Heringman. Albany: State University of New York Press, 2003, pp. 223–54.

Kelley, Theresa. "Romantic Histories: Charlotte Smith and 'Beachy Head.'" *Nineteenth-Century Literature* 59.3 (2004): 281–314.

Kelley, Theresa. "Romantic Interiority and Cultural Objects." *Romanticism and Philosophy in an Historical Age*. Ed. Karen Weisman. Romantic Praxis: http://www.rc.umd.edu/praxis/index.html. Accessed 23 February 2011.

Keen, Paul. *The Crisis of Literature in the 1790s: Print Culture and the Public Sphere*. Cambridge: Cambridge University Press, 1999.

Knoepflmacher, U. C. "Editor's Preface: Hybrid Forms and Cultural Anxiety." *SEL* 48.4 (2008: 745–54.

Kroeber, Karl. *The Artifice of Reality: Poetic Style in Wordsworth, Foscolo, Keats, and Leopardi*. Madison and Milwaukee: University of Wisconsin Press, 1964.

Labbe, Jacqueline. *Charlotte Smith: Romanticism, Poetry and the Culture of Gender*. Manchester: Manchester University Press, 2003.

Labbe, Jacqueline. "Gentility in Distress: A New Letter by Charlotte Smith." *The Wordsworth Circle* XXXV (2004): 91–3.

Labbe, Jacqueline. "The Seductions of Form in the Poetry of Ann Batten Cristall and Charlotte Smith." *Romantic Form*. Ed. Alan Rawes. Basingstoke: Palgrave Macmillan, 2007, pp. 154–70.

Labbe, Jacqueline. "'The absurdity of animals having the passions and the faculties of man': Charlotte Smith's fables (1807)." *European Romantic Review* 19 (2008): 157–62.

Landry, Donna. "Green Languages? Women Poets as Naturalists in 1653 and 1807." *Forging Connections: Women's Poetry from the Renaissance to Romanticism*. Eds. Anne K. Mellor, Felicity Nussbaum, and Jonathan Post. *Huntington Library Quarterly* 7 (2002): 39–61.

Langan, Celeste. *Romantic Vagrancy: Wordsworth and the Simulation of Freedom*. Cambridge: Cambridge University Press, 1995.

Langbaum, Robert. *The Poetry of Experience: The Dramatic Monologue in Modern Literary Experience*. London: Chatto and Windus, 1957.

Lau, Beth. "Placing Jane Austen in the Romantic Period: Self and Solitude in the Works of Austen and the Male Romantic Poets." *European Romantic Review* 15 (2004): 255–67.

Leader, Zachary. *Revision and Romantic Authorship*. Oxford: Oxford University Press, 2002.

Levinson, Marjorie. *Wordsworth's Great Period Poems: Four Essays*. Cambridge: Cambridge University Press, 1986.

Liu, Alan. *Wordsworth: The Sense of History*. Stanford: Stanford University Press, 1989.

Liu, Alan. "Local Transcendence: Cultural Criticism, Postmodernism, and the Romanticism of Detail." *Representations* 32 (1990): 75–113.

Lokke, Kari. "Charlotte Smith and Literary History: 'Dark Forgetfulness' and the 'Intercession of St. Monica.'" *Women's Studies* 27.3 (1998): 259–80.

Lokke, Kari. "'The Mild Dominion of the Moon': Charlotte Smith and the Politics of Transcendence." *Rebellious Hearts: British Women Writers and the French Revolution*. Eds. Adriana Craciun and Kari Lokke. Albany: State University of New York Press, 2001, pp. 85–108.

Makdisi, Saree. *Romantic Imperialism: Universal Empire and the Culture of Modernity*. Cambridge: Cambridge University Press, 1998.

Makdisi, Saree. *William Blake and the Impossible History of the 1790s*. Chicago: University of Chicago Press, 2003.

Mayo, Robert. "The Contemporaneity of the *Lyrical Ballads*." *PMLA* 69 (1954): 486–522.

Mazzeo, Tilar. *Plagiarism and Literary Property in the Romantic Period*. Philadelphia: University of Pennsylvania Press, 2007.

McFarland, Thomas. *Paradoxes of Freedom: The Romantic Mystique of a Transcendence*. Oxford: Clarendon Press, 1996.

McGann, Jerome. "Romantic Responses to the Death of Beauty." *Repossessing the Romantic Past*. Eds. Heather Glen and Paul Hamilton. Cambridge: Cambridge University Press, 2006, pp. 226–43.

McLane, Maureen. "Ballads and Bards: British Romantic Orality." *Modern Philology* 98.3 (2001): 423–43.

Mee, Jon. *Dangerous Enthusiasm: William Blake and the Culture of Radicalism in the 1790s*. Oxford: Oxford University Press, 1992.

Mee, Jon. *Romanticism, Enthusiasm and Regulation: Poetics and the Policing of Culture in the Romantic Period*. Oxford: Oxford University Press, 2003.

Miller, Christopher. *The Invention of Evening: Perception and Time in Romantic Poetry*. Cambridge: Cambridge University Press, 2006.

Moretti, Franco. *Atlas of the European Novel, 1800–1900*. London: Verso, 1998.

Nagle, Christopher C. *Sexuality and the Culture of Sensibility in the British Romantic Era*. Basingstoke: Palgrave Macmillan, 2007.

[Newbery, John.] *The Art of Poetry on a New Plan*. London: for J. Newbery, 1762.

O'Neill, Michael. *Romanticism and the Self-Conscious Poem*. Oxford: Clarendon, 1997.

Onorato, Richard J. *The Character of the Poet: Wordsworth in* The Prelude. Princeton: Princeton University Press, 1971.

Parrish, Stephen Maxfield. "Dramatic Technique in the Lyrical Ballads." *PMLA* 74.1 (1959): 85–97.

Parrish, Stephen Maxfield. *The Art of the Lyrical Ballads*. Cambridge: Harvard University Press, 1973.

Pascoe, Judith. "Female Botanists and the Poetry of Charlotte Smith." *Re-Visioning Romanticism: British Women Writers, 1776–1837*. Eds. Carol Shiner Wilson and Joel Haefner. Philadelphia: University of Pennsylvania Press, 1994, pp. 193–209.

Pascoe, Judith. *Romantic Theatricality: Gender, Poetry and Spectatorship*. Ithaca: Cornell University Press, 1997.

Pascoe, Judith. *The Hummingbird Cabinet: A Rare and Curious History of Romantic Collectors*. Ithaca: Cornell University Press, 2006.

Peer, Larry H. "The Name and Nature of Romanticism Revisited." *Prism(s)* 7 (1999): 175–86.

Perkins, David. *Wordsworth and the Poetry of Sincerity*. Cambridge: Belknap Press of Harvard University Press, 1964.

Pfau, Thomas. *Wordsworth's Profession: Form, Class, and the Logic of Early Romantic Cultural Production*. Stanford: Stanford University Press, 1997.

Philp, Mark. *Godwin's Political Justice*. London: Duckworth, 1986.

Plug, Jan. "Romanticism and the Invention of Literature." *Idealism without Absolutes: Philosophy and Romantic Culture*. Eds. Tilottama Rajan and Arkady Plotnisky. Albany: State University of New York Press, 2004, pp. 15–38.

Porter, Dahlia. "Scientific Analogy and Literary Taxonomy in Darwin's *Loves of the Plants*." *European Romantic Review* 18.2 (2007): 213–21.

Porter, Dahlia. "From Nosegay to Specimen Cabinet: Charlotte Smith and the Labour of Collecting." *Charlotte Smith in British Romanticism*. Ed. Jacqueline Labbe. London: Pickering and Chatto, 2008, pp. 29–44.

Potts, Abbie Findlay. *Wordsworth's* Prelude*: A Study of its Literary Form*. Ithaca: Cornell University Press, 1953.

Pratt, Kathryn. "Charlotte Smith's Melancholia on the Page and Stage." *Studies in English Literature* 41.3 (2001): 563–81.

Richardson, Alan. "British Romanticism as a Cognitive Category." *Romanticism on the Net* 8 (1997). http://www.erudit.org/revue/ron/1997/v/n8/005767ar.html. Accessed 5 July 2010.

Richardson, Alan. *British Romanticism and the Science of the Mind*. Cambridge: Cambridge University Press, 2001.

Robinson, Daniel. "*Elegiac Sonnets*: Charlotte Smith's Formal Paradoxy." *Papers on Language and Literature* 39.2 (2003): 185–220.

Roe, Nicholas. "Renewing *Lyrical Ballads*." *1800: The New Lyrical Ballads*. Eds. Nicola Trott and Seamus Perry. Basingstoke: Palgrave, 2001, pp. 224–38.

Roe, Nicholas. "Politics, History and Wordsworth's Poems." *The Cambridge Companion to Wordsworth*. Ed. Stephen Gill. Cambridge: Cambridge University Press, 2003, pp. 196–212.

Romantic Science: The Literary Forms of Natural History. Ed. Noah Heringman. Albany: State University of New York Press, 2003.

Romantic Sociability. Eds. Clara Tuite and Gillian Russell. Cambridge: Cambridge University Press, 2002.

Rosenblatt, Paul C. *Metaphors of Family Systems Theory: Toward New Constructions*. New York and London: Guilford Press, 1994.

Rovee, Christopher. "Solitude and Sociability: *Wordsworth on Helvellyn*." *Literature Compass* 1 (2004).

Ruwe, Donelle. "Charlotte Smith's Sublime: Feminine Poetics, Botany, and *Beachy Head*." *Prism(s): Essays in Romanticism* 7 (1999): 117–32.

Ryskamp, Charles. "Wordsworth's *Lyrical Ballads* in Their Time." *From Sensibility to Romanticism: Essays Presented to Frederick A. Pottle*. London: Oxford University Press, 1965, pp. 357–72.

Sanders, Charles Richard. "Carlyle and Wordsworth." *Browning Institute Studies* 9 (1981): 115–22.

Scrivener, Michael. "Literature and Politics." *The Cambridge Companion to English Literature, 1740–1830*. Eds. Thomas Keymer and Jon Mee. Cambridge: Cambridge University Press, 2004, pp. 43–60.

Simpson, David. *Wordsworth and the Figurings of the Real*. Basingstoke: Macmillan, 1982.

Simpson, David. *Wordsworth's Historical Imagination: The Poetry of Displacement*. New York: Methuen, 1987.

Sinfield, Alan. *The Dramatic Monologue*. London: Methuen, 1977.

Siskin, Clifford. *The Historicity of Romantic Discourse*. New York: Oxford University Press, 1988.

Siskin, Clifford. "The Year of the System." *1798: The Year of the* Lyrical Ballads. Ed. Richard Cronin. Basingstoke: Macmillan, 1998, pp. 9–31.

Siskin, Clifford. *The Work of Writing: Literature and Social Change in Britain, 1700–1830*. Baltimore: Johns Hopkins University Press, 1998.

Siskin, Clifford. "Novels and Systems." *Novel* 34.2 (2001): 202–16.

Slinn, E. Warwick. "Poetry and Culture: Performativity and Critique." *New Literary History* 30 (1999): 57–74.

Smith, Charlotte. *Poems of Charlotte Smith*. Ed. Stuart Curran. Oxford: Oxford University Press, 1993.

Smith, Charlotte. *Poetry*. Ed. Jacqueline Labbe. London: Pickering and Chatto, 2007.

Stafford, Barbara. "Romantic Systematics and the Genealogy of Thought: The Formal Roots of a Cognitive History of Images." *Configurations* 12 (2004): 315–48.

St. Clair, William. *The Reading Nation in the Romantic Period*. Cambridge: Cambridge University Press, 2004.

St. Cyres (Viscount). "The Sorrows of Mrs. Charlotte Smith." *The Cornhill Magazine* 15 (1903): 683–96.

Stokes, Christopher. "Lorn Subjects: Haunting, Fracture and Ascesis in Charlotte Smith's *Elegiac Sonnets.*" *Women's Writing* 16.1 (2009): 143–60.

Stork, Charles Wharton. "The Influence of the Popular Ballad on Wordsworth and Coleridge." *PMLA* 29.3 (1914): 299–326.

Sullivan, Heather I. "Collecting the Rocks of Time: Goethe, the Romantics and Early Geology." *European Romantic Review* 10.3 (1999): 341–70.

Sussman, Charlotte. "The Art of Oblivion: Charlotte Smith and Helen of Troy." *Studies in Eighteenth-Century Culture* 27 (1998): 131–46.

Swingle, L. J. "The Romantic Emergence: Multiplication of Alternatives and the Problem of Systematic Entrapment." *Modern Language Quarterly* 39 (1978): 264–83.

Tayebi, Kandi. "Charlotte Smith and the Quest for the Romantic Prophetic Voice." *Women's Writing* 11.3 (2004): 421–38.

Thomas, Sophie. "'Things on Holiday': Collections, Museums, and the Poetics of Unruliness." *European Romantic Review* 20.2 (2009): 167–75.

Thorslev, Peter. "German Romantic Idealism." *The Cambridge Companion to British Romanticism*. Ed. Stuart Curran. Cambridge: Cambridge University Press, 1993, pp. 74–94.

Trilling, Lionel. *Sincerity and Authenticity*. London: Oxford University Press, 1972.

Venis, Linda. "The Problem of Broadside Balladry's Influence on the *Lyrical Ballads.*" *Studies in English Literature* 24.4 (1984): 617–32.

Waldoff, Leon. *Wordsworth in his Major Lyrics: The Art and Psychology of Self-Representation*. Columbia: University of Missouri Press, 2001.

Wallace, Anne D. *Walking, Literature and English Culture: The Origins and Uses of Peripatetic in the Nineteenth Century*. Oxford: Clarendon Press, 1993.

Wallace, Anne D. "Picturesque Fossils, Sublime Geology? The Crisis of Authority in Charlotte Smith's *Beachy Head.*" *European Romantic Review* 13 (2002): 77–93.

Wallace, Anne D. "Home at Grasmere Again: Revising the Family in Dove Cottage." *Literary Couplings: Writing Couples, Collaborators, and the Construction of Authorship*. Eds. Marjorie Stone and Judith Thompson. Madison: University of Wisconsin Press, 2006, pp. 100–23.

Warton, Thomas. *The History of English Poetry, from the Close of the Eleventh to the Commencement of the Eighteenth Century*. London: J. Dodsley; J. Walter; T. Becket; J. Robson; G. Robinson, and J. Bew; and Messrs. Fletcher, at Oxford, 1774–81. 4 vols.

Wheeler, Maxwell. "Charlotte Smith's Historical Narratives and the English Subject." *Prism(s): Essays in Romanticism* 10 (2002): 7–18.

White, Daniel. *Early Romanticism and Religious Dissent*. Cambridge: Cambridge University Press, 2006.

Wiley, Michael. *Romantic Geography: Wordsworth and Anglo-European Spaces*. Basingstoke: Macmillan, 1998.

Wolfson, Susan. "The Language of Interpretation in Romantic Poetry: 'A Strong Working of the Mind.'" *Romanticism and Language*. Ed. Arden Reed. London: Methuen, 1984, pp. 22–49.

Wolfson, Susan. "Charlotte Smith's *Emigrants*: Forging Connections at the Borders of a Female Tradition." *Forging Connections: Women's Poetry from the Renaissance to Romanticism*. Eds. Anne K. Mellor, Felicity Nussbaum, and Jonathan Post. *Huntington Library Quarterly* 7 (2002): 81–118.

Woodring, Carl. "Wordsworth and the Victorians." *The Age of William Wordsworth: Critical Essays on the Romantic Tradition.* Eds. Kenneth R. Johnston and Gene W. Ruoff. New Brunswick: Rutgers University Press, 1987, pp. 261–75.

Woolford, John. "The Critique of Romantic Solipsism in Tennyson's 'The Palace of Art.'" *Review of English Studies* 57 (2006): 707–20.

Wordsworth, William. *Wordsworth: Poems, in Two Volumes 1807.* Ed. Helen Darbishire. 1952; Oxford: Clarendon Press, 1914.

Wordsworth, William. *The Salisbury Plain Poems of William Wordsworth.* Ed. Stephen Gill. Ithaca: Cornell University Press, 1975.

Wordsworth, William. *William Wordsworth: The Poems, Volume One.* Ed. John O. Haydon. Harmondsworth: Penguin, 1977.

Wordsworth, William. The Ruined Cottage *and* The Pedlar. Ed. James Butler. Ithaca: Cornell University Press, 1979.

Wordsworth, William. Poems, in Two Volumes, *and Other Poems, 1800–1807.* Ed. Jared Curtis. Ithaca: Cornell University Press, 1983.

Wordsworth, William. *The Letters of William Wordsworth: A New Selection.* Ed. Alan G. Hill. 1990; Oxford: Oxford University Press, 1984.

Wordsworth, William. *An Evening Walk.* Ed. James Averill. Ithaca: Cornell University Press, 1984.

Wordsworth, William. *Descriptive Sketches.* Ed. Eric Birdsall. Ithaca: Cornell University Press, 1984.

Wordsworth, William. *Lyrical Ballads.* Eds. R.L. Brett and A.R. Jones. London: Routledge, 1991.

Wordsworth, William. Lyrical Ballads, *and Other Poems, 1797–1800.* Eds. James Butler and Karen Green. Ithaca: Cornell University Press, 1992.

Wordsworth, William. *Early Poems and Fragments, 1785–1797.* Eds. Carol Landon and Jared Curtis. Ithaca: Cornell University Press, 1997.

Wu, Duncan. *Wordsworth's Reading 1770–1799.* Cambridge: Cambridge University Press, 1993.

Wu, Duncan. "Wordsworth's Poetry to 1798." *The Cambridge Companion to Wordsworth.* Ed. Stephen Gill. Cambridge: Cambridge University Press, 2003, pp. 22–37.

Zimmerman, Sarah. *Romanticism, Lyricism, and History.* Albany: State University of New York Press, 1999.

Index

Note: An "n." after a page reference number refers to a note on that page.

Lightning Source UK Ltd.
Milton Keynes UK
UKOW05f1557091014

239854UK00008B/102/P

9 781137 465108